The best of Mrs BEETON'S British Cooking

The best of Mrs BEETON'S British Cooking

MARKS & SPENCER

Designed by seagulls and cbdesign
Index prepared by Chris Bell
Production by Omnipress Ltd, Eastbourne
Printed in Spain

Marks and Spencer p.l.c.
PO Box 3339 Chester CH99 9QS

shop online

www.marksandspencer.com

Contents

British Cooking

The cornerstones of British cooking, including
hearty breakfasts, the attractive rituals of
afternoon tea and picnics, and
of course, the traditional
Sunday roast.

BREAKFAST

Mrs Beeton said that 'to begin the day well is a grand thing, and a good breakfast at a reasonable hour is an excellent foundation for a day's work, or even a pleasure'.

A traditional English breakfast comprises of sausages, crisply-grilled bacon, mushrooms fried in butter with a little oil (parsley and garlic are optional), slow-grilled tomato halves, fried slices of black pudding (optional), baked beans (optional), fried eggs, fried bread or buttered toast, ketchup or brown sauce, salt and pepper.

AFTERNOON / HIGH TEA

High tea is said to have been invented by Anna, the 7th Duchess of Bedfordshire around 1840, to fill the hungry gap between lunch and dinner. Served around 4pm, the best silver cake tongs and cutlery, fine bone china, pretty linen tablecloths, napkins, runners and doilies, and cake stands were showcased to create a strong impression.

Hot, freshly-brewed tea (Earl Grey is especially suitable), milk and fine lemon slices (served with tongs from a pretty arrangement on a saucer) should be provided. For those who do not like tea, fresh coffee and a light soft drink such as fresh, iced lemonade or elderflower cordial may be made available. Soft drinks are best served in jugs with citrus slices, borage flowers or sprigs of mint as garnishes. If the weather is very cold, warm, spiced apple juice may be served as the soft alternative.

A large bowl or basket of fresh fruit and several small arrangements of flowers and foliage make good table adornments.

A mixture of savoury and sweet dishes comprise the food for this civilised social occasion.

SAVOURY ITEMS

Cucumber sandwiches made with fresh, good white sliced bread with the crusts removed and crisp cucumber. Butter both sides, not too thinly, and add salt and freshly ground pepper. Do not use margarine under any circumstances – butter provides a much superior flavour and is essential on both inner surfaces of such items as cucumber sandwiches to prevent the bread absorbing water from the filling. Seasoning can make the difference between bland and delicious.

Note: Assemble all sandwiches just before consumption to avoid limpness.

- Smoked salmon slices served with wedges of lemon, freshly ground pepper and soft wholemeal or Irish Soda Bread (page 155) and butter
- Cheese Straws (page 50), served warm
- Cheese Scones (page 204), served warm with butter
- Gentleman's Relish (an anchovy spread available from delicatessens and good supermarkets) on toast
- Scotch Woodcock (page 45) or Welsh Rarebit (page 47)
- Scotch Eggs (page 42)

SWEET ITEMS

- Toasted Crumpets (page 154) or English Muffins (page 12) with butter and jam. These are particularly good if guests are allowed to toast the bread themselves (on a long-handled silver toasting fork) over the flames of an open fire.
- Pastries – Pastry Horns (page 159), other patisserie
- Cakes – particularly plain cakes such as Madeira Cake (page 182), Victoria Sponge (page 183) or Battenberg Cake (page 198)
- Scones (page 204), butter, strawberry jam and clotted cream

PICNICS

The word picnic seems to have entered the English language in about 1748, but there are no clear explanations about its origins. At first, it meant a feast to which all members of the party contributed a dish. In the early nineteenth century, it came to mean trifling or inconsequential, but soon became associated with outdoor eating parties.

Al fresco celebrations had been popular for hundreds of years, and in the eighteenth century the fashion for elaborate gardens and parks laid out with pavilions, follies, grottoes, temples and arbours, increased the popularity of elegant parties in the fresh air.

By Queen Victoria's reign, the desire to enjoy open countryside encouraged expeditions to rugged moorland, archaeological ruins and beauty spots quite far from home. Improved rail services and increased wealth allowed many to experience the pleasure of travel, and picnics became all the rage. On their visits to places of interest, the travelling public usually took their lunch with them, and hampers were filled with elaborate dishes of meat and fish, pies, cakes, wines and spirits.

Shooting parties also became very popular among the Victorian landed gentry. Such outings had originally been restricted to farmers, whose lunch would have been simply bread and cheese. When gentlemen developed a taste for the sport, their midday meal took on the proportions of a banquet. Silver, china and linen were sometimes brought from the main house and laid out on long trestle tables. Vast quantities of food were consumed at these five-course luncheons that often lasted for about an hour and a half.

As long ago as the 1870s, some of the railway companies offered luncheon hampers and three shillings purchased chicken, ham, salad, bread, cheese, butter, and a bottle of wine in a sturdy, returnable wicker basket. Early picnic hampers tended to contain a teapot and burner as well as a cutlery, crockery and containers for food.

Today's picnics can take advantage of chiller bags, vacuum flasks, ice packs and airtight containers so that our meals in the fresh air are easier to transport and can be as sumptuous as those extravagant Victorian repasts.

PACKING A PICNIC

When deciding on a picnic menu, choose dishes that are reasonably easy to transport, and follow these basic tips:

- Pack any spillable items such as salads, pasta dishes and casseroles, into rigid containers with tightly-fitting lids and transport in an upright position.
- Pack salad dressing separately in airtight, screw-topped bottles. Just before serving, shake vigorously and pour over salad.
- Wrap cold meats and fish in cling film or foil.
- Carry hot soups in wide-necked vacuum flasks.
- Transport tarts and quiches on sturdy plates covered with cling film or foil and packed inside a box or tin.
- Leave meat loaves, mousses and pâtés in the containers in which they were made.
- Wrap breads and sandwiches tightly in two layers of cling film.
- Carry cakes and biscuits in airtight tins or boxes.
- Transport bottles in a rigid container and surround with ice packs.

PICNIC ESSENTIALS

As well as all the food, the following are essential:

- Plates, knives, forks, spoons, serving spoons, serving knives, salad servers and large salad bowl, wine glasses, tumblers or beakers, cups and saucers
- A bottle opener
- Stoppers for unfinished bottles
- Salt, pepper and mustard, and any other sauces and chutneys
- Tea, coffee, a vacuum flask of boiling water, milk, sugar
- Garnishes for food
- Ice cubes in a wide-necked thermos flask
- Linen or paper napkins
- Damp flannels or towels to wipe sticky fingers
- Ice packs to keep the food cool in transit
- Waterproof sheeting and blankets to sit in, and a few cushions
- A pretty tablecloth on which to display the food
- Insect repellent and antihistamine cream
- A rubbish bag

ADVICE FROM MRS BEETON

Bill of Fare for a picnic for 40 persons:

A joint of cold roast beef, a joint of cold boiled beef, 2 ribs of lamb, 4 roast fowls, 2 roast ducks, 1 ham, 1 tongue, 2 veal and ham pies, 2 pigeon pies, 6 medium-sized lobsters, 1 piece of collared calf's head, 18 lettuces, 6 baskets of salad, 6 cucumbers.

Stewed fruit, well sweetened, 3 or 4 dozen plain pastry biscuits, 2 dozen fruit turnovers, 4 dozen cheesecakes, 2 cold cabinet puddings, 2 blancmanges, a few jam puffs, 1 large cold plum pudding, a few baskets of fresh fruit, 3 dozen plain biscuits, a piece of cheese, 6 lbs of butter, 4 quartern loaves, 3 dozen rolls, 6 loaves of tin bread, 2 plain plum cakes, 2 pound cakes, 2 sponge cakes, a tin of mixed biscuits, ½ lb of tea.

Things not to be forgotten at a picnic:

A stick of horseradish, a bottle of mint sauce well corked, a bottle of salad dressing, a bottle of vinegar, made mustard, pepper, salt, good oil, and pounded sugar. If it can be managed, take a little ice. It is scarcely necessary to say that plates, tumblers, wine-glasses, knives, forks and spoons must not be forgotten; as also teacups and saucers, 3 or 4 teapots, some lump sugar and milk. Take three corkscrews.

Beverages:
3 dozen quart bottles of ale, ginger beer, soda water, and lemonade, of each 2 dozen bottles; 6 bottles of sherry, 6 bottle of claret, champagne, and any other light wine that may be preferred, and 2 bottles of brandy.

Mrs Beeton, *Book of Household Management*, 1861

THE PERFECT SANDWICH

The sandwich is said to have been invented in 1764 by John Montague, the 4th Earl of Sandwich. During one of his 24-hour sessions at the gambling table, he asked his servant to bring him two slices of bread with a slice of beef between so that he would not have to leave the game.

For perfect sandwiches:
- Always use bread that is 12–24 hours old (use rolls as fresh as possible) and chill for 30 minutes before slicing.
- Soften butter before spreading and spread right up to the edges of each slice.
- Fill sandwiches generously and add salt and pepper to taste.
- Press each sandwich well together and place a hand on top to hold firm; slip the knife between hand and sandwich and cut into the required shape.
- Store in cling film or foil until needed. The best results are obtained when the sandwiches are made as near to the time of eating as possible.

SUNDAY ROAST

During the first half of the nineteenth century the pattern of meal times for the wealthy began to change. The poor, working classes continued to breakfast, lunch and dine on whatever food they could get, but by the mid 1860s, meals for the increasingly wealthy upper classes became larger and more elaborate. Breakfast, which had in previous centuries been taken at 9 or 10 in the morning was now eaten at 8, and was a hearty affair. Lunch remained a fairly light meal at about 1 o'clock. If a lady was alone she sometimes ate with her children, or had soup and a sandwich on her own. If she was entertaining, dishes would have been dainty rather than filling.

Dinner until the first decade of the nineteenth century had usually been served at 5 or 6 o'clock in the evening, but because of the demands of the work routine, the establishment of gentlemen's clubs which kept the men from their homes until well into the evening, and because of the amount of visiting done, dinner was now served at 8, 9 or 10 o'clock. In the eighteenth century, a family dinner would have consisted of three or four savoury dishes and two desserts. A formal dinner, however, consisted of two complete meals. One set out after the other, from which guests selected a variety of sweet and savoury foods. This changed in Victorian times to a grand repast where dishes of the same type were served together – soups and fish, then roast meats and made-up dishes, then vegetables and sweets and finally dessert. There were up to seven courses, and even a modest dinner for six or seven people could involved thirteen or fourteen dishes plus desserts.

Supper dances and receptions were also popular and played a major part in Victorian nightlife. The food at these was generally a cold buffet of salmon mayonnaise, lobster patties, poultry, tongue, fancy sandwiches, trifles, jellies, creams and cakes. In contrast a family supper would have been a simple affair of cold meats, stewed fruit, cheese and biscuits.

In all these eating activities the servants obviously played a major part – setting tables, folding napkins, polishing silver, arranging flowers, cooking the food, serving the food and attending at table. Their work started well before breakfast and ended when the last family member had retired for the night. But, on Sunday afternoons they were usually given a free half-day, so a full meal was cooked and served for the family at lunchtime, and then the servants disappeared to enjoy their short time of freedom. Cook left ready a cold supper which the family could manage without help, and so the tradition of Sunday lunch began. Many families around Britain still sit down together at Sunday lunchtime to enjoy a roast meal and all the traditional trimmings.

SELECTING GOOD MEAT

Beef – look for red, marbled meat with as little fat as possible; any fat should be a pale creamy colour, and the meat should be firm and elastic and scarcely moisten the fingers.

Veal – choose white or very pale pink, firm meat with bubbly tissue between the muscles. Any fat should be firm and white.

Mutton – fresh meat should be a cherry red and firmer than beef; fast should be white, firm and waxy; if the flesh remains creased when pinched it is old and will be tough.

Lamb – look for lean, firm meat with pearly, white fat.

Pork – this should be smooth, form and pale pink with firm fat and a smooth, thin rind; reject all meat with a tinge of red.

Ham – choose a ham that does not have too much fat, and what fat there is should be white, not yellow; the lean should not be too dark or too soft.

Poultry – the flesh should be firm and thick, look for small-boned, plump birds with some fat; the breast bone, wing tips and feet should be pliable, the legs smooth and the skin white and soft. Frozen poultry must be completely thawed before cooking.

CARVING

For successful carving it is most important to have a sharp knife. The cuts should be direct, sharp and incisive. It is also very important that the joint is served on a plate that is big enough to give the carver ample room for manoeuvre.

Meat is usually cut across the grain except with a saddle of lamb or mutton, which is carved at right angles to the rib bones.

Here are some hints for the more difficult joints of meat:

Ribs of beef – cut slices off the side, starting at the thick end and cutting through to the other end.

Leg of pork – cut down to the bone and run the knife between bone and meat to ease the slices out.

Loin of pork – always ensure the crackling is well-scored.

Leg of lamb – start in the middle and cut down to the bone.

Chicken – insert the fork into the breast and cut down between the body and the thigh. Detach the leg by twisting the knife. Remove the wings, lifting off with them some of the breast meat. Slice the breast.

Breakfast

A variety of ways to cook an egg, plus recipes ranging from the simple (porridge) to those verging on full meals (kedgeree).

EGGS

BOILED

Bring the eggs to room temperature to avoid cracking. An extra precaution is to make a very small hole at the rounded end with a skewer or a sharp knife point. Care must be taken not to make the hole too large. Egg-prickers can also be purchased.

Bring a small saucepan of water to the boil, allowing enough water to cover the eggs. Place an egg on a spoon and lower it into the water. Begin timing as soon as the egg is in the water. Regulate the heat so that the water is just boiling. Timing for boiled eggs is very personal, but the following provides a guide when cooking average sized eggs (medium, sizes 3–4): soft-boiled (soft set white) 3¼ minutes, medium (soft yolk, firm white) 4–4¾ minutes, hard (firm white, just firm yolk) 10 minutes.

FRIED

Heat a thin layer of oil or half oil and half butter in a frying pan. Bacon fat may be used instead or this may be combined with oil. Crack an egg into a saucer then slide it into the hot fat. Cook over moderate heat, spooning the fat over the egg, until the white is set and the yolk is covered with a lightly set white film. For a firmer set, baste and cook for longer or use a fish slice to turn the egg over as soon as the white is set firmly underneath, Cook for a further 30–60 seconds before serving – this gives a yolk which is set. A soft fried egg is usually ready in 2–3 minutes; slightly sooner if basted often.

POACHED

Pour 5 cm / 2 inches water into a pan – a frying pan is ideal. Add 15 ml / 1 tbsp cider vinegar and bring just to simmering point. Crack a fresh egg on to a saucer. Use a draining spoon to swirl the water in the pan, then slide the egg into the middle of the gentle swirl. (The swirling water gives the egg a good shape.) Simmer for about 3 minutes, or until the egg is set. Spoon the simmering water over the egg to set it evenly. Up to four eggs may be cooked at the same time in a frying pan. Use a slotted spoon to drain the eggs as they are cooked. Trim the edges of the whites and serve at once.

SCRAMBLED

Allow two eggs per person. Put the requisite number of eggs in a bowl. Add 15–30 ml / 1–2 tbsp milk or cream for each pair of eggs. Season to taste and beat the mixture lightly.

Melt a little butter in a small saucepan over a low heat. There should be just enough butter to cover the bottom of the saucepan. Pour in the eggs. Cook gently, stirring or whisking all the time, until the eggs are lightly set and creamy. Remove from the heat and serve at once. If the eggs are allowed to stand in the hot pan, or are left on the heat, they will become hard and rubbery, eventually separating into curds and a thin liquid.

MRS BEETON'S TIP

*Half a finely chopped onion may be fried in
the butter until golden, before adding the eggs.
A little grated cheese makes an excellent topping.
Cold smoked salmon goes famously well with
scrambled eggs, served with lemon wedges
and hot wholemeal toast.*

ENGLISH MUFFINS

*The correct way to serve muffins is to split each one open around
the edges almost to the centre. Toast slowly on both sides so that
the heat penetrates to the centre, then pull the muffin halves apart,
butter thickly, put together again and serve at once.*

**400 g / 14 oz strong white flour
5 ml / 1 tsp salt
25 g / 1 oz butter or margarine
225 ml / 7½ fl oz milk
10 ml / 2 tsp dried yeast
1 egg
fat for frying**

Sift the flour and salt into a large bowl. Rub in the butter or margarine. Place
the milk in a saucepan and warm gently. It should be just hand-hot. Pour the
milk into a small bowl, sprinkle the dried yeast on top and leave for 10–15
minutes until frothy. Beat in the egg.

Add the yeast liquid to the flour to make a very soft dough. Beat the dough by
hand or with a wooden spoon for about 5 minutes until smooth and shiny. Cover
the bowl with a large lightly oiled polythene bag and leave in a warm place for
1–2 hours or until doubled in bulk. Beat again lightly.

Roll out on a well floured surface to a thickness of about 1 cm / ½ inch. Using
a plain 7.5 cm / 3 inch cutter, cut the dough into rounds. Place the rounds on
a floured baking sheet, cover with polythene and leave to rise for about
45 minutes or until light and puffy.

Heat a griddle or heavy-bottomed frying pan, then grease it. Cook the muffins
on both sides for about 8 minutes until golden.

MAKES TWENTY

GRILLED KIPPERS

4 kippers, preferably naturally smoked
20 ml / 4 tsp butter
4 pats of butter, chilled, to serve
chopped parsley to garnish

Lay the kippers flat, skin side up, in the base of the grill pan. Do not place on a rack. Grill under high heat for 3 minutes. Turn the kippers over, dot each one with 5 ml / 1 tsp butter and grill for 3 minutes more. A crispier fish can be achieved by longer grilling. Serve on warmed plates, topping each portion with a pat of chilled butter and a sprinkling of chopped parsley.

SERVES FOUR

JUGGED KIPPERS

4 kippers
4 pats of butter, ½ a lemon and chopped parsley to garnish

Put the kippers, tail end up, in a tall, heatproof jug. Pour boiling water into the jug to cover all but the tails of the fish. Cover the jug with a cloth and leave to stand for 5 minutes. Tilt the jug gently over a sink and drain off the water (see Mrs Beeton's Tip). Put each kipper on a warmed plate and serve topped with a pat of butter, a squeeze of lemon juice and a sprinkling of chopped parsley.

SERVES FOUR

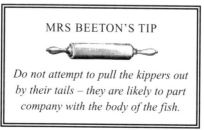

MRS BEETON'S TIP

Do not attempt to pull the kippers out by their tails – they are likely to part company with the body of the fish.

KEDGEREE

No Victorian country-house breakfast would have been complete without kedgeree. Hard-boiled egg and parsley are the traditional garnish, sometimes arranged in the shape of the cross of St Andrew.

150 g / 5 oz long-grain rice
125 ml / 4 fl oz milk
450 g / 1 lb smoked haddock
50 g / 2 oz butter
15 ml / 1 tbsp curry powder
2 hard-boiled eggs, roughly chopped
cayenne pepper to taste
salt and pepper

GARNISH
15 g / ½ oz butter
1 hard-boiled egg, white and yolk sieved separately
15 ml / 1 tbsp chopped parsley

Bring a saucepan of salted water to the boil. Add the rice and cook for 12 minutes. Drain thoroughly, rinse under cold water and drain again. Place the strainer over a saucepan of simmering water to keep the rice warm.

Put the milk in a large shallow saucepan or frying pan with 125 ml / 4 fl oz water. Bring to simmering point, add the fish and poach gently for 4 minutes. Using a slotted spoon and a fish slice, transfer the haddock to a wooden board. Discard the cooking liquid. Remove the skin and any bones from the haddock and break up the flesh into fairly large flakes. Melt half the butter in a large saucepan. Blend in the curry powder and add the flaked fish. Warm the mixture through. Remove from the heat, lightly stir in the chopped eggs; add salt, pepper and cayenne.

Melt the remaining butter in a second pan, add the rice and toss until well coated. Add more salt, pepper and cayenne if required. Add the rice to the fish mixture and mix well. Pile the kedgeree on to a warmed dish, dot with the butter, garnish with sieved hard-boiled egg yolk, egg white and parsley and serve at once.

SERVES FOUR

TRADITIONAL DARK COARSE-CUT MARMALADE

1.5 kg / 3¼ lb Seville oranges (in season January and February)
2 lemons
3 kg / 6½ lb sugar
15 ml / 1 tbsp black treacle

Wash the oranges and lemons. Squeeze the fruit and strain the juice into a preserving pan. Reserve the fruit shells, pulp and pips. Slice the peel into medium-thick shreds, then add it to the pan.

Scrape all the pith from the shells and tie it loosely in a muslin bag with the pulp and the pips. Add to the preserving pan with 4 litres / 8 pints water. Bring the liquid to simmering point and simmer for 1½–2 hours or until the peel is tender and the liquid has reduced by at least one third. Remove from the heat. Squeeze the muslin bag gently over the pan.

Add the sugar and treacle. Return to a low heat and stir until the sugar has dissolved, then bring to the boil and and boil fast until setting point is reached. Remove from the heat and skim quickly.

Leave to cool slightly until a skin forms on the surface of the marmalade. Then stir, pot, and top with waxed paper discs. Cover and label when cold.

MAKES ABOUT 5 kg / 11 lb

MRS BEETON'S TIP

The quickest method of preparing fruit for marmalade is to opt for a chunky style preserve, then simply wash and chop the whole fruit, discarding pips as you work.

PRATIE OATEN

These Irish potato cakes are ideal at breakfast time.

2 cups warm mashed potatoes
1 cup (approx.) fine oatmeal
½ cup melted butter or warm bacon fat / salt

Mix mashed potatoes mixed with fine oatmeal to make a soft dough. Add salt and enough fat to bind. Scatter oatmeal on a board and roll out the dough. Cut into shapes and cook on both sides in a frying pan. Serve hot.

MAKES ABOUT FIFTEEN

PORRIDGE

1 pint / 600 ml water, or half water and half milk
3 oz / 75 g medium-ground oats
pinch of salt / sprinkling of sugar / golden syrup to taste / tot of whisky

Bring the water (or water and milk) to a good rolling boil, preferably in a non-stick pan. Slowly add the oats, stirring vigorously with a wooden spoon all the time. Keep stirring until it returns to the boil, reduce heat, cover pan and simmer very gently for 15 minutes, stirring frequently. Add the salt and simmer, stirring, for a further 5–10 minutes (timing depends on the quality of the oats). It should be a thick but pourable consistency. Serve hot in wooden bowls if you have them.

SERVES THREE

MRS BEETON'S TIP

Scottish tradition requires porridge to be stirred clockwise with a horn spoon and to be eaten standing up. The porridge would be served with communal bowls of cream.

Soups

Economical and easy to make, the soups here range from classic starters to comforting meals-in-a-bowl.

LEEK AND OAT BROTH

The oatmeal is not as evident a flavour in the soup as the recipe might suggest. However, any cook unaccustomed to using oatmeal as a soup thickener may be surprised to discover how well it works, giving a pleasing texture and contributing a slightly nutty flavour.

**1 litre / 1¾ pints pale Chicken (page 229)
or Vegetable Stock (page 232)
3 leeks, trimmed, sliced and washed
1 bay leaf
60 ml / 4 tbsp fine or medium oatmeal
150 ml / ¼ pint single cream
salt and pepper**

Bring the stock and leeks to the boil in a large saucepan. Add the bay leaf and salt and pepper to taste. Lower the heat and simmer for 20 minutes.

Sprinkle the oatmeal into the simmering soup, whisking all the time and simmer for 5 minutes more. Then cover pan and simmer gently for a further 15–20 minutes, until thickened.

Stir in the cream, reheat without boiling and serve at once.

SERVES FOUR

MRS BEETON'S TIP

Quick-cook porridge oats may be substituted for oatmeal and the soup simmered for just 5 minutes before adding the cream.

PARSNIP SOUP

25 g / 1 oz butter
1 onion, chopped
450 g / 1 lb parsnips, sliced
1 litre / 1¾ pints Chicken Stock (page 229) or
Vegetable Stock (page 232)
150 ml / ¼ pint single cream
30 ml / 2 tbsp pine nuts (optional)
salt and cayenne pepper

Melt the butter in a large saucepan, add the onion and parsnips, and cook over gentle heat for 10 minutes, turning frequently to coat them in the butter.

Add the stock, with salt and cayenne pepper to taste. Bring to the boil, lower the heat and simmer for 20 minutes until the parsnips are very soft.

Purée the soup in a blender or food processor, or rub through a sieve into a clean pan. Reheat it to just below boiling point, then stir in most of the cream, reserving about 30 ml / 2 tbsp for the garnish.

Meanwhile spread out the pine nuts (if used) in a grill pan and toast them under a hot grill until golden. Ladle the soup into individual bowls and top each portion with a swirl of cream and a sprinkling of toasted pine nuts.

SERVES FOUR

VARIATION

- **Spiced Parsnip Soup** Add 5 ml / 1 tsp good-quality curry powder to the onion and parsnips when cooking in the butter. Substitute plain yogurt for the cream and use roughly chopped cashew nuts instead of the pine nuts. Sprinkle with chopped fresh coriander leaves, if liked.

CABBAGE SOUP

Cabbage and bacon go wonderfully well together,
a fact that is celebrated in this hearty soup.

15 ml / 1 tbsp oil
175 g / 6 oz rindless streaky bacon rashers
2 carrots, thinly sliced
1 large onion, thinly sliced
1 large cabbage, shredded
1. 1 litres / 2 pints pale Chicken (page 229)
or Vegetable Stock (page 232)
pepper to taste
croûtons to serve (optional)

Heat the oil in a large heavy-bottomed saucepan or flameproof casserole. Add the bacon and cook, stirring, for 5 minutes. Add the carrots and onion, then cook gently for 10 minutes. Stir in the cabbage and add the stock. Bring to the boil, lower the heat and cover the pan. Simmer for 45 minutes, until the vegetables are tender and the soup well flavoured.

Taste the soup for seasoning and add pepper. The bacon usually makes the soup sufficiently salty, depending on the stock. Skim off any excess surface fat, then serve the soup very hot, with croûtons, if liked.

SERVES EIGHT

MRS BEETON'S TIP

If the soup is sightly too salty
when cooked, add 2 peeled and
diced potatoes and simmer for
20–30 minutes, keeping the pan
closely covered.

CARROT SOUP

Grating the vegetables speeds up the cooking time considerably,
making this an ideal soup for those occasions
when time is short.

600 ml / 1 pint Chicken Stock (page 229)
or Vegetable Stock (page 232)
3 carrots, grated
1 onion, finely chopped
1 potato, grated
25 g / 1 oz butter
25 g / 1 oz plain flour
300 ml / ½ pint milk
salt and pepper
grated nutmeg

Combine the stock, carrots, onion and potato in a saucepan. Bring to the boil, lower the heat and simmer for about 15 minutes or until the vegetables are tender.

Meanwhile melt the butter in a separate saucepan, add the flour and cook for 1 minute. Gradually stir in the milk, then add the stock and vegetables. Heat, stirring constantly, until the mixture boils and thickens. Add salt, pepper and nutmeg to taste. Serve at once, with triangles of hot toast, if liked.

SERVES FOUR

VARIATION

- **Carrot and Orange Soup** Cut the carrot into matchstick strips and use a parsnip, cut into similar strips, instead of the potato. Use 900 ml / 1½ pints stock and add 60 ml / 4 tbsp fresh orange juice. Omit the milk and do not thicken the soup.

CREAM OF TOMATO SOUP

25 g / 1 oz butter
2 rindless back bacon rashers, chopped
1 small onion, chopped
1 carrot, chopped
900 g / 2 lb tomatoes, chopped
600 ml / 1 pint pale Chicken (page 229) or
Vegetable Stock (page 232)
1 bouquet garni
10 ml / 2 tsp sugar
300 ml / ½ pint double cream
salt and pepper
chopped parsley or snipped chives to garnish

Melt the butter in a large saucepan, add the bacon and fry for 2–3 minutes. Stir in the onion and carrot and fry over gentle heat for 5 minutes, then add the tomatoes and cook for 5 minutes more.

Add the stock and bouquet garni, with salt and pepper to taste. Bring to the boil, lower the heat and simmer for about 20 minutes, until the vegetables are soft.

Remove the bouquet garni. Purée the soup in a blender or food processor, then rub through a sieve to remove traces of skin and seeds.

Return the soup to the rinsed-out pan. Stir in the sugar and reheat to just below boiling point. Stir in the cream, heat briefly but do not allow to simmer or the soup will curdle. Taste and adjust the seasoning, then serve at once, topped with chopped parsley or snipped chives.

SERVES SIX

CAULIFLOWER SOUP

1 large cauliflower
25 g / 1 oz butter
1 onion, finely chopped
900 ml / 1½ pints milk
2 egg yolks
150 ml / ¼ pint single cream
salt and pepper
50 g / 2 oz flaked almonds, toasted

Steam the cauliflower whole for 20–30 minutes until tender. Cut it into florets, reserving any leaves or tender stems.

Melt the butter in a small frying pan. Add the onion and cook over gentle heat for about 10 minutes, until soft but not coloured. Purée the cauliflower and the onion mixture with 250 ml / 8 fl oz of the milk in a blender or food processor, then rub through a fine sieve into a clean pan.

Stir the remaining milk into the pan, with salt and pepper to taste. Heat the soup to just below boiling point, then lower the heat so that it barely simmers. In a small bowl, mix the egg yolks with the cream. Stir a little of the hot soup into the egg mixture, mix well, then add the contents of the bowl to the soup, stirring over low heat until it thickens. Serve at once, topping each portion with toasted almonds.

SERVES FOUR

MRS BEETON'S TIP

To make a quick cauliflower soup, break the vegetable into florets and place in a saucepan with 1 diced potato and 1 chopped onion. Add 600ml / 1 pint Chicken Stock (page 229) and bring to the boil. Simmer, covered, for 30 minutes, then purée. Add 300 ml / ½ pint milk and seasoning to taste. Heat without boiling.

BEAN SOUP

The perfect warmer for a chilly winter's night,
this soup is a meal in itself.

450 g / 1 lb haricot beans, soaked overnight in water to cover
100 g / 4 oz fat bacon, diced
2 onions, sliced
10 ml / 2 tsp dried thyme
salt and pepper
15 ml / 1 tbsp chopped parsley

Drain the beans. Put them in a large heavy-bottomed saucepan. Add 2.25 litres / 4 pints water and bring to the boil. Boil vigorously for 10 minutes, then lower the heat and simmer for 45 minutes or until the beans are almost tender. Drain, reserving the bean stock.

Put the bacon in the clean pan and heat gently until the fat runs. Add the onions and fry over moderate heat for 3–4 minutes. Stir in the beans with the thyme. Add the reserved bean stock, with salt and pepper to taste. Simmer for 1 hour, stirring occasionally to prevent the soup from sticking to the pan.

Check the seasoning and add more salt and pepper if required. Stir in the parsley and serve at once, with chunks of wholemeal bread.

SERVES SIX TO EIGHT

VARIATIONS

- **Two-bean Soup** Use half red kidney beans instead of haricot beans alone. Add 1 diced green pepper with the onions.
- **Vegetarian Bean Soup** Omit the bacon and fry the onion in 25 g / 1 oz butter with 1 crushed garlic clove. Stir in 45 ml / 3 tbsp tahini with the parsley.

YELLOW SPLIT PEA SOUP

30 ml / 2 tbsp oil
6 rindless streaky bacon rashers, chopped
1 large onion, finely chopped
100 g / 4 oz yellow split peas, soaked overnight in water to cover
2 litres / 3½ pints Chicken Stock (page 229)
or Vegetable Stock (page 232)
60 ml / 4 tbsp chopped celery leaves
2 parsley sprigs & 2 bay leaves
5 ml / 1 tsp chopped summer savory or 2.5 ml / ½ tsp dried savory
salt and pepper

Heat the oil in a large saucepan. Add the bacon and onion. Fry for 10 minutes over gentle heat, until the onion is soft but not coloured.

Drain the split peas and add them to the pan with the stock, celery leaves, parsley, bay leaves and savory. Add salt and pepper to taste. Bring to the boil, lower the heat and simmer for about 2 hours, or until the peas are very tender. If the soup becomes too thick, add water or extra stock.

Remove the parsley sprigs and bay leaves. Serve the soup as it is, or purée in a blender or food processor. Alternatively, rub through a sieve into a clean pan. Reheat, stirring frequently to prevent the soup from sticking to the pan, and serve at once.

SERVES FOUR TO SIX

FRESH ASPARAGUS SOUP

450 g / 1 lb fresh asparagus
salt and white pepper
1.4 litres / 2 pints Chicken Stock (page 229)
or Vegetable Stock (page 232)
50 g / 2 oz butter
1 small onion, chopped
50 g / 2 oz plain flour
1 egg yolk
150 ml / 1 pint double cream

Cut off asparagus tips and place in a saucepan. Add salted water to cover, bring to the boil, then simmer for about 5 minutes or until tender. Drain and set aside.

Slice the asparagus stalks and cook them in 600 ml / 1 pint of the stock for about 15 minutes or until tender. Purée in a blender or food processor, or rub through a sieve into a bowl or large jug.

Melt the butter in a large saucepan, add the onion and fry over gentle heat for about 10 minutes until soft but not coloured. Stir in the flour and cook for 1 minute, stirring constantly.

Gradually add the remaining stock, stirring until the mixture boils and thickens. Stir in the asparagus purée, with salt and pepper to taste. Reheat.

In a small bowl, mix the egg yolk with the cream. Stir a little of the hot soup into the egg mixture, mix well, then add the contents of the bowl to the soup, stirring over low heat until the mixture thickens slightly. Add the reserved asparagus tips and heat through without boiling. Serve at once.

SERVES SIX

SPINACH SOUP

25 g / 1 oz butter
1 large onion, finely chopped
1. 1 litres / 2 pints Chicken Stock (page 229)
or Vegetable Stock (page 232)
2 potatoes, diced
900 g / 2 lb spinach, washed, trimmed and roughly chopped
2.5 ml / ½ tsp grated nutmeg
salt and pepper
150 ml / ¼ pint single cream
2 rindless back bacon rashers, grilled and crumbled,
to garnish (optional)

Melt the butter, add the onion and cook over gentle heat for 10 minutes until soft but not coloured. Add the stock and potatoes and cook for 15 minutes.

Add the spinach and cook for 10 minutes more or until both potatoes and spinach are tender. Purée the soup in a blender or food processor, or rub through a sieve into a clean pan. Add the nutmeg, with salt and pepper to taste.

Stir in the cream and reheat without boiling. Serve the soup in individual bowls, topping each portion with crumbled bacon, if liked.

SERVES FOUR

VARIATION

- **Green and Gold Soup** Fry the onion in the butter as described above. Meanwhile cook the spinach with just the water that clings to the leaves after washing. Drain thoroughly, pressing the spinach against the sides of the colander with a wooden spoon to extract as much liquid as possible, then mix the spinach with the onion mixture. Form into egg-sized balls. Bring the stock to the boil. Spoon a few spinach balls into each soup bowl, add the boiling stock and serve at once.

SOUTHWOLD COD SOUP

25 g / 1 oz butter
20 ml / 4 tsp olive oil
2 large onions, thinly sliced
1 large carrot, thinly sliced
2 celery sticks, thinly sliced
225 g / 8 oz potatoes, peeled and diced
5 ml / 1 tsp curry powder
1 bouquet garni
575 g / 1¼ lb cod fillet, skinned and cut into small pieces
45 ml / 3 tbsp white wine (optional)
25 g / 1 oz cornflour
125 ml / 4 fl oz milk
75 ml / 5 tbsp single cream
salt and pepper

Melt the butter in the oil in a deep saucepan. Add the vegetables and fry for 10 minutes.

Stir in the curry powder and cook for 3 minutes. Stir in 750 ml / 1¼ pints boiling water. Add the bouquet garni, with salt and pepper to taste. Add the fish and bring the soup back to simmering point. Cover and simmer for 3–5 minutes until the fish is tender.

Using a slotted spoon, transfer the best pieces of fish to a bowl. Ladle in a little of the soup stock and keep hot.

Reduce the remaining soup by simmering, uncovered, for 15 minutes. Remove the bouquet garni. Rub the soup through a sieve into a clean pan, or process in a blender or food processor. Add the wine, if used, and reheat.

Meanwhile, blend the cornflour with a little of the milk in a bowl. Stir in the rest of the milk. Add the mixture to the soup, stirring constantly. Bring to the boil and cook for 2–3 minutes, stirring constantly. Add the fish, remove the pan from the heat and stir in the cream. Serve at once.

SERVES SIX

COCK-A-LEEKIE

100 g / 4 oz dried prunes
450 g / 1 lb leeks, trimmed, sliced and washed
1 x 1.4 kg / 3 lb chicken
3 rindless streaky bacon rashers, chopped
2.5 ml / ½ tsp salt
1 bouquet garni
1.25 ml / ¼ tsp pepper

Soak the prunes overnight in a small bowl of water, then drain them and remove the stones. Set aside, with about one-third of the drained leek slices.

Put the chicken, with its giblets if available, and bacon in a deep saucepan. Add cold water to cover (about 2 litres / 3½ pints). Stir in the salt and bring slowly to simmering point.

Add the remaining leeks to the pan, with the bouquet garni and pepper. Cover, then simmer gently for about 3 hours or until the chicken is cooked through and tender.

Carefully remove the chicken, discard the skin and giblets, if used, then carve off the meat and cut it into fairly large serving pieces. Return the chicken meat to the soup and add the reserved prunes and leeks. Simmer gently for about 30 minutes, until the prunes are cooked but not broken. Skim off surface fat and check seasoning before serving.

SERVES SIX TO EIGHT

MRS BEETON'S TIP

Ready-to-eat dried prunes
may be used. There is no
need to presoak them.

HODGE-PODGE

450 g / 1 lb shin of beef, diced
300 ml / ½ pint bitter beer or mild ale
2 onions, chopped
2 carrots, diced
2 turnips, diced
1 head of celery, sliced
salt and pepper
40 g / 1½ oz butter
25 g / 1 oz plain flour

Place the beef, beer and 1.25 litres / 2¼ pints water in a large saucepan and bring to the boil. Skim the surface, then add the vegetables and plenty of seasoning. Reduce the heat and cover the pan. Simmer gently for 3 hours, until the meat is thoroughly tender.

Cream the butter and flour to a paste. Stir into the soup and bring to the boil. Simmer for 3 minutes, check the seasoning and serve.

SERVES SIX

SCOTCH BROTH

This economical soup was originally intended to furnish two meals:
the meat was removed after cooking and served separately.
Today it is more usual to cut up the meat and add it to the soup.

25 g / 1 oz pearl barley
450 g / 1 lb middle neck of lamb, trimmed of excess fat
1.4 litres / 2½ pints pale Chicken Stock (page 229) or
Vegetable Stock (page 232)
1 onion, chopped
1 leek, trimmed, sliced and washed
2 carrots, sliced
1 swede, cubed
salt and pepper

Put the barley in a small saucepan with water to cover. Bring to the boil, then drain off the water and transfer the barley to a large pan with the meat and stock. Bring the mixture to the boil, skim off any scum on the surface, then lower the heat and simmer gently for 2 hours.

Add the vegetables with plenty of salt and pepper. Simmer for a further 45–60 minutes. Lift out the meat, remove it from the bones, and roughly chop it. Skim off any fat from the broth, add more salt and pepper if required, then replace the chopped meat. Serve very hot.

SERVES FOUR

PRESSURE COOKER TIP

It is not necessary to blanch the barley. Simply
combine the ingredients in the cooker, reducing the
amount of stock to 900ml / 1½ pints. The cooker should
not be more than half full. Put the lid on, bring to
15 lb pressure and cook for 10 minutes. Reduce the
pressure slowly. Continue as above, reheating the soup
in the open pan, and adding more stock if liked.

OXTAIL SOUP

Prepare this soup a day ahead and refrigerate it overnight.
This will not only allow the full flavour to develop, but will also
permit the removal of the fat that solidifies on the surface.

1.4 kg / 3 lb oxtail, jointed
25 g / 1 oz beef dripping or 30 ml / 2 tbsp oil
1 onion, sliced
2 large carrots, sliced
1 small turnip, diced
2 celery sticks, sliced
2 litres / 3¼ pints Rich Strong Stock (page 227),
Vegetable Stock (page 232), or water
5 ml / 1 tsp salt
6 black peppercorns
1 bouquet garni
15g / ½ oz butter
15 ml / 1 tbsp plain flour
chopped parsley to garnish

Wash the oxtail, dry it thoroughly and trim off any excess fat. Cut it into joints, if not already jointed by the butcher, and divide the thick parts in half. Heat the fat in a large saucepan, add the oxtail and fry until the meat is browned.

Remove the oxtail pieces and set them aside. Add the vegetables to the fat remaining in the pan and fry, stirring occasionally, for about 10 minutes until lightly browned. Drain off excess fat from the pan.

Return the oxtail pieces to the pan. Add the stock, salt, peppercorns and bouquet garni. Bring to the boil, skim the surface, then lower the heat and simmer the soup for 3–4 hours. Strain into a clean pan, discarding the bouquet garni and flavouring vegetables. Return the meat and bones to the pan. Cool quickly, then refrigerate overnight.

Next day, lift off the fat from the surface of the soup. Remove the oxtail meat from the bones, chop it finely and return it to the pan. Heat the soup to simmering point, taste and add salt and pepper if required.

In a cup, blend the butter with the flour. Gradually add small pieces of the mixture to the soup, stirring thoroughly after each addition and for about 5 minutes after all the butter mixture has been added. Serve in individual bowls, garnished with chopped parsley.

SERVES SIX TO EIGHT

VARIATION

• **Mrs Beeton's Rich Oxtail Soup** Dice 225 g / 8 oz raw gammon and add with the vegetables. Add 3 cloves with the peppercorns. Finally, stir in 30 ml / 2 tbsp Mushroom Ketchup (page 239) and 60–90 ml / 4–6 tbsp port before serving the soup.

MRS BEETON'S MULLIGATAWNY SOUP

25 g / 1 oz butter
30 ml / 2 tbsp oil
1 chicken, skinned and jointed, or 900 g / 2 lb chicken portions
4 rindless back bacon rashers, chopped
3 onions, sliced
1 garlic clove, crushed
15 ml / 1 tbsp mild curry powder
25 g / 1 oz ground almonds
2 litres / 3 ½ pints Chicken Stock (page 229)
75 g / 6 oz red lentils
salt and pepper
hot boiled rice to serve

Heat the butter and oil in a large, heavy-bottomed saucepan. Add the chicken and brown the joints all over, then remove them from the pan and set aside. Add the bacon, onions and garlic to the fat remaining in the pan and cook over gentle heat for 5 minutes, then stir in the curry powder and cook for 2 minutes more.

In a small bowl, mix the ground almonds to a paste with a little of the stock. Set aside. Add the remaining stock to the pan and return the chicken joints. Bring to the boil, lower the heat and simmer for 1 hour or until the chicken is tender.

Remove the chicken and cut the meat off the bones, then set aside. Skim any fat off the soup. Add the lentils and bring back to the boil. Reduce the heat, cover and simmer the soup for 30 minutes.

Stir the almond paste into the pan and replace the chicken meat. Simmer for a further 5–10 minutes. Taste for seasoning before serving very hot, with boiled rice.

SERVES EIGHT

Starters
& Savouries

*Potted delicacies, canapés, variations
on toasted cheese and satisfying
snacks for busy people.*

POTTED BEEF

*Before the days of refrigerators, potted meat was something of a preserve.
Mrs Beeton actually pointed out that 'if much gravy' was added to the meat
it would keep for only a short time, whereas 'if a large portion of butter is
used, it may be preserved for some time.' Potted beef can be stored in the
refrigerator for up to a week and is served like a pâté for a first course or
as a light meal. It also makes an extremely tasty sandwich filling.*

**900 g / 2 lb lean braising steak
pinch of cayenne pepper
2.5 ml / ½ tsp ground mace
100 g / 4 oz Clarified Butter (see Mrs Beeton's Tip)
salt and black pepper**

Cut the steak into cubes and place in a large pudding basin which is suitable for
boiling. Sprinkle with plenty of salt and pepper, a good pinch of cayenne and the
mace. Add a quarter of the butter to the meat with 15 ml / 1 tbsp water.

Cover the basin with double-thick foil, folding it firmly around the rim to make
a good seal. Stand the basin in a large saucepan and pour in boiling water from
a kettle to come about two-thirds of the way up the outside of the basin. Bring
the water to the boil, then reduce the heat so that the water boils steadily, but
not so vigorously that it knocks the basin off balance. Cover the pan. Cook the
beef for 3½ hours, topping up with water as necessary.

Remove the basin from the pan and set it aside to cool, covered, for about
30 minutes. When the meat is cool enough, mince or process in a food processor
until very fine. Add the cooking juices from the bowl as you process the meat.

MRS BEETON'S TIP

*To clarify butter, heat gently until melted, then stand
for 2–3 minutes. Carefully pour the clear yellow liquid
on top into a clean bowl, leaving the residue behind.*

Melt the remaining clarified butter and stir it into the beef. Taste the mixture for seasoning before dividing it between ramekins or small pots, or turning it into a single dish. Press the meat down well with a palette knife or the back of a spoon, then cover and leave to cool. Chill overnight before using.

SERVES SIX TO EIGHT

MRS BEETON'S TIP

Originally, Mrs Beeton cooked the meat in one piece. The butter and seasonings were added to the pounded or minced and sieved cooked meat, with sufficient cooking liquor to give the required texture. Cooking the seasonings with the meat gives it an excellent flavour as they can otherwise taste quite harsh.

POTTED SALMON

450 g / 1 lb cold cooked salmon, skinned and boned
pinch of cayenne pepper
pinch of ground mace
anchovy essence
50 g / 2 oz softened Clarified Butter,
plus extra for sealing (page 36)
salt and pepper

Pound the salmon flesh in a mortar or process roughly in a blender or food processor. Add salt, pepper, cayenne, mace and anchovy essence to taste. Blend in the softened clarified butter thoroughly. Rub the mixture through a fine sieve into a bowl. Turn into small pots. Cover with a layer of clarified butter and refrigerate until the butter is firm.

MAKES ABOUT 450 g / 1 lb

POTTED SHRIMPS

225 g / 8 oz unsalted butter
450 g / 1 lb peeled cooked shrimps or prawns
1.25 ml / ¼ tsp ground white pepper
1.25 ml / ¼ tsp ground mace
1.25 ml / ¼ tsp ground cloves
dill sprigs to garnish

Melt the butter in a saucepan, add the shrimps or prawns and heat very gently, without boiling. Add the pepper, mace and cloves. Using a slotted spoon, transfer the shrimps or prawns to small pots. Pour a little of the hot spiced butter into each pot. Set the remaining spiced butter aside until the residue has settled, then pour over the shrimps or prawns. Chill until the butter is firm. Store in a refrigerator for no more than 48 hours. Garnish with dill.

MAKES ABOUT 675 g / 1½ lb

HOT CRAB

1 dressed crab or about 150 g / 5 oz crab meat
100 g / 4 oz fresh white breadcrumbs
grated nutmeg
75 g / 3 oz butter
30 ml / 2 tbsp cider vinegar
salt and pepper

Flake the crab meat and mix it with the breadcrumbs. Season the mixture with freshly grated nutmeg, salt and pepper. Dice the butter and mix it into the crab with the cider vinegar. Divide the mixture between four clean, dry shells or gratin dishes. Place the dishes under the grill, keeping them well away from the heat source, then turn the grill down to a medium setting. Grill the crab mixture from cold, until it has heated through and is crisp and brown on top. Serve at once.

SERVES FOUR

VARIATION

- **Crab-filled Mushrooms** The hot crab can be served as a filling for open cup mushrooms. Remove the stalks from four large mushroom caps and brush the curved tops with a little melted butter. Grill the tops for about 3 minutes, then turn them over and divide the crab mixture between them. Continue grilling them slowly, as in the main recipe, until the filling is crisp and browned on top and the mushrooms cooked. A little warm crusty bread may be served to mop up the juices from the mushrooms.

PRINCESS SANDWICHES

175 g / 6 oz cooked chicken, finely chopped
75 g / 3 oz cooked ham, finely chopped
15 ml / 1 tbsp grated cheese
2 hard-boiled yolks
2.5 ml / ½ tsp lemon juice
prepared mustard
olive oil
salt and pepper
thin slices of buttered white bread, to serve

Pound the chicken and ham in a mortar with the cheese and egg yolks, adding lemon juice, mustard, salt and pepper to taste, and sufficient oil to moisten the mixture. Spread on slices of bread and butter, press together well, trim neatly, and cut into required shapes.

SERVES FOUR TO SIX

SPORTSMAN'S SANDWICHES

Toast some 5 mm / ¼ inch thick slices of bread lightly, split them and butter the plain sides. On half of them lay thin slices of cold game, chicken, or meat, spread in a little Tartare Sauce (page 241) seasoned with French mustard, and cover with the remaining slices of bread. Press together well, trim neatly, and cut into squares. Wrap them in lettuce leaves, and finally in cling film or foil.

OTHER SUGGESTED SANDWICH FILLINGS

- Thin slices of cold roast beef, topped with a thin layer of horseradish sauce.
- A slice of boiled ham spread with red tomato chutney.
- Softened cream cheese mixed with canned crushed pineapple and finely chopped preserved ginger.
- Thick slices of banana sprinkled with coarsely grated chocolate.
- A layer of cottage cheese, covered with a layer of fresh strawberries or raspberries sprinkled with caster sugar.

SAVOURY BUTTERS

Spread the slices of bread with savoury butters to complement the filling:

- **Anchovy** – cream 100 g / 4 oz butter well with 5 ml / 1 tsp anchovy essence and season lightly with cayenne.
- **Green** – cream 100 g / 4 oz butter well, then beat in 15–30 ml / 1–2 tbsp finely chopped parsley, 15 ml / 1 tbsp lemon juice, anchovy essence and salt and pepper to taste.
- **Mustard** – cream 100 g / 4 oz butter well, then mix in 5 ml / 1 tsp prepared mustard and a little salt.

Also see page 6 for tips on making the perfect sandwich.

ASPARAGUS WITH HOT BUTTER SAUCE

48 asparagus spears, trimmed
175 g / 6 oz butter
white pepper
lemon juice

Cook the asparagus in simmering water in a tall narrow saucepan or on a rack over boiling water in a roasting tin for about 5 minutes, until just tender. Meanwhile, melt the butter. Add pepper and lemon juice to taste and pour over the drained asparagus. Serve eight spears per person.

SERVES SIX

ASPARAGUS ROLLS

12 thin slices of white or brown bread, crusts removed
50 g / 2 oz butter, softened
12 cold cooked asparagus spears
salt and pepper

Flatten the bread slices lightly with a rolling pin. Spread them with butter. Lay an asparagus spear diagonally across each slice of bread. Season to taste, then roll up. Arrange the rolls in a shallow dish, seams underneath. Cover with cling film until required.

SERVES FOUR

SCOTCH EGGS

4 rindless back bacon rashers, finely chopped or minced
50 g / 2 oz shredded suet
175 g / 6 oz fresh white breadcrumbs
grated rind ½ lemon
5 ml / 1 tsp finely chopped parsley
5 ml / 1 tsp finely chopped fresh thyme, marjoram or oregano
generous pinch of ground mace
salt
cayenne pepper
2 eggs, beaten
4 hard-boiled eggs
plain flour for coating
oil for deep frying

Mix the bacon with the suet, half the breadcrumbs, the lemon rind, parsley and thyme, marjoram or oregano. Season the mixture with mace, salt and cayenne to taste, then mix well until thoroughly combined. Stir in about half the beaten egg, or slightly less, to make a forcemeat which binds together and can be shaped by hand. Lightly whisk 10 ml / 2 tsp water into the remaining beaten egg.

Divide the forcemeat into quarters. Dust the hard-boiled eggs with a little flour. Flatten a portion of forcemeat into a circle on the palm of one hand. Place an egg on top and gently mould the forcemeat around the egg to enclose it completely. Try to make the coating as even as possible and ensure that it clings to the egg.

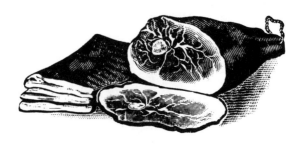

Place the remaining breadcrumbs in a large, shallow dish. Coat the Scotch eggs in a little flour, then roll them in the beaten egg and coat them with breadcrumbs. Press the breadcrumbs on neatly.

Heat the oil for deep frying to 160°C / 325°F or until it will brown a cube of day-old bread in 2 minutes. Fry the Scotch eggs until they are crisp and golden, turning them in the oil, if necessary, so that they cook evenly. They will need about 10 minutes cooking.

Drain the Scotch eggs on absorbent kitchen paper and allow them to stand for 5 minutes. They can be served hot or cold. Cut them lengthways in half or quarters, leaving them until completely cold before cutting if they are to be served cold.

MAKES FOUR

VARIATION

- **Anchovy-crusted Eggs** Substitute anchovies for the bacon in the main recipe. Drain a 50 g / 2 oz can of anchovy fillets, then chop them finely. The grated rind of a whole lemon can be added for a more pronounced flavour, to balance the strength of the anchovy fillets.

MRS BEETON'S TIP

Scotch eggs will keep for a day if chilled when cold; however, do not freeze them as the cooked egg becomes unpleasant, watery and rubbery during freezing and thawing.

BAKED MUSHROOMS

*Baked mushrooms are delicious on slices of hot buttered toast
for breakfast or lunch. For a starter, medium-thick fried croûtes
of bread would be more suitable, or the mushrooms can be served
in individual dishes, sprinkled with parsley and accompanied
by thin slices of wholemeal bread and butter.*

**16 open cup mushrooms
salt and pepper
about 50 g / 2 oz butter**

Set the oven at 200°C / 400°F / gas 6. Trim the tops of the stalks off the mushrooms, leaving only a short length in each cap. Use a piece of absorbent kitchen paper and a little salt to wipe the tops of the mushroom caps, ridding them of any dirt, then stand them, stalks up, in an ovenproof dish.

Season the mushrooms with pepper and place a small knob of butter on top of each cap. Bake the mushrooms for about 20 minutes, until they are well cooked, reduced in size and moist with buttery juices. Towards the end of the cooking time, warm a serving dish for the mushrooms. As soon as they are ready, pile the mushrooms in the dish and pour the cooking juices over the top. Sprinkle lightly with salt and serve at once.

SERVES FOUR

MRS BEETON'S TIP

*Select your mushrooms carefully for
this recipe – they should be large
enough to have lots of flavour. The
very small, partially open mushrooms
that are pale and delicate are better
prepared by other methods.*

SCOTCH WOODCOCK

50 g / 2 oz can anchovy fillets, drained
50 g / 2 oz butter, softened
freshly ground black pepper
150 ml / ¼ pint single cream
3 egg yolks
4 slices hot thick toast

Mash the anchovies with the butter, adding pepper to taste. Heat the cream in a small saucepan but do not let it boil.

Beat the egg yolks, then stir in the cream. When mixture is well combined, return to the pan and cook it over gentle heat, stirring constantly, for a few minutes, until slightly thickened. Remove the saucepan from the heat.

Trim the crusts off the toast and spread it with the anchovy butter. Pour the sauce over and serve at once.

SERVES FOUR

POTTED CHEESE

225 g / 8 oz cheese
40 g / 1½ oz butter
2.5 ml / ½ tsp prepared English mustard

Grate the cheese finely. Soften the butter, if necessary, by beating it. Pound the cheese with the back of a mixing spoon, gradually adding the butter to make a smooth paste. Mix in the mustard and pack the cheese into a pot. Smooth the top of the cheese, cover the pot and chill the cheese until required.

The pounded cheese will keep as well as fresh cheese. Any slightly dry cheese or scraps that are beyond their best will keep for 2–3 days once pounded.

SERVES FOUR TO SIX

CHEESE RAMEKINS

75 g / 3 oz butter, melted
50 g / 2 oz fresh white breadcrumbs
60 ml / 4 tbsp milk
4 eggs, separated
100 g / 4 oz Cheddar cheese, grated
100 g / 4 oz Parmesan cheese, grated
salt and pepper

Set the oven at 190°C / 375°F / gas 5. Grease four ramekin dishes or individual soufflé dishes with a little of the melted butter. Place the breadcrumbs in a mixing bowl, sprinkle them with the milk and set them aside for 5 minutes.

Beat the egg yolks into the breadcrumb mixture with a little seasoning. Beat in both types of cheese.

Whisk the egg whites until they stand in stiff peaks; do not whisk them for too long or they will become dry. Beat the remaining melted butter into the cheese mixture, then beat in about a quarter of the egg whites. Fold in the remaining egg whites lightly but evenly.

Divide the mixture between the prepared dishes and bake the ramekins for about 30 minutes. The mixture should be risen and golden brown. The ramekins must be served immediately they are cooked.

SERVES FOUR

MRS BEETON'S TIP

These are similar to soufflés, but have a slightly firmer texture than creamy, sauce-based soufflés. They make an excellent first course.

WELSH RAREBIT

25 g / 1 oz butter
15 ml / 1 tbsp plain flour
75 ml / 5 tbsp milk or 30 ml / 2 tbsp milk and
45 ml / 3 tbsp ale or beer
5 ml / 1 tsp French mustard
few drops Worcestershire sauce
175 g / 6 oz Cheddar cheese, grated
salt and pepper

Melt the butter in a saucepan, stir in the flour and cook over gentle heat for 2–3 minutes, stirring constantly. Do not let the flour colour. Stir in the milk and blend to a smooth, thick mixture, then stir in the ale or beer, if used. Add the mustard and Worcestershire sauce.

Gradually add the cheese, stirring after each addition. Remove from the heat as soon as the mixture is smooth. Add salt and pepper to taste. Place in a covered container and chill when cool.

To use the rarebit, spread the mixture on buttered toast and place under a preheated hot grill for 2–3 minutes until bubbling and lightly browned. Serve at once.

SERVES FOUR TO SIX

VARIATIONS

- **Buck Rarebit** Make as for Welsh Rarebit, but top each slice with a poached egg.
- **Yorkshire Rarebit** Make as for Welsh rarebit, but add 4 grilled rindless back bacon rashers.

SCOTCH RAREBIT

100 g / 4 oz mature Cheddar cheese, grated
5 ml / 1 tsp prepared English mustard
30 ml / 2 tbsp port
salt and pepper
4 slices of bread

Mix the cheese, mustard and port in a small saucepan. Add seasoning, particularly pepper, as the quantity of salt required will depend on the flavour of the cheese. Stir the mixture over a low heat until the cheese has melted and all the ingredients are fully combined.

Toast the bread completely on one side and lightly on the second side. Trim off the crusts, if liked, and spread the cheese on the lightly toasted side. Grill the topping until it is golden and bubbling, then serve the Scotch rarebit immediately.

SERVES FOUR

CHEESE PASTRIES

oil for greasing
225 g / 8 oz Puff Pastry (page 148)
175 g / 6 oz Cheshire, Stilton or Parmesan cheese, or a
mixture of Parmesan and any mild hard cheese, grated
1 egg yolk

Grease one or two baking sheets. Set the oven at 220°C / 425°F / gas 7.

Roll out the pastry into a rectangle measuring about 25 x 15 cm (10 x 6 inches). Sprinkle half the cheese over the middle of the pastry. Fold the bottom third of the pastry over the cheese, then fold the top third down. Give the pastry a quarter turn clockwise, then press the edges together firmly with the rolling pin and roll it out into a rectangle as before. Repeat with the remaining cheese.

Roll out the pastry to a thickness of about 2.5 mm / ⅛ inch or slightly thicker. Use cutters to stamp out pastry shapes and place them on the baking sheets. Alternatively, cut the pastry into strips, diamond shapes or triangles. Use a palette knife to transfer the pastry shapes to the baking sheets.

Stir 5 ml / 1 tsp water into the egg yolk, then brush it over the pastry shapes. Bake them for 7-10 minutes, until puffed and golden. Serve freshly baked.

MAKES ABOUT TWENTY-FOUR

HOT PEPPER CHEESES

When freshly cooked, these savouries are inclined to crumble and break easily. For this reason it is best to allow them to cool completely, then reheat gently until warm.

butter for greasing
200 g / 7 oz plain flour
200 g / 7 oz butter
200 g / 7 oz Lancashire cheese, grated
few drops of hot pepper sauce
1.25 ml / ¼ tsp salt
flour for rolling out

Grease four baking sheets. Sift the flour into a mixing bowl. Rub in the butter until the mixture resembles fine breadcrumbs. Add the cheese and seasonings. Work the mixture thoroughly by hand to make a smooth dough. Use a few drops of water if necessary, but the dough will be shorter and richer without it. Chill for 30 minutes.

Meanwhile, set the oven at 180°C / 350°F / gas 4. Roll out the dough on a floured surface to a thickness of 5 mm / ¼ inch. Cut into rounds or shapes.

Using a palette knife, transfer the shapes to the prepared baking sheets and bake for 10–12 minutes until light brown and crisp. Cool on the baking sheets.

MAKES FORTY TO FIFTY

CHEESE STRAWS

butter for greasing
100 g / 4 oz plain flour
pinch of mustard powder
pinch of salt
pinch of cayenne pepper
75 g / 3 oz butter
75 g / 3 oz grated Parmesan cheese
1 egg yolk
flour for rolling out

Grease four baking sheets. Set the oven at 200°C / 400°F / gas 6.

Sift the flour, mustard, salt and cayenne into a bowl. In a mixing bowl, cream the butter until soft and white, then add the flour mixture with the cheese. Stir in the egg yolk and enough cold water to form a stiff dough.

Roll out on a lightly-floured surface to a thickness of about 5 mm / ¼ inch and cut into finger, each measuring about 10 x 1 cm / 4 inches x ½ inch. From the pastry trimmings make several rings, each about 4 cm / 1½ inches in diameter.

With a palette knife, transfer both rings and straws to the prepared baking sheets and bake for 8–10 minutes or until lightly browned and crisp. Cool on the baking sheets.

To serve, fit a few straws though each ring and lay the bundles in the centre of a plate with any remaining straws criss-crossed around them.

MAKES FORTY-EIGHT TO SIXTY

Fish
& Seafood

The British Isles provide extensive coastlines
of delicious fresh produce. Serve a whole
salmon at a party, or present a tasty
fish pie at a family supper.

MACKEREL

Mackerel are deep sea fish which migrate between the Mediterranean and Atlantic waters as far north as Iceland. They have a reputation for being voracious eaters and attacking large objects during the spring after near hibernation in deep waters over winter.

The mackerel has a striking appearance, with bold dark stripes on vivid green-blue skin. It tastes delicious. The fish visit British shores from spring through summer; small fish caught early in the season have fine flesh with a superior flavour.

The oily flesh deteriorates rapidly in quality, so it is important to look for mackerel with bright eyes and avoid any dull-skinned, stale specimens. Historically, because of the rapidity with which this fish decays, fishermen were allowed to sell mackerel on a Sunday.

BAKED MACKEREL

4 medium mackerel
50 g / 2 oz butter
1 small onion, very finely chopped
1 rindless bacon rasher, finely diced or chopped
100g / 4 oz fresh white breadcrumbs
15ml / 1 tbsp chopped parsley
15ml / 1 tbsp chopped fresh dill, fennel or tarragon
25g / 1 oz suet
a little grated nutmeg
1 small egg, beaten
salt and pepper

Clean the mackerel, removing the heads and tails. Bone them following the instructions for boning herrings. Set the oven at 200°C / 400°F / gas 6.

Melt half the butter in a small saucepan. Add the onion and cook for 5 minutes. Stir in the bacon, cook for 1–2 minutes, then allow to cool slightly. Put the breadcrumbs in a bowl and stir in the herbs and suet. Add the onion and bacon, with the butter from the pan, a little nutmeg and seasoning to taste. Mix in the egg to bind this stuffing or forcemeat.

Divide the stuffing into four. Press one portion together into a neat sausage shape and place it on one mackerel fillet. Fold the mackerel over the stuffing and secure the edges of the fillet with a wooden cocktail stick. Repeat with the remaining stuffing and mackerel.

Place the stuffed mackerel in an ovenproof dish and season lightly, then dot with the remaining butter. Cover and cook for 35–40 minutes, until the mackerel and stuffing are cooked through. Serve piping hot, with the cooking juices poured over.

SERVES FOUR

MRS BEETON'S TIP

Originally, the mackerel were stuffed with heads and tails on, but they are easy to bone and far more pleasant to eat when this has been done. Mrs Beeton suggested that the fish could be cooked in a little wine – about 60 ml (4 tbsp) dry white wine can be poured into the dish.

MACKEREL WITH CREAMED GOOSEBERRY SAUCE

1 onion, thinly sliced
1 bay leaf
4 large fennel sprigs
4 small mackerel, cleaned
salt and pepper
fennel sprigs to garnish

GOOSEBERRY SAUCE
450 g / 1 lb gooseberries
50 g / 2 oz butter
15 ml / 1 tbsp plain flour
50 g / 2 oz sugar
45 ml / 3 tbsp single cream
a little grated nutmeg

Place the onion, bay leaf and fennel in a fairly deep frying pan or saucepan large enough to hold the mackerel. A roasting tin can be used, with foil for a cover instead of a lid. Pour in water to a depth of about 2.5 cm / 1 inch and stir in a generous seasoning of salt and pepper. Heat the water gently until it boils, then cover the pan and remove it from the heat. Leave the water and flavourings to infuse for 15 minutes.

Meanwhile, make the sauce: place the gooseberries in a pan and add 150 ml / ¼ pint water. Heat gently until the water is boiling, then cover the pan and reduce the heat. Cook the gooseberries for about 20 minutes or until they are soft, stirring occasionally. Rub the cooked fruit through a fine sieve.

Melt the butter in a saucepan and stir in the flour. Gradually add the gooseberry purée, stirring continuously. Stir in the sugar and bring the sauce to the boil. Simmer the sauce, stirring occasionally, for 3–4 minutes.

Arrange the mackerel in the cooled water in the pan or roasting tin and cook over medium heat until just boiling. Then reduce the heat, cover and poach the fish for 5 minutes. Turn the mackerel, replace the cover and continue to cook gently for a further 5–7 minutes, or until the flesh is firm and opaque. Lift out the mackerel, draining them thoroughly and place them on a heated serving dish. Remove the skin from the fish. Add the cream and a little nutmeg to the sauce and heat it gently, if necessary, but do not let it boil. Garnish the mackerel with fennel sprigs and serve the sauce separately.

SERVES FOUR

SAUCES FOR MACKEREL

As well as the gooseberry sauce described above, which is based on stewed fruit with a small quantity of creamy Béchamel sauce, Mrs Beeton suggested serving these richer fennel and caper sauces.

- **Fennel Sauce** Cut 100 g / 4 oz unsalted butter into small pieces and place them in a saucepan with 30 ml / 2 tbsp plain flour. Whisk in 300 ml / 2 tbsp plain flour. Whisk in 300 ml / ½ pint water and heat the sauce gently, whisking continuously, until the butter has melted. Bring the sauce to a full boil, whisking until it is smooth. Add 30 ml / 2 tbsp finely chopped fennel and simmer the sauce gently for 1–2 minutes.
- **Caper Sauce** Finely chop 45 ml / 3 tbsp drained capers. Follow the recipe for Fennel Sauce, but add capers instead of fennel. Stir in 15 ml / 1 tbsp liquid from the capers. Add 15 ml / 1 tbsp anchovy essence if you like. Bring the sauce to simmering point and then serve it at once.

MRS BEETON'S TIP

Both the cooking method for the mackerel and the unusual milk-based gooseberry sauce are surprisingly successful in the above recipe: the sauce perfectly complements the poached fish and the result is delicious. However, the sauce does not go well with grilled mackerel, one of the various ways Mrs Beeton generally recommended for cooking the fish. She also suggested frying fillets in a coating of egg and breadcrumbs. Fennel and Caper Sauce are better suited to grilled or fried fish.

SOLE WITH MUSHROOMS

*Plaice fillets can be used instead of sole for equally good results.
The plain, creamy dish benefits from a contrasting accompaniment,
such as slightly crunchy carrots and broccoli. Firm little new
potatoes complement the dish; alternatively, the fish can be served
in a gratin dish edged with a piped border of mashed potatoes.
Brown the piped potatoes under a hot grill before arranging the
fish in the gratin dish.*

8 sole fillets
25 g / 1 oz butter
25 g / 1 oz plain flour
300 ml / ½ pint Fish Stock (page 231)
150 ml / ¼ pint milk
175 g / 6 oz small button mushrooms
300 ml / ½ pint single cream
salt and pepper
a little lemon juice
parsley sprigs and lemon slices to garnish

Season the sole fillets. Starting at the head end, roll up the fillets and secure them with wooden cocktail sticks. Place them in a flameproof casserole or saucepan. Cream the butter and flour to a paste and set this beurre manié aside. Warm a serving dish for the sole, have a piece of foil ready to cover the dish and warm the grill compartment or oven to keep the sole hot while the sauce is prepared.

Check the fish for seasoning, then pour the stock and milk over the rolls. Heat the liquid until it just simmers, then cover the pan and reduce the heat to poach the sole gently for 5–7 minutes, or until the rolls are just cooked.

Use a slotted spoon to drain the fish rolls and transfer them to the warm dish. Cover the fish and keep it hot. Bring the cooking liquid to the boil and boil it for 2 minutes to reduce it slightly. Reduce the heat and whisk knobs of the beurre manié into the simmering liquid to make a thick sauce – the sauce will be too thick at this stage, but juices from the mushrooms will thin it. Stir in the mushrooms and simmer the sauce for 2 minutes stirring occasionally.

Add the cream to the sauce and heat it gently without boiling. Taste the sauce for seasoning and add a little lemon juice to taste. Pour the sauce over the sole and garnish the dish with parsley and lemon.

SERVES FOUR

MRS BEETON'S TIP

Originally, this was a recipe for whole soles, poached in a mixture of milk and water (which was then discarded) and served with a mushroom sauce. Either Dover or lemon sole can be used; fillets are easier to cook and serve than the whole fish in the original recipe. Dover sole is often cooked whole as its fillets are quite small. The fishmonger will remove the tough skin, leaving the fish ready for grilling or baking. These alternative methods can be used instead of poaching, if preferred, and the sauce prepared while the fish is cooking. Brush with melted butter and season it lightly before grilling or baking.

NATIVE OYSTERS

Britain is famous for flat oysters, known as native oysters, which are renowned for their sweet taste compared to the Pacific oysters, introduced to Europe and America from Japan, or other types found in Mediterranean waters.

The taste and texture of the oysters depend on the waters in which they are reared. Colchester, in particular, has a reputation for the high quality of its oysters; also on the east coast, Whitstable is known for its oyster beds. In the south-west, Cornwall is another region where oysters thrive. Freshly harvested Irish oysters are traditionally slipped down as an accompaniment to creamy Guinness stout.

British oysters are in season during months with an 'r' in their names, that is from September through to April.

OYSTERS FRIED IN BATTER

This is a good way of making the most of oysters as the batter makes them more substantial and preserves their succulent texture without masking their flavour. The speedy cooking method is perfect for firming the oysters to perfection and enhancing their flavour to the full. The quantities given are sufficient for a light meal or starter.

20 oysters
100 g / 4 oz plain flour, plus extra for coating
grated nutmeg
1 egg
100 ml / 3½ fl oz milk
salt and pepper
oil for deep frying
lemon wedges to serve

Shell the oysters, reserving the liquor from the shells. Remove their dark, slightly frilly edges. Pour the liquor into a small saucepan and add the oysters. Heat them gently until the liquor just begins to simmer and the oysters are opaque and barely firm. Remove them from the heat at once, drain them on absorbent kitchen paper. Dust the oysters lightly with flour.

Sift the flour into a bowl and add seasoning, with a little grated nutmeg. Make a well in the middle of the flour and break in the egg. Pour in a little of the milk, then gradually beat the egg and milk together, incorporating the flour and adding the remaining milk in stages to make a smooth, fairly thick batter. Beat the batter thoroughly until it is smooth and light.

Heat the oil for deep frying to 190°C / 375°F. Dip the oysters individually into the batter to coat them; deep fry them briefly until the batter is crisp and light brown. Use a slotted spoon to remove the oysters from the pan and drain them thoroughly on absorbent kitchen paper. Serve immediately with lemon wedges, so that a little lemon juice can be squeezed over the oysters before they are eaten.

SERVES FOUR

DEVILLED WHITEBAIT

450 g / 1 lb whitebait
60 ml / 4 tbsp plain white flour
10 ml / 2 tsp curry powder
1.25 ml / ¼ tsp chilli powder
freshly ground black pepper
lemon wedges
sunflower oil for frying

Wash the whitebait and dry with a clean tea-towel or kitchen paper. Mix the flour, curry powder, chilli powder and freshly ground black pepper in a bowl.

Heat enough oil in a frying pan to just cover the whitebait. Coat the whitebait in the seasoned flour and fry in batches until crisp. This should only take 2–3 minutes. Remove from the oil with a spatula and drain on kitchen paper.

Keep the batches hot in a heated, covered dish until all the whitebait are prepared. Serve with lemon wedges.

SERVES FOUR TO SIX

SOUSED HERRINGS

6 herrings, gutted, heads removed and boned
2 bay leaves
6 cloves
6 allspice berries
1 blade of mace
salt
cayenne pepper
about 600 ml / 1 pint vinegar

Set the oven at 160°C / 325°F / gas 3. Lay three herrings in an ovenproof dish, placing them skin sides down. Arrange the bay leaves, cloves, allspice and mace on the fish. Sprinkle with salt to taste and add a pinch of cayenne. Place the remaining herrings on top, laying them skin side up.

Pour in enough vinegar to just cover the herrings. Cover the dish and bake the herrings for 1 hour, until they are just cooked. Leave them to cool in their cooking liquid, then chill them for several hours or overnight.

Drain the herrings and pat them dry on absorbent kitchen paper. Serve them cold, with bread and butter and a salad of thinly sliced cucumber.

SERVES SIX

MRS BEETON'S TIP

The herrings can be stored in an airtight container, submerged in the vinegar in which they were cooked, for 4–5 days. Ordinary malt vinegar can be used, but, for a finer flavour, use wine vinegar. The exact quantity required will depend upon the shape and size of the dish. In addition to the flavourings used above, sliced onion is a popular ingredient. Mackerel can also be soused by this method.

BONING HERRINGS

You do not have to be skilled or brave to bone small round fish, like herrings and mackerel. It is a simple, comparatively clean, task. It works particularly well for mackerel, but removing all the fine bones from herrings is fiddly and time consuming.

1 The fish should be gutted and the head should be removed. Lay it skin side up on a board and rub it firmly along the length of the backbone, from the tail towards the head. Repeat this, rubbing outwards from the bone towards both sides of the fillet. The aim is to press the bones away from the flesh of the fin.

2 Turn the fish over and snip the backbone at the tail end. Then carefully lift it off the fish, removing it from the tail towards the head. As the main bone is removed, the small bones will come away with it.

3 Pick out any remaining bones. A pair of tweezers is useful for removing the fine bones from herrings.

FISH CAKES

1 small onion, sliced
1 bouquet garni
450 g / 1 lb white fish, preferably cod fillet
450 g / 1 lb potatoes cut into 2.5 cm / 1 inch chunks
30 ml / 2 tbsp finely chopped parsley
50 g / 2 oz fresh white breadcrumbs
2 eggs
plain flour for coating
100 g / 4 oz dried white breadcrumbs
salt and pepper
oil for frying

Place the onion and bouquet garni in a saucepan. Sprinkle in a little salt and pour in 600 ml / 1 pint water. Partially cover the pan and bring the water to the boil. Reduce the heat and simmer the flavoured liquid for 5 minutes. Add the fish and poach it gently, just below simmering point, for 5 minutes, until it is opaque and the flakes separate easily. Remove the pan from the heat, cover it and leave the fish in its cooking liquid until it is cool enough to handle.

Meanwhile, cook the potatoes in boiling salted water for about 10 minutes, until they are tender. Drain and mash them, then press them through a sieve or beat them well until they are smooth.

Remove the fish from the cooking liquid, discard the skin and bones, then use two forks to break up the flesh into fine flakes. Mix the fish and parsley with the potatoes. Add the fresh white breadcrumbs and mix well, adding salt and pepper to taste. Beat in 1 egg.

Lightly beat the remaining egg with 15 ml / 1 tbsp water in a large shallow dish. Pile a little flour on a plate and sprinkle some dried white breadcrumbs on to a third plate or shallow dish.

Divide the fish mixture into quarters, then divide each quarter in half. Take a portion of the mixture and drop it on the flour in one neat spoonful. Using the flour to prevent the mixture from sticking to your hands, press the mixture into a neat round cake. Alternatively, use two palette knives to pat and shape the mixture.

Dip the floured fish cake into the beaten egg, turning it once and spooning the egg over it, then transfer it to the plate of breadcrumbs. Spoon the breadcrumbs over the fish cake, then gently pat them into place all over. Dust off the excess breadcrumbs and transfer the coated fish cake to a plate, ready for cooking. Repeat with the remaining mixture.

Chill the fish cakes for about 15 minutes to set the coating. Heat a little oil in a frying pan and fry the fish cakes for 3–4 minutes, until crisp and golden. Turn them over and cook the second side. Drain the fish cakes on absorbent kitchen paper and serve them freshly cooked.

MAKES EIGHT

VARIATION

- **Fresh Salmon Fish Cakes** Poach a 450 g / 1 lb portion of thick fresh salmon fillet or enclose it completely in foil and bake it in the oven at 180°C / 350°F / gas 4 for 20 minutes. Leave the salmon to cool in its poaching liquid or wrapped in foil. When cool, use the salmon to make the fish cakes. The left-overs from a poached salmon can be used in fish cakes, alone or combined with white fish.

MRS BEETON'S TIP

Chopped parsley, a little thyme and grated lemon rind is a tasty combination for flavouring fish cakes. Alternatively, a little chopped tarragon may be combined with snipped chives.

COD PIE

*In Mrs Beeton's day, oysters were an economical ingredient,
widely used in sauces, stuffings and fish mixtures for pies or bakes.
As an inexpensive alternative in the following recipe, and in the
following recipe for potato-topped fish pie, add chopped hard-boiled
eggs or lightly sautéed, sliced mushrooms to the sauce.
Chopped parsley, chives and tarragon can be added to
the sauce, either singly or as a mixture.*

Short Crust Pastry made with 175 g / 6 oz plain flour (page 146)
450 g / 1 lb cod fillet, skinned and cut into chunks
2.5 ml / ½ tsp grated nutmeg
1.25 ml / ¼ tsp ground mace
10 oysters
25 g / 1 oz butter
30 ml / 2 tbsp plain flour
300 ml / ½ pint Fish Stock (page 231)
grated rind of 1 lemon
150 ml / ¼ pint single cream
salt and pepper
milk or beaten egg to glaze

Set the oven at 180°C / 350°F / gas 4. Roll out the short crust pastry to the same shape as a 900 ml / 1½ pint pie dish, but about 4 cm / 1½ inches larger all around. Cut a strip from around the edge of the pastry, dampen the rim of the dish and press the pastry strip on to it.

Place the cod chunks in the dish and sprinkle them with the nutmeg, mace and seasoning. Open the oysters, reserving the liquor from their shells. Melt the butter in a small saucepan. Stir in the flour and cook the mixture gently for 1 minute. Stir in the stock and the reserved liquor from the oysters, then cook, stirring, until the sauce comes to the boil. Remove from the heat and stir in the lemon rind, cream and oysters, with seasoning to taste. Pour the oyster mixture into the dish and mix it lightly with the seasoned cod chunks. Dampen the pastry rim and cover the pie with the lid.

Trim off the excess pastry, knock up the edge and pinch it into decorative flutes or scallops. Roll out the pastry trimmings and cut out leaves or other decorative shapes to place on top of the pie. Brush the pastry with a little milk or beaten egg and bake the pie for 45 minutes or until golden brown.

SERVES FOUR

VARIATIONS

- **Scallops** These are delicious in a special fish pie, made with a light puff pastry topping instead of the homely short crust pastry. Separate the bright corals and slice the white nuggets of flesh. Add both to the sauce as in the main recipe. To make this filling even more special, use dry white wine instead of the fish stock.
- **Prawns** Peeled cooked prawns can be added to the sauce instead of oysters.

POTATO-TOPPED FISH PIE

Unlike modern recipes for fish pies, in which the fish is coated with a Béchamel or cheese sauce, in this case the fish is simply moistened with the milk in which it was poached. The result is a pie which is lighter than usual and it makes a pleasing change. As the liquid in this pie is thinner than the now-popular sauce, it will bubble over more easily during cooking. So be sure to use a dish which is deep enough to prevent the milk from boiling out from under the potato topping.

Oysters are not an essential ingredient in the pie – Mrs Beeton used them for the economical ingredient they were in her day – but good-quality, thick cod will give by far the best results as both the flavour and texture of the fish contribute to the quality of the cooked pie. It is also important to season the fish well or the result will be rather bland.

250 ml / 8 fl oz milk
450 g / 1 lb cod fillet
12 oysters (optional)
900 g / 2 lb potatoes, boiled until tender
50 g / 2 oz butter
salt and pepper

Set the oven at 200°C / 400°F / gas 6. Pour 175 ml / 6 fl oz of the milk into a frying pan or large saucepan and heat it gently to just below simmering point. Add the fish fillet and poach it gently for 2 minutes, or until it is half- to three-quarters cooked and the flakes can be separated. Remove from the heat and cool slightly.

Open the oysters, if using, and set them aside in the reserved liquor from their shells. Drain and mash the potatoes with half the butter, the remaining milk and salt and pepper to taste. Drain the fish, reserving the cooking liquid, and flake it, discarding the skin and any bones.

Place the fish in a deep ovenproof dish and top it with the oysters and their liquor, if using. Season the fish well with salt and pepper before pouring in the reserved cooking liquid. Melt the remaining butter and pour it over the fish mixture. Spread the mashed potatoes evenly over the top and score them with a fork. Bake the pie for about 30 minutes, or until golden brown on top.

SERVES FOUR

MRS BEETON'S TIP

Topping any type of moist base with mashed potato can be difficult as the sauce or liquid tends to rise around the edge or between the portions of potato as they are added. The trick is to start by placing modest spoonfuls of potato all around the edge – this helps to prevent the liquid rising just inside the rim of the dish. Then cover the middle with potato before filling in with any remaining potato. Do not be tempted to smooth the top until the pie is completely covered. Use a fork to press the potato down lightly, working very gently at first, and fill any tiny gaps around the edge of the dish.

SALMON WITH CAPER SAUCE

*Tomato sauce is given as an alternative to caper sauce to dress
the baked salmon fillets. The quantities given in the recipe are based
on one of Mrs Beeton's original sauces – the result bears little
resemblance to the type of rich tomato sauce we might make today,
but it is good with the salmon.*

**4 x 175–225 g / 6–8 oz salmon fillet portions
75 g / 3 oz butter
2 parsley sprigs, finely chopped
1 shallot, finely chopped
grated nutmeg
12.5 ml / 2½ tsp plain flour
250 ml / 8 fl oz Fish Stock (page 231) or water
30 ml / 2 tbsp drained capers, roughly chopped
10 ml / 2 tsp vinegar from capers
2.5 ml / ½ tsp anchovy essence (optional)
salt and pepper**

Set the oven at 200ºC / 400ºF / gas 6. Lay the salmon in an ovenproof dish and
dot with a third of the butter. Sprinkle the parsley, shallot, salt, pepper and
nutmeg over the fish and cover the dish. Bake the salmon for 20–30 minutes, or
until it is cooked and the flesh flakes easily.

Cut the remaining butter into dice and place these in a saucepan. Sprinkle the
flour over the butter. Pour in the stock or water. Whisk the mixture over medium
heat, reducing the heat as the water gets hotter, until the butter has melted and
combined with the other ingredients. Bring to a full boil, then remove the pan
from the heat. Stir the capers, vinegar and anchovy essence (if liked) into the
sauce.

Transfer the salmon to serving plates, then stir the cooking juices from the dish
into the caper sauce. Pour the sauce over the salmon and serve immediately.
New potatoes or creamy mashed potatoes and broccoli, carrots and French
beans are excellent accompaniments.

SERVES FOUR

VARIATION

- **Tomato Sauce** Cut 900 g / 2 lb ripe tomatoes into quarters and place them in a saucepan with 4 chopped shallots, 2 cloves and a blade of mace. Add 300 ml / ½ pint White Stock (page 230). Season to taste. Bring to the boil, then reduce the heat and cover the pan. Simmer the sauce gently for 1 hour. Rub the sauce through a fine sieve. Alternatively, purée it in a blender or food processor, then sieve it to remove the seeds. Return the sauce to a large saucepan, bring it to the boil and boil hard for 5 minutes to reduce it and concentrate the flavours slightly. Taste the sauce for seasoning and add 5 ml / 1 tsp sugar, if you like. Serve instead of the caper sauce in the main recipe.

MRS BEETON'S TIP

The combination of ingredients is unusual, as is the method used to make the sauce but the results are highly successful. At first, it seems as though the sauce cannot possibly work, but as the butter melts the ingredients blend together beautifully. It is important to bring the sauce to a full boil and to whisk it all the time. Do taste the sauce before adding the anchovy essence, particularly if fish stock is used, as it completely alters the nature of the mixture and you may prefer to leave it out. A proportion of dry white wine can be used instead of all water or stock – about half would be appropriate.

HOT POACHED SALMON

Court Bouillon is the traditional cooking liquid for poached fish and
is discarded after use. Serve hot poached salmon with a Hollandaise sauce.
Cold poached salmon may be garnished with cucumber slices.
See Garnishing Salmon, page 72.

1 x 1.6–3.25 kg / 3½–7 lb salmon

COURT BOUILLON
1 litre / 1¾ pints dry white wine or dry cider
60 ml / 4 tbsp white wine vinegar
4 large carrots, sliced
4 large onions, sliced
4–5 celery sticks, chopped
12 parsley stalks, crushed
1 bouquet garni
20 peppercorns, lightly crushed
salt and pepper

First make the Court Bouillon. Put the wine in a large stainless steel or enamel saucepan. Add 2 litres / 3½ pints water, with the remaining ingredients. Bring to the boil, lower the heat and simmer for 30 minutes. Cool, then strain.

Cut the fins from the fish, remove the scales and thoroughly wash the body cavity. Tie the mouth of the fish shut. Tie the body of the fish loosely to keep it in shape during cooking – two or three bands of string around the fish to prevent the body cavity from gaping are usually sufficient. Weigh the fish and calculate the cooking time. Allow 5 minutes per 450 g / 1 lb for salmon up to 2.25 kg / 5 lb in weight; 4 minutes per 450 g / 1 lb plus 5 minutes for salmon up to 3.25 kg / 7 lb.

Put the fish in a fish kettle and pour over the Court Bouillon. Bring the liquid gently to just below boiling point. Lower the heat and simmer for the required cooking time. The Court Bouillon should barely show signs of simmering; if the liquid is allowed to bubble then it may damage the delicate salmon flesh. If serving the salmon cold, simmer for 5 minutes only, then leave the fish to cool in the cooking liquid.

Drain the salmon well and untie the body. Slide the salmon on to a large, heated platter. Slit the skin around the body immediately below the head and just above the tail of the fish. Carefully peel back the skin from the head towards the tail. Carefully turn the fish over and remove the skin from the second side. Remove the string from the mouth.

Garnish the salmon with lemon slices and parsley sprigs. Freshly cooked vegetables (new potatoes and baby carrots) may be arranged around the fish. Serve at once.

SERVINGS FROM SALMON

Hot salmon served as a main course will yield the following servings. Served cold and dressed, as part of a buffet with other main dishes, it will yield about 2 extra portions.

1.6 kg / 3½ lb salmon	4 portions
2.25 kg / 5 lb salmon	6 portions
3.25 kg / 7 lb salmon	10 portions

MICROWAVE TIP

Provided it can be curled into a circular dish that will fit into your microwave, salmon may be cooked by this method. Prepare the fish, tuck 2 bay leaves, some peppercorns and a small sprig of parsley into the body cavity, then curl the fish into the dish (a 25 cm / 10 inch quiche dish works well). Cover fish and dish with two layers of microwave-proof film to hold the fish securely and prevent it from losing its shape. Cook on High. A 2.25 kg / 5 lb salmon will take about 12 minutes. If you do not have a turntable turn the dish three times while cooking. Allow to stand, covered, for 5 minutes. To serve hot, drain, remove the herbs from the body cavity and skin as suggested above. Allow to cool in the wrapping if serving cold.

BONING POACHED SALMON

Follow the recipe for Hot Poached Salmon (page 70). Cool the fish in the Court Bouillon, following the instructions for serving cold and removing the skin.

Using a sharp, pointed knife, cut the flesh around the head down to the bone. Cut the flesh down to the bone around the tail. Make a cut into the flesh along the length of the fish as far as the bone (above).

Cut horizontally into the flesh, along the backbone of the fish, from head to tail to loosen the top fillet.

Have a piece of foil on the work surface beside the fish ready to hold the fillets. You need a long palette knife or two fish slices to remove the fillet. Carefully slide the knife or slices under the fillet and lift it off in one piece. If the fish is large, cut the fillet in half or into three portions, then remove each piece neatly.

Carefully cut the flesh off the bone over the belly of the fish and lift it off, in one piece or several pieces, as before.

Now remove all the bones from the fish. If serving a salmon trout, snip the backbone at the head and tail end. The bones of salmon come away easily in sections.

When all the bones have been removed, carefully replace the fillets in their original position. There will be small gaps and untidy-looking areas but these will be covered by the garnish.

If the fish has been curved for cooking, it should be garnished with the bones in place.

GARNISHING SALMON

The final dressing: cut the finest possible slices of cucumber. Thick slices will not do – they have to be thin enough to curve to the shape of the fish. Dip each slice in lemon juice and lay it on the salmon. Start at the tail, overlapping each row of cucumber to mimic scales.

Pipe mayonnaise stars or shells around the tail and head of the fish, also along the top and base of the body if liked. Small triangles of lemon slices or sliced stuffed olives may be used to cover the eye of the fish. Sprigs of parsley may also be used as a garnish.

Poultry & Game

*Make the most of a roast chicken or try
a recipe using one of our finest
British game birds.*

ROAST TURKEY WITH CHESTNUTS

1 x 4.5–5.5 kg / 10–12 lb turkey
salt and pepper
225 g / 8 oz rindless streaky bacon rashers

HERB FORCEMEAT
50 g / 2 oz margarine
100 g / 4 oz fresh white breadcrumbs
pinch of grated nutmeg
15 ml / 1 tbsp chopped parsley
5 ml / 1 tsp chopped fresh mixed herbs
grated rind of ½ lemon
salt and pepper
1 egg, beaten

CHESTNUT STUFFING
1 kg / 2¼ lb chestnuts
275 ml / 9¾ fl oz turkey or Chicken Stock (page 229)
50 g / 2 oz butter
1 egg, beaten
single cream or milk (see method)

First make the chestnut stuffing. Shell and skin the chestnuts. Put them in a saucepan, add the stock and simmer for 20 minutes or until tender. Drain the chestnuts and chop them finely, or press through a sieve into a clean bowl. Melt the butter in a small saucepan. Remove from the heat and add to the bowl containing the chestnuts. Stir in the beaten egg, with enough cream or milk to moisten the mixture.

Make the forcemeat. Melt the margarine in a small saucepan. Add the breadcrumbs, nutmeg, herbs and lemon rind. Stir in salt and pepper to taste and sufficient beaten egg to bind the mixture.

Set the oven at 180°C / 350°F / gas 4. Trim the turkey and wash it inside and out in cold water. Pat dry with absorbent kitchen paper and season inside with salt and pepper. Immediately before cooking, fill the neck end of the bird with chestnut stuffing and the body with the forcemeat. Truss if wished, and cover the bird with the bacon.

Place the bird in a roasting tin and roast for 4½–5 hours or until cooked through, removing the bacon towards the end to allow the breast to brown. Serve with giblet gravy.

SERVES FOURTEEN TO SIXTEEN

MRS BEETON'S TIP

*Lemons, cut in half and with all flesh
and pulp removed, make ideal containers for
individual portions of cranberry sauce.
Arrange them around the turkey.*

ROAST STUFFED CHICKEN WITH GRAVY

50 g / 2 oz gammon or rindless bacon, finely chopped
50 g / 2 oz shredded suet
grated rind of ½ lemon
5 ml / 1 tsp finely chopped parsley
5 ml / 1 tsp finely chopped mixed fresh herbs
cayenne pepper
pinch of ground mace
175 g / 6 oz fresh white breadcrumbs
2 eggs, lightly beaten
1 x 1.5–1.8 kg / 3½–4lb oven-ready chicken
50 g / 2 oz plain flour, plus a little extra for dusting
25 g / 1 oz butter
900 ml / 1½ pints vegetable cooking water
salt and pepper

Set the oven at 180°C / 350°F / gas 4. Mix the gammon or bacon, suet, lemon rind and herbs, then add salt, cayenne and mace to taste. Stir in the breadcrumbs and add enough beaten egg to bind the ingredients into a moist forcemeat. Use a small, pointed knife to loosen the skin over the breast of the chicken: cut the membrane under the skin at the vent end (between the legs) of the chicken to form a gap under the skin. Carefully insert the point of the knife into the gap and ease the skin away from the meat without cutting through the skin. When there is sufficient space, use your fingers, or a teaspoon or dessertspoon, to continue loosening the skin up over the breast.

Use a small spoon to push the forcemeat between the skin and the breast of the chicken. As the forcemeat is packed in, it can be eased over and around the top of the bird by gently pushing from outside the skin. Insert enough forcemeat to cover the breast evenly and make the bird look extremely plump.

Truss the chicken neatly and dust it with a little plain flour. Place the bird in a roasting tin and sprinkle it generously with salt and pepper. Dot the butter on the top of the chicken and roast it for 30 minutes. Cover the top of the breast with foil and continue cooking for a further 1–1½ hours. Baste the chicken occasionally during cooking, replacing the foil each time, but taking it off the breast for the final 15–20 minutes.

Transfer the chicken to a warmed serving platter, cover it with foil and keep it hot. If there is a lot of fat in the tin, pour off the excess but retain a shallow layer (sufficient to absorb the flour). Stir in the flour over medium heat. Cook the mixture, stirring, for 2–3 minutes, to brown the paste slightly. If the meat juices in the roasting tin are already well browned this may not be necessary. Gradually pour in the vegetable cooking water and bring the gravy to the boil, stirring continuously to incorporate roasting residue from the tin. Simmer the gravy for 3–5 minutes, then taste it and season if necessary. Serve the piping hot gravy with the roast chicken and forcemeat.

SERVES FOUR TO SIX

MRS BEETON'S TIP

When the chicken is cooked the meat will be white and firm, not pink and soft. It is important to check the thick area of meat around the thigh area by making a discreet slit with a small pointed knife. Any sign of blood in the juices – or uncooked meat – indicates that the chicken is not cooked through. Check both sides of the bird to be sure.

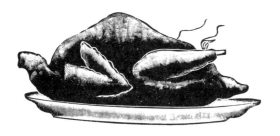

CHICKEN PIE

50 g / 2 oz gammon or rindless bacon,
finely chopped
50 g / 2 oz shredded suet
grated rind of ½ lemon
5 ml / 1 tsp finely chopped parsley
5 ml / 1 tsp finely chopped mixed herbs
cayenne pepper
ground mace
175 g / 6 oz fresh white breadcrumbs
2 eggs, lightly beaten
3 skinless boneless chicken breasts
6 slices lean cooked ham
3 hard-boiled eggs
(optional – see Mrs Beeton's Tip)
grated nutmeg
175 g / 6 oz Puff Pastry (page 148)
salt and pepper

Set the oven to 220°C / 425°F / gas 7. Mix the gammon or bacon, suet, lemon rind and herbs, then add salt, cayenne, and mace to taste. Stir in the bread-crumbs, and add three-quarters of the beaten egg to bind the forcemeat.

Slice the chicken breasts in half at a slant. Layer the chicken, ham, forcemeat and hard-boiled eggs (if using) in a 1.5 litre / 2¾ pint pie dish. Season each layer with mace, nutmeg, salt and pepper. Pour in 300 ml / ½ pint water.

Roll out the pastry on a lightly floured surface to the same shape as the dish but about 2.5 cm / 1 inch larger all round. Cut off a 1 cm / ½ inch strip from around the edge of the pastry, dampen the rim of the dish and press the pastry strip on to it. Dampen the strip and lay the lid on top. Trim off the excess pastry, knock up and flute the edge, then use any trimmings to decorate the crust with pastry leaves. Brush the pastry with the reserved beaten egg and make a small hole in the centre of the pie.

MRS BEETON'S TIP

Originally, this pie was made with a jointed chicken, including the bones. The remnants of the carcass were boiled to make a stock and this was poured into the cooked pie before serving. However, the pie is quite full, so it is easier to make the gravy to serve separately: melt 50 g / 2 oz butter in a saucepan and cook 1 finely chopped onion with 1 finely diced carrot, 1 diced celery stick and 1 bay leaf until softened and lightly browned. Gradually stir in 900 ml / 1½ pints Chicken Stock (page 229) and bring the gravy to the boil. Reduce the heat, cover the pan and simmer the gravy for 15 minutes. Remove the bay leaf. Taste and adjust the seasoning before serving the gravy. The hot pie tastes slightly odd with hard-boiled eggs in the filling, especially when served with gravy, but the eggs were an excellent addition when the pie was served cold.

Bake the pie for 15 minutes to set the pastry, then reduce the oven temperature to 180°C / 350°F / gas 4 and bake it for a further 30 minutes. Cover the pastry loosely with foil and continue to bake the pie for 45 minutes. Serve the pie hot or cold.

SERVES SIX TO EIGHT

ROAST DUCK WITH SAGE AND ONION STUFFING

1 x 1.8 kg / 4 lb oven-ready duck with giblets
5 onions
1 carrot, sliced
1 celery stick, sliced
1 bay leaf
2 parsley sprigs
10 large fresh sage leaves
50 g / 2 oz butter, cut into small pieces
100 g / 4 oz fresh white breadcrumbs
1 egg yolk
45 ml / 3 tbsp plain flour
salt and pepper

Place the giblets from the duck in a saucepan. Thickly slice 1 onion and add the slices to the pan with the carrot, celery, bay leaf and parsley. Add water to cover and bring it to the boil. Reduce the heat, cover the pan and simmer the stock gently for 1 hour. Strain the duck stock and boil it further, if necessary, until it is reduced to 600 ml / 1 pint.

Cook the remaining onions whole in simmering water for 2 minutes. Add the sage leaves just before draining the onions, to blanch them for a few seconds. Chop the drained onions and sage finely, then mix the butter into them until it

has melted. Stir in the breadcrumbs. Add seasoning to taste and bind the stuffing with egg yolk.

Set the oven to 190°C / 375°F / gas 5. Spoon the stuffing into the duck and truss it. Put the duck on a wire rack in a roasting tin and prick the skin all over with a fork or skewer to release the fat. Sprinkle the duck generously with salt, then roast it for 1¾ hours, basting it occasionally with the pan juices and pouring away the excess fat if necessary. Test by piercing the thickest part of the thigh with the point of a sharp knife. The juices should run clear.

Transfer the duck to a heated platter, remove the trussing string and keep hot. Pour off most of the fat from the roasting tin, sprinkle the flour and cook, stirring for 2 minutes. Gradually stir in the stock and bring the gravy to the boil, then lower the heat and simmer, stirring, for 3–4 minutes. Add salt and pepper to taste and serve the gravy with the duck.

SERVES FOUR

ACCOMPANIMENTS

Fresh peas are the classic accompaniment to roast duck. Try frozen petits pois dressed with butter and tossed with chopped tarragon or mint. Slightly crisp carrots, sugar snap peas or French beans are all suitable vegetables, with new potatoes or boiled potatoes topped with a little chopped parsley.

Apple Sauce (page 237) is another traditional accompaniment or a tangy jelly, such as crab apple, redcurrant or rowanberry, can be served. Sweet-sour flavours complement the richness of duck.

MRS BEETON'S TIP

*If the duck is sold without giblets,
the cooking water from boiling
vegetables can be used to make gravy.*

ROAST GOOSE

1 goose with giblets
5 onions
1 carrot, sliced
1 celery stick, sliced
1 bay leaf
2 parsley sprigs
10 large fresh sage leaves
75 g / 3 oz butter, cut into small pieces
100 g / 4 oz fresh white breadcrumbs
salt and pepper
1 egg yolk
½ lemon
5 ml / 1 tsp prepared English mustard
250 ml / 8 fl oz port
cayenne pepper
30 ml / 2 tbsp plain flour

Place the giblets from the goose in a saucepan. Thickly slice 1 onion and add the slices to the pan with the carrot, celery, bay leaf and parsley. Add water to cover the ingredients generously and bring to the boil. Reduce the heat, cover the pan and simmer the stock gently for 1 hour. Strain the stock and boil it further, if necessary, until it is reduced to 600 ml / 1 pint.

Cook the remaining onions whole in simmering water for 2 minutes. Add the sage leaves just before draining the onions, to blanch them for a few seconds. Chop the drained onions and sage finely, then mix two-thirds of the butter into them until it has melted. Stir in the breadcrumbs. Add seasoning to taste and bind the stuffing with the egg yolk.

Set the oven to 230°C / 450°F / gas 8. Weigh the goose and calculate the cooking time at 20 minutes per 450 g / 1 lb. Remove the excess fat usually found around the vent. Rinse the inside of the bird, then rub the skin with lemon and season the bird with salt and pepper.

Stuff the body of the bird with the sage and onion stuffing and truss the legs and wings neatly.

Put the goose on a rack in a roasting tin, place it in the oven and immediately lower the temperature to 180°C / 350°F / gas 4. Roast for the calculated time. Drain fat away from the roasting tin occasionally. About 20 minutes before the end of the cooking time, mix the mustard with the port, a pinch of cayenne and a little salt.

Drain off the excess fat from the roasting tin, then slowly trickle the port mixture over the goose. Continue to roast the bird until it is cooked.

Transfer the goose to a serving platter, cover it with tented foil and keep it hot. Stir the giblet stock into the pan juices and bring it to the boil. Reduce the hat and simmer the gravy for 2–3 minutes, scraping the sediment off the roasting tin. Cream the remaining butter with the flour to a smooth paste, then whisk knobs of this into the simmering gravy, continuing to whisk until the gravy thickens. Simmer the gravy for a further 2 minutes, stirring occasionally, then taste it for seasoning. Serve the gravy with the roast goose.

SERVES SIX TO EIGHT

MRS BEETON'S TIP

Goose fat was put to many uses in the Victorian household, where nothing was wasted. Apart from being an excellent medium for cooking, in particular for roasting potatoes, goose fat was an ingredient in furniture polish when beeswax was not available. It was also used to protect against illness by being rubbed into the chest of anyone, children in particular, who showed the first signs of developing a cold or cough.

PIGEON PIE

1 onion, sliced
50 g / 2 oz butter
450 g / 1 lb rump steak, cubed
salt and pepper
ground mace
2 oven-ready pigeons (see Mrs Beeton's Tip)
1 thin gammon steak
250 ml / 8 fl oz Beef Stock (page 228) or
Chicken Stock (page 229)
175 g / 6 oz Puff Pastry (page 148)
beaten egg to glaze

Set the oven to 220°C / 425°F / gas 7. Cook the onion in half the butter for about 5 minutes, until it is slightly softened, but not browned.

Place the steak in a pie dish and sprinkle the onion on top. Season the meat well and sprinkle it with a generous pinch of mace. Cut the remaining butter in half and place a piece in the body cavity of each pigeon. Place the pigeons on the steak, nestling them in neatly. Sprinkle with seasoning and a little mace. Trim the rind from the gammon, then cut the gammon steak in half and lay one piece over each bird. Pour in the stock.

Roll out the pastry to the same shape as the pie dish, but 4 cm / 1½ inches larger all around. Cut a 2.5 cm / 1 inch strip from around the edge. Dampen the rim of the dish and press the pastry strip on to it, then dampen the pastry. Lay the pastry lid in place, trim off the excess pastry and knock up the edges. Flute the rim of the pie and use the pastry trimmings to make a garnish of leaves.

Cut a small hole in the middle of the pie and glaze it with beaten egg. Bake the pie for 15 minutes, then reduce the temperature to 160°C / 325°F / gas 3 and cook the pie for a further 2 hours. Cover the top of the pie loosely with foil after 1 hour to prevent the pastry from overbrowning. Serve the pie piping hot.

SERVES SIX

MRS BEETON'S TIP

*Pigeon pie has a superb flavour, but making it with
whole birds does present difficulties when it comes to
cutting and serving. It is far better to use the breast
fillets from three pigeons, boiling the remainder
of the birds to make a delicious stock for the pie.
If you use breasts, dice the gammon and sprinkle
it evenly over the top of the filling. Omit the
second portion of butter.*

ROAST GUINEAFOWL

1 oven-ready guineafowl
salt and pepper
25 g / 1 oz butter
2–3 rindless streaky bacon rashers
a little flour
Bread Sauce (page 236) to serve

Set the oven at 180°C / 350°F / gas 4. Place the guineafowl in a roasting tin.
Sprinkle the bird with seasoning, then dot it with butter, spreading some over
the thighs as well as on the breast. Lay the bacon rashers over the breast.

Roast the guineafowl for 1–1½ hours or until cooked through, basting
frequently. About 20 minutes before the end of the cooking time, remove the
bacon, baste the bird and dredge the breast with flour. Serve with bread sauce.

SERVES TWO TO THREE

STEWED VENISON

225 g / 8 oz pork fat or fatty belly of pork, thinly sliced
salt and pepper
2.5 ml / ½ tsp ground allspice
300 ml / ½ pint port
1.6 kg / 3½ lb haunch or shoulder of venison joint
50 g / 2 oz butter
1 large onion
1 carrot, diced
1 celery stick, diced
1 bay leaf
900 ml / 1½ pints hot Beef Stock (page 228),
Chicken Stock (page 229) or Game Stock (page 229)
2.5 ml / ½ tsp black peppercorns
2.5 ml / ½ tsp allspice
25 g / 1 oz plain flour
redcurrant jelly to serve

Lay the pork fat or belly slices in a large shallow dish and season them well. Sprinkle the ground allspice over, then pour in the port. Turn the slices in the port and seasoning to coat both sides, then cover the dish and chill the fat or pork for 2–3 hours.

Set the oven to 160°C / 325°F / gas 3. Trim any fat and membrane off the venison. Drain the marinated slices or fat or pork, reserving the marinade, and wrap them around the joint, tying them on. Place the joint in a large casserole.

Melt half the butter in a small saucepan and fry the onion, carrot and celery until lightly browned. Add the bay leaf and stir in some of the stock – enough to allow the cooking residue to be scraped off the pan and incorporated. Bring the mixture to the boil, stirring, then add it to the casserole with the remaining stock and reserved marinade. Tie the whole peppercorns and allspice berries in a small piece of muslin and add them to the casserole.

Cover the casserole tightly and cook the venison for 3–3½ hours. Baste the meat occasionally, if necessary, and turn the joint halfway through cooking. Cream the flour with the remaining butter. Stir knobs of this beurre manié into the cooking juices about 30 minutes before the end of the cooking time. Stir until all the paste has melted, then replace the casserole in the oven.

When the venison is tender, lift it out of the casserole, remove the barding fat and carve the meat into thick slices. Discard the bay leaf and the spices in the muslin bag, then ladle the cooking juices over the venison. Serve with redcurrant jelly.

SERVES SIX TO EIGHT

MRS BEETON'S TIP

Instead of a whole joint of venison, the same ingredients and method may be used for steaks. Alternatively, the joint may be cut into serving portions before cooking.

JUGGED HARE

1 hare, jointed with liver and blood reserved
60 ml / 4 tbsp plain flour
75 g / 3 oz butter
900 ml / 1½ pints Beef Stock (page 228)
1 lemon
1 onion
6 cloves
1 bouquet garni
1.25 ml / ¼ tsp ground allspice
300 ml / ½ pint port
salt and pepper
redcurrant jelly to serve

FORCEMEAT
50 g / 2 oz gammon or rindless bacon, finely chopped
50 g / 2 oz shredded suet
grated rind ½ lemon
5 ml / 1 tsp finely chopped parsley
5 ml / 1 tsp finely chopped fresh mixed herbs
cayenne pepper
pinch of ground mace
175 g / 6 oz fresh white breadcrumbs
1 egg, lightly beaten

Set the oven to 180°C / 350°F / gas 4. Dust the portions of hare with the flour and season them well. Melt 50 g / 2 oz of the butter in a frying pan and brown the hare joints all over, reserving any flour left over from coating them. Transfer the joints to a casserole. Stir the reserved flour into the fat remaining in the pan, then gradually stir in about half the stock and bring it to the boil, stirring. Stir in salt and pepper to taste, then turn off the heat under the pan.

Cut the lemon into quarters and add these to the hare. Stud the onion with the cloves and add it to the casserole with the bouquet garni and allspice. Add the thickened stock from the pan and stir in the remaining stock. Cover the casserole tightly and place it in the oven. Cook the hare for 3 hours.

For the forcemeat, mix the gammon or bacon, suet, lemon rind and herbs, adding salt, cayenne and mace to taste. Stir in the breadcrumbs and add the beaten egg to bind the mixture. Mould small balls of this forcemeat and fry them in the remaining butter until lightly browned.

Remove the bouquet garni and lemon quarters from the casserole. Reduce the oven temperature to 150°C / 300°F / gas 2. Finely chop the liver, place it in a bowl and add a little of the cooking liquid from the casserole, Mash the liver into the hot liquid. Add the port and the hare's blood, then stir this mixture into the casserole. Top with the forcemeat balls and cover the casserole, then return it to the oven and cook for a further 10–15 minutes.

Serve the hare garnished with the forcemeat balls, with the cooking juices ladled over the joints. Offer redcurrant jelly as an accompaniment.

SERVES SIX

MRS BEETON'S TIP

Traditionally, the point of jugged hare was to thicken the casserole with the reserved blood. The butcher will reserve the blood and liver for you if the hare is ordered in advance. To prevent the blood from coagulating, 5 ml / 1 tsp vinegar must be added to it and it must be stored in a covered container in the refrigerator. In her original recipe, Mrs Beeton did not add the blood, which was legitimate because the title referred to recipes cooked in a deep pot or 'jug'. If you do not add blood to the sauce, do not boil it or cook it at too high a temperature after the blood has been added as this will curdle the mixture.

PHEASANT WITH MUSHROOM STUFFING

2 pheasants
½ onion
50 g / 2 oz butter

MUSHROOM STUFFING
25 g / 1 oz butter or margarine
100 g / 4 oz finely chopped onion
100 g / 4 oz mushrooms, chopped
50 g / 2 oz cooked ham, chopped
75 g / 3 oz fresh white breadcrumbs
salt and pepper
15 ml / 1 tbsp game or Chicken Stock
(optional) (page 229)
watercress sprigs, to garnish

Wash the pheasant giblets. Place in a saucepan and cover with cold water. Add the half onion and simmer gently for 40 minutes to make stock for the gravy.

Make the stuffing. Melt the butter or margarine in a frying pan and cook the onion until soft. Add the mushrooms to the onion; cook for a few minutes. Stir in the ham and breadcrumbs, then add salt and pepper. If the stuffing is too crumbly, add the stock.

Set the oven at 190°C / 375°F / gas 5. Divide the stuffing between the birds, filling the body cavities only. Truss the birds neatly and put them in a roasting tin; spread with the butter. Roast for 45–60 minutes, depending on the size of the birds. Baste occasionally while roasting. Transfer the birds to a heated serving dish and remove the trussing strings. Garnish with watercress and serve with gravy made from the giblet stock (see page 234). Wild mushrooms, tossed in butter, are good with this dish.

SERVES SIX

Meat Dishes

*From grand roasts to comforting stews and
other one-dish meals, these recipes
produce delicious, rich flavours.*

ROAST RIBS OF BEEF
WITH YORKSHIRE PUDDING

This impressive joint is also known as a standing rib roast.
Ask the butcher to trim the thin ends of the bones so that the
joint will stand upright. The recipe below, as in Mrs Beeton's
day, uses clarified dripping for cooking, but the roast
may be cooked without any additional fat, if preferred.
There will be sufficient fat from the meat for basting.

2.5 kg / 5½ lb forerib of beef
50–75 g / 2–3 oz beef dripping
salt and pepper
Vegetable Stock (page 232) or water (see method)

YORKSHIRE PUDDING
100 g / 4 oz plain flour
1 egg, beaten
150 ml / ¼ pint milk

Set the oven at 230°C / 450°F / gas 8. Wipe the meat but do not salt it. Melt 50 g / 2 oz of the dripping in a roasting tin, add the meat and quickly spoon some of the hot fat over it. Roast for 10 minutes.

Lower the oven temperature to 180°C / 350°F / gas 4. Baste the meat thoroughly, then continue to roast for a further 1¾ hours for rare meat; 2¼ hours for well-done meat. Baste frequently during cooking.

Meanwhile make the Yorkshire pudding batter. Sift the flour into a bowl and add a pinch of salt. Make a well in the centre of the flour and add the beaten egg. Stir in the milk, gradually working in the flour. Beat vigorously until the mixture is smooth and bubbly, then stir in 150 ml / ¼ pint water.

About 30 minutes before the end of the cooking time, spoon off 30 ml / 2 tbsp of the dripping and divide it between six 7.5-cm / 3-inch Yorkshire pudding tins. Place the tins in the oven for 5 minutes or until the fat is very hot, then carefully divide the batter between them. Bake above the meat for 15–20 minutes (or see Mrs Beeton's Tip).

When the beef is cooked, salt it lightly, transfer it to a warmed serving platter and keep hot. Pour off almost all the water in the roasting tin, leaving the sediment. Pour in enough vegetable stock or water to make a thin gravy, then heat to boiling point, stirring all the time. Season with salt and pepper and serve in a heated gravyboat with the roast and Yorkshire puddings.

SERVES SIX TO EIGHT

MRS BEETON'S TIP

Yorkshire pudding is traditionally cooked in a large tin below the joint, so that some of the cooking juices from the meat fall into the pudding to give it an excellent flavour. In a modern oven, this means using a rotisserie or resting the meat directly on the oven shelf. The pudding should be cooked in a large roasting tin, then cut into portions and served as a course on its own before the meat course. Gravy should be poured over the portions of pudding.

BEEF WELLINGTON

This classic Beef Wellington differs from beef en croûte in
that the meat is covered with fine pâté – preferably
pâté de foie gras – before it is wrapped.

800 g–1 kg / 1¾ lb–2¼ lb fillet of beef
freshly-ground pepper
25 g / 1 oz butter
15 ml / 1 tbsp oil
100 g / 4 oz button mushrooms, sliced
5 ml / 1 tsp chopped fresh mixed herbs
5ml / 1 tsp chopped parsley
75 g / 3 oz fine liver pâté

PUFF PASTRY
225 g / 8 oz plain flour
2.5 ml / ½ tsp salt
225 g / 8 oz butter
3.75 ml / ¾ tsp lemon juice
beaten egg for glazing

Make the pastry. Sift the flour and salt into a mixing bowl and rub in 50 g / 2 oz of the butter. Add the lemon juice and mix to a smooth dough with cold water. Shape the remaining butter into a rectangle on greaseproof paper. Roll out the dough on a lightly floured surface to a strip a little wider than the butter and rather more than twice its length. Place the butter on one half of the pastry, fold the other half over it, and press the edges together with the rolling pin. Leave in a cool place for 15 minutes to allow the butter to harden.

Roll out the pastry into a long strip. Fold the bottom third up and the top third down, press the edges together with the rolling pin and turn the pastry so that the folded edges are on the right and left. Roll and fold again, cover and leave in a cool place for 15 minutes. Repeat this process until the pastry has been rolled out six times. Chill the pastry well between each rolling, wrapping it in cling film to prevent it drying on the surface. After the final rolling, leave wrapped pastry in the refrigerator until required.

Set the oven at 230°C / 450°F / gas 8. Wipe, trim and tie the meat into a neat shape. Season with pepper. Melt the butter in the oil in a large frying pan, add the fillet and brown it quickly all over. Carefully transfer the fillet to a roasting tin, reserving the fat in the pan, and roast it for 10–20 minutes (for a rare to medium result). Remove and cool. Leave the oven on.

Heat the fat remaining in the frying pan, add the mushrooms and fry over moderate heat for 2–3 minutes. Remove from the heat, add the herbs and leave to cool.

Roll out the pastry on a lightly floured surface to a rectangle large enough to enclose the fillet. Using a slotted spoon, transfer the mushroom mixture to one half of the pastry. Lay the beef on top and spread the pâté over the meat. Wrap the pastry around the beef to form a neat parcel, sealing the edges well. Place on a baking sheet with the join underneath. Top with leaves and / or a lattice of strips cut from the pastry trimmings, glaze with beaten egg and bake for about 30 minutes. Serve hot or cold.

SERVES SIX

MRS BEETON'S TIP

To make individual Beef Wellingtons, use six portions of raw fillet. Wrap individually, including mushrooms and pâté, bringing up the pastry sides to make neat parcels. Glaze and bake, allowing 15–20 minutes for rare beef; 25–30 minutes for medium-cooked beef.

ROASTED ROLLED STEAK

50 g / 2 oz gammon or rindless bacon, finely chopped
50 g / 2 oz shredded suet
grated rind of ½ lemon
5 ml / 1 tsp finely chopped parsley
5 ml / 1 tsp finely chopped mixed herbs
cayenne pepper
pinch of ground mace
175 g / 6 oz fresh white breadcrumbs
1 egg, lightly beaten
900 g / 2 lb thick-cut rump steak, in one or two pieces
50 g / 2 oz Clarified Butter (page 36)
25 g / 1 oz plain flour
750 ml / 1¼ pints vegetable cooking water
salt and pepper

Set the oven at 200°C / 400°F / gas 6. Mix the gammon or bacon, suet, lemon rind and herbs, adding salt, cayenne and mace to taste. Stir in the breadcrumbs and add the beaten egg to bind the ingredients into a forcemeat.

Lay the steak between two sheets of greaseproof paper and beat it with a rolling pin or steak mallet to thin it out slightly so that it is the same thickness all over. Season the steak well and spread the forcemeat over half of it, if it is in one piece, or over one portion if it is two pieces. Roll up the steak to enclose the forcemeat; wrap the unfilled piece around the filled steak if there are two portions. Tie the steak firmly to keep it in shape and place it in a roasting tin.

Dot the clarified butter over the steak and roast it for 10 minutes. Reduce the heat to 180°C / 350°F / gas 4 and continue roasting the steak for 1¼ hours. Baste the roll frequently during cooking.

Transfer the cooked steak to a serving plate, cover it and keep it warm. Stir the flour into the pan juices and cook the paste, stirring it often, until the flour browns lightly. Stir in the vegetable cooking water and bring the gravy to the boil, stirring continuously. Boil the gravy for about 3 minutes, until it has reduced and all the cooking residue from the pan has been incorporated. Taste and season the gravy before serving it with the rolled stuffed steak.

SERVES FOUR

VARIATION

• **Beef Olives** These are now the more familiar version of rolled steak. Mrs Beeton's method for making beef olives was simple and successful. Beat out small slices of lean beef steak (braising steak works well) until thin. Brush the steaks with beaten egg, then sprinkle them with seasoning and finely chopped mixed herbs (parsley, thyme and marjoram or your favourite combination). Roll up the steaks and secure them with skewers or wooden cocktail sticks.

Place the rolls in a casserole and pour in 600 ml / 1 pint Beef Stock (page 228). Lay 2 or 3 rashers of bacon over the top and cover the casserole. Cook the beef olives gently for 2 hours, either by simmering them on the hob or cooking them in the oven at 160°C / 325°F / gas 3. Thicken the cooking juices by stirring in a few pieces of beurre manié (made by creaming equal quantities of softened butter and plain flour together). Pour the sauce over the beef olives.

SCOTCH COLLOPS

*Collop is said to be derived from escalope, meaning slice. It was also used
as an everyday term for veal, so sliced veal could equally well have
been used in this old-fashioned dish. Minced collops, a less extravagant
variation on this recipe, uses chopped steak in place of sliced meat.*

50 g / 2 oz dripping, lard or butter
675 g / 1½ lb rump steak, beaten and cut into
thin slices, about 7.5 cm / 3 inches long
25 g / 1 oz plain flour
½ small onion or 1 shallot, finely chopped
250 ml / 8 fl oz good Beef Stock (page 228)
5 ml / 1 tsp chopped capers
1 pickled walnut, chopped
salt and pepper

Heat the fat in a deep frying pan. In a bowl or stout polythene bag, toss the meat
with the flour, salt and pepper, then add the slices to the hot fat and fry until
browned on all sides. With a slotted spoon, remove the meat from the pan. Add
the onion or shallot to the fat remaining in the pan and fry gently until softened
but not browned. Stir in any flour left from dusting the meat and cook for about
5 minutes, stirring all the time, until the flour begins to brown.

Gradually add the stock, stirring constantly, then add the capers, pickled walnut
and salt and pepper to taste. Bring to the boil, stirring constantly, then lower the
heat and replace the meat. Simmer very gently for 10 minutes and serve hot.

SERVES FOUR TO SIX

VARIATION

- **Minced Collops** Braising steak may be used instead of rump. Trim and
finely chop the meat by hand (minced beef is too fine). Fry 1 chopped onion
in the fat, then add the beef tossed in flour and cook until browned. Add the
stock and seasoning, as above, without removing the meat from the pan.
Omit the capers and walnut but add a bouquet garni and a dash of
Worcestershire sauce or Mushroom Ketchup (page 239) instead. Bring just
to the boil, then cover and simmer gently for 1–1½ hours, until tender.

BRAISED BRISKET

1.25 kg–1.5 kg / 2¾ lb–3¼ lb brisket of beef, trimmed
25 g / 1 oz dripping or 30 ml / 2 tbsp oil
25g / 1 oz rindless streaky bacon rashers, chopped
1 large carrot, thickly sliced
1 small turnip, thickly sliced
1 large onion, chopped, or 15 button onions
2 celery sticks, thickly sliced
1 bouquet garni
250–300 ml / 8–10 fl oz Beef Stock (page 228)
salt and pepper

GRAVY
30 ml / 2 tbsp dripping or oil
10 ml / 2 tsp plain flour
450 ml / ¾ pint Beef Stock (page 228)
10 ml / 2 tsp tomato purée

Tie the meat into a neat shape if necessary. Heat the dripping or oil in a large flameproof casserole, add the meat and brown it on all sides. Remove the meat and set it aside. Add the bacon and vegetables, and fry gently until beginning to soften. Tuck in the bouquet garni and add salt and pepper to taste. Place the meat on top of the vegetables and pour the stock over. Cover with a tight-fitting lid and cook over gentle heat for 2 hours or until the meat is tender. Baste occasionally and add more stock if required. Alternatively, cook in a preheated 160°C / 325°F / gas 3 oven for about 2 hours.

To make the gravy, heat the dripping or oil in a saucepan. Stir in the flour and cook gently until pale brown. Gradually add the stock, stirring constantly, then add the tomato purée. Bring to the boil, stirring all the time, then lower the heat and simmer uncovered for 15–20 minutes.

When the meat is cooked, transfer it to a heated serving dish, remove the string, if used, and keep hot. Strain any stock remaining in the casserole into the gravy. Garnish the meat with the vegetables and serve the gravy separately.

SERVES TEN TO TWELVE

STEWED BEEF

25 g / 1 oz butter
900 g / 2 lb stewing beef or braising steak, cut into
2.5–5 cm / 1–2 inch chunks
3 onions, thinly sliced
3 carrots, thinly sliced
2 turnips, diced
15 ml / 1 tbsp Mushroom Ketchup (page 239), liquid from
pickled walnuts or Worcestershire sauce
30 ml / 2 tbsp plain flour
salt and pepper

Melt the butter in a flameproof casserole or heavy-bottomed saucepan and fry the beef or steak until the chunks are browned on both sides. Use a slotted spoon to remove the meat, then fry the vegetables in the fat remaining in the pan. Stir the vegetables until the onions are slightly softened.

Replace the meat and add plenty of seasoning. Pour in 600 ml / 1 pint water, or enough to just cover the ingredients, then bring the stew slowly to simmering point. Cover the pan tightly and simmer the stew very gently for 2½–3 hours, or until the meat is tender.

Add the ketchup, walnut liquid or sauce and additional seasoning if necessary. Blend the flour to a smooth paste with a little cold water, then stir in a few spoonfuls of the hot liquid from the stew. Stir the flour mixture into the stew and bring it to the boil, stirring to thicken the cooking liquid smoothly. Reduce the heat and simmer for 1–2 minutes before serving.

Note The stew will be less rich if it is cooked the day before it is required, then cooled and chilled. This allows and fat to be lifted off the surface, so that the stew merely needs to be heated before being served.

SERVES SIX

MRS BEETON'S TIP

YEAST DUMPLINGS
These were made using a basic bread dough, mixed with milk
instead of water, and served with meat gravy or as a sweet dish,
with melted butter and sugar.

To make yeast dumplings, take small portions of dough, about 50 g
(2 oz), and roll them into neat balls, then place these on a floured baking
sheet. Cover the dumplings loosely with greased polythene or foil and
leave them in a warm place until they have doubled in size.

The dumplings must be served as soon as they are cooked or they will
become heavy. Bring a large saucepan of water to the boil and gently
add the dumplings, using a slotted spoon. Cover the pan and simmer
them for 20 minutes. Turn the dumplings halfway through cooking, but
take care not to knock the air out of the mixture or the dumplings will be
leaden. Remove them with a slotted spoon and serve at once, breaking
the dumplings open with two forks.

BRAISED STUFFED SHOULDER OF LAMB

50 g / 2 oz gammon or rindless bacon, finely chopped
50 g / 2 oz shredded suet
grated rind of ½ lemon
5 ml / 1 tsp finely chopped parsley
5 ml / 1 tsp finely chopped mixed herbs
cayenne pepper
pinch of ground mace
175 g / 6 oz fresh white breadcrumbs
1 egg, lightly beaten
1 shoulder of lamb, boned
2 onions, sliced
½ head of celery, sliced
1 bouquet garni
1.1 litres / 2 pints lamb stock or Chicken Stock (page 229)
2 streaky bacon rashers
salt and pepper

Set the oven at 180°C / 350°F / gas 4. Mix the gammon or bacon, suet, lemon rind and herbs, then add salt, cayenne and mace to taste. Stir in the breadcrumbs and add enough of the beaten egg to bind the ingredients into a forcemeat.

Fill the boned shoulder of lamb with the forcemeat and sew up the joint with a trussing needle and string or heavy buttonhole thread (used double). Place the onions, celery and bouquet garni in a large casserole and put the shoulder of lamb on top. Pour in the stock, leaving the top of the meat exposed. Season the lamb well. Lay the streaky bacon over the lamb. Cover the casserole and place it in the oven.

Cook the lamb for 30 minutes, then remove the lid. Cook for 1 hour more, then lift off the bacon and continue to cook the lamb for a further 30–40 minutes. Transfer the lamb to a serving dish and spoon the celery and onions around it.

SERVES SIX

VARIATION

• **Mushroom Stuffing** A well-flavoured mushroom stuffing is delicious with lamb. Chop 225 g / 8 oz open-cup mushrooms fairly finely and fry them in 50 g / 2 oz butter in a large saucepan. Continue to cook until the liquid which runs from the mushrooms evaporates completely. Stir the mushrooms towards the end of cooking to prevent them from sticking to the pan.

Mix 100 g / 4 oz fresh white breadcrumbs, 60 ml / 4 tbsp chopped parsley, 15 ml / 1 tbsp chopped fresh tarragon, thyme or savory and a little grated nutmeg with the mushrooms. Add salt and pepper to taste. Bind the stuffing with 30 ml / 2 tbsp dry sherry and a little beaten egg, if necessary. The stuffing should be quite dry for braised lamb but moist if the joint is to be roasted.

MRS BEETON'S TIP

Peas and stewed cucumbers with onions were among the original accompaniments suggested for the stuffed shoulder of lamb. New potatoes would complete the menu.

HERBED SHOULDER
OF LAMB

*This recipe maybe used for leg as well
as for shoulder of lamb.*

**1 shoulder of lamb, boned
4 garlic cloves, peeled and quartered lengthways
about 6 small sprigs each fresh
rosemary and thyme
4 bay leaves
2 oranges
60 ml / 4 tbsp olive oil
salt and pepper
300 ml / ½ pint red wine**

GARNISH
**orange slices
fresh herbs**

Trim any lumps of fat from the lamb, then tie it in a neat shape if the butcher
has not already done this. Weigh the joint and calculate the cooking time at
30 minutes per 450 g / 1 lb plus 30 minutes. Use a small pointed knife to make
short cuts into the lamb, at an angle running under the skin, all over the joint.
Insert pieces of garlic and the rosemary and thyme sprigs into the cuts. Place
the joint in a deep dish, with two bay leaves underneath and two on top.

Pare two long strips of rind off one orange and add them to the dish, placing
them next to or on top of the lamb. Squeeze the juice from the oranges, then
mix it with the olive oil, salt and pepper. Pour this mixture over the lamb, cover
and marinate for several hours or overnight. Turn the joint at least once during
the marinating time.

Set the oven at 180°C / 350°F / gas 4. Transfer the joint to a roasting tin, adding
the bay leaves and orange rind but reserving the marinade. Cook for half the
calculated time, brushing occasionally with the reserved marinade and basting
with cooking juices from the tin. Pour the remaining marinade and the wine
over the joint and continue roasting. Baste the lamb occasionally and add a little

water to the juices in the tin if they begin to dry up – if the roasting tin is large they will evaporate more speedily.

Transfer the cooked joint to a serving dish, cover with foil and set aside. Pour 300 ml / ½ pint boiling water or vegetable cooking water into the roasting tin. Boil the cooking juices rapidly, stirring and scraping the sediment off the base and sides of the pan, until they are reduced by half. Taste for seasoning, then strain the sauce into a heated sauceboat.

Garnish the lamb with orange slices and fresh herbs and serve at once, carving it into thick slices. Offer the sauce separately.

SERVES SIX

MRS BEETON'S TIP

Once it has been reduced, the sauce may be thickened by whisking in small knobs of beurre manié, then boiling for 2 minutes, whisking all the time. To make beurre manié cream 25 g / 1 oz butter with 30–45 ml / 2–3 tbsp plain flour.

COTTAGE PIE

50 g / 2 oz butter
575 g / 1¼ lb minced beef
1 onion, chopped
2 carrots, finely chopped
100 g / 4 oz mushrooms, chopped
30 ml / 2 tbsp plain flour
300 ml / ½ pint Beef Stock (page 228)
5 ml / 1 tsp Worcestershire sauce
900 g / 2 lb potatoes, halved
30 ml / 2 tbsp milk
pinch of grated nutmeg
salt and pepper

Melt half the butter in a saucepan and fry the minced beef until browned, stirring to break up any lumps. Add the chopped onion, carrots and mushrooms and cook for 10 minutes or until softened slightly.

Stir in the flour, then pour in the beef stock and Worcestershire sauce, with salt and pepper to taste. Bring to the boil, stirring, then cover the pan and simmer for 30 minutes.

Cook the potatoes in a saucepan of salted boiling water for about 20 minutes or until tender. Drain thoroughly and mash with a potato masher. Beat in the remaining butter and the milk to make a creamy consistency. Add salt, pepper and nutmeg to taste.

Set the oven to 200°C / 400°F / gas 6. Spoon the meat mixture into an ovenproof dish. Cover with the potato and mark the top with a fork. Bake for about 25 minutes until the potato topping is browned.

SERVES FOUR TO SIX

SHEPHERD'S PIE

butter for greasing
50 g / 2 oz butter
2 onions, roughly chopped
15 ml / 1 tbsp plain flour
250 ml / 8 fl oz well-flavoured lamb stock
575 g / 1¼ lb lean cooked lamb, minced
5 ml / 1 tsp Worcestershire sauce
675 g / 1½ lb potatoes, halved
15–30 ml / 1–2 tbsp milk
pinch of grated nutmeg
salt and pepper

Melt half the butter in a saucepan and fry the onions until softened but not coloured. Stir in the flour and cook gently for 1–2 minutes, stirring all the time. Gradually add the stock. Bring to the boil, stirring until the sauce thickens.

Stir in the lamb, with salt and pepper and Worcestershire sauce to taste. Cover the pan and simmer for 30 minutes.

Meanwhile cook the potatoes in a saucepan of salted boiling water for about 30 minutes or until tender. Drain thoroughly and mash with a potato masher, or beat them with a handheld electric whisk until smooth. Beat in the rest of the butter and the milk to make a creamy consistency. Add salt, pepper and nutmeg to taste.

Set the oven at 220°C / 425°F / gas 7. Spoon the meat mixture into a greased pie dish or shallow oven-to-table dish. Cover with the potato, smooth the top, then flick it up unto small peaks or score a pattern on the surface with a fork. Bake for 10–15 minutes until browned on top. Serve at once.

SERVES FOUR TO SIX

LANCASHIRE HOT POT

oil for greasing
1 kg / 2¼ lb potatoes
1 kg / 2¼ lb middle neck of lamb or mutton,
trimmed and cut into neat cutlets
3 lamb's kidneys, skinned, cored and sliced
2 large onions, sliced
250 ml / 8 fl oz hot lamb or Vegetable Stock (page 232)
25 g / 1 oz lard or dripping
salt and pepper

Set the oven to 180°C / 350°F / gas 4. Slice half the potatoes and cut the rest into chunks. Arrange half the sliced potatoes in the bottom of a greased, large and deep casserole. Layer the meat, kidneys, onions and potato chunks on top, seasoning each layer lightly with salt and pepper. Finish with the remaining potato slices.

Pour in the hot stock. Melt the lard or dripping and brush it over the top layer of potatoes. Cover the casserole with a tight-fitting lid and bake for about 2 hours or until the meat and potatoes are tender.

Remove the lid, increase the oven temperature to 220°C / 425°F / gas 7 and cook for 20 minutes more or until the top layer of potatoes is brown and crisp. Serve from the casserole.

SERVES SIX

IRISH STEW

**1 kg / 2¼ lb middle neck or scrag end
of neck of lamb
2 large onions, thinly sliced
1 kg / 2¼ lb potatoes, thinly sliced
salt and pepper
well-flavoured lamb or Chicken Stock (page 229)
30 ml / 2 tbsp chopped parsley to garnish**

Set the oven to 190°C / 375°F / gas 5. Cut the meat into neat cutlets or pieces, trimming off any excess fat. Layer the meat, onions, and potatoes in a casserole, sprinkling each layer with salt and pepper, and ending with potatoes.

Add enough stock to half-fill the casserole. Cover with a lid and bake for about 2—2½ hours, removing the lid for the last 30 minutes of the cooking time, to allow the potato topping to brown. Sprinkle with chopped parsley to serve.

SERVES FOUR TO SIX

TOAD-IN-THE-HOLE

450 g / 1 lb pork sausages

BATTER
100 g / 4 oz plain flour
1.25 ml / ¼ tsp salt
1 egg beaten
300 ml / ½ pint milk, or milk and water

Make the batter. Sift the flour and salt into a bowl, make a well in the centre and add the beaten egg. Stir in half the milk (or all the milk if using a mixture of milk and water), gradually working in the flour.

Beat vigorously until the mixture is smooth and bubbly, then stir in the rest of the milk (or water). Pour the batter into a jug and set aside.

Set the oven to 220°C / 425°F / gas 7. Arrange the sausages, spoke-fashion. In a shallow 1.1 litre / 2 pint circular dish. Stand the dish on a baking sheet and cook the sausages for 15 minutes.

Pour the batter over the sausages and bake for 40–45 minutes more until golden brown and well risen. Serve at once with a rich gravy.

SERVES FOUR

TO MOULD A RAISED PIE

Hot Water Crust Pastry (page 150)
lard for greasing
flour

Use a jar, round cake tin or similar container, as a mould: grease and flour the sides and base of the mould and invert it.

Reserve a quarter of the warm pastry for the lid and leave in the bowl in a warm place, covered with a greased polythene bag. Roll out the remainder to about 5 mm / ¼ inch thick, in a round or oval shape. Lay the pastry over the mould, then ease the pastry around the sides. Take care not to pull the pastry and make sure that the sides and base are of an even thickness. Leave to cool.

When cold, remove the pastry case from the mould and put in the filling. Roll out the pastry reserved for the lid, dampen the rim of the case, put on the lid, pressing the edges firmly together. Tie 3 or 4 folds of greaseproof paper round the pie to hold it in shape during baking and to prevent it from becoming too brown.

MAKES ONE 13-cm / 5-inch PIE

USING A RAISED PIE MOULD

Decorative pie moulds may be purchased from cookshops. Usually oval in shape, they range in size from those which provide up to 6 servings, to others which make pies large enough to feed 40 people.

The two sides of the mould fit into a base and they are secured with clips. The sides should be secured and the inside of the mould should be well greased. The pastry should be rolled out to about two-thirds of the required size.

Lift the pastry into the mould and secure its edge just below the rim of the mould. Use your fingers to press the pastry into the mould, easing it upwards at the same time so that it comes above the rim of the mould when the lining is complete. The pie may be filled at once.

The sides of the mould should be removed about 15–30 minutes before the end of the cooking time. Brush the pastry with beaten egg immediately and return the pie to the oven promptly to prevent the sides from collasping.

RAISED VEAL PIE

If preferred, these ingredients can be made into 6 individual pies.
The eggs should be sliced and divided between the smaller pies.

Hot Water Crust Pastry (page 150),
using 400 g / 14 oz flour
400 g / 14 oz pie veal
400 g / 14 oz lean pork
25 g / 1 oz plain flour
7.5 ml / 1½ tsp salt
1.25 ml / ¼ tsp ground pepper
3 hard-boiled eggs
beaten egg for glazing
about 125 ml / 4 fl oz well-flavoured, cooled
and jellied stock or canned consommé

Set the oven at 230°C / 450°F / gas 8. Line a 20 cm / 8 inch round pie mould with three-quarters of the pastry, or use a round cake tin to mould the pie as described opposite. Use the remaining quarter for the lid.

Cut the meat into small pieces, removing any gristle or fat. Season the flour with the salt and pepper, then toss the pieces of meat in it. Put half the meat into the pastry case and put in the whole eggs. Add the remaining meat and 30 ml / 2 tbsp water. Put on the lid and brush with beaten egg. Make a hole in the centre to allow steam to escape. Bake for 15 minutes, then reduce the oven temperature to 140°C / 275°F / gas 1. Continue baking 2½ hours. Remove the greaseproof paper or mould for the last 30 minutes of the cooking time and brush the top and sides of the pastry with beaten egg.

Heat the stock or consommé until melted. When the pie is cooked, pour it through the hole in the lid using a funnel until the pie is full. Leave to cool.

SERVES SIX

RAISED PORK PIES

about 400 g / 14 oz pork bones
1 small onion, finely chopped
300 ml / ½ pint stock or cold water
Hot Water Crust Pastry (page 150), using 400 g / 14 oz flour
500 g / 18 oz lean pork, minced
1.25 ml / ¼ tsp dried sage
beaten egg for glazing
salt and pepper

Simmer the pork bones, onion, salt, pepper and stock or water, covered, for 2 hours. Strain and cool. Make one 15 cm / 6 inch pie (as described page 111) or divide three-quarters of the pastry into 6 portions. Mould each piece using a jam jar, keeping the pastry about 5 mm / ¼ inch thick. Use the remainder for the lids. Set the oven at 220°C / 425°F / gas 7.

Season the pork with salt, pepper and sage. Divide between the prepared pie case or cases and add 10 ml / 2 tsp of the jellied stock to each. Put on the lids, brush with beaten egg, and make holes in the centres. Bake for 15 minutes, then reduce the oven temperature to 180°C / 350°F / gas 4. Continue baking for 45 minutes (1 hour for a large pie). Remove the greaseproof paper for the last 30 minutes and brush the top and sides of the pastry with egg.

When cooked, remove from the oven and leave to cool. Warm the remainder of the jellied stock. Using a funnel, pour the stock through the hole in the pastry lids until the pies are full. Leave to cool.

SERVES SIX

STEAK AND KIDNEY PUDDING

100 g / 4 oz shredded beef suet
275 g / 10 oz self-raising flour
175–200 ml / 6–7 fl oz milk
150 g / 5 oz lamb's kidneys
575 g / 1¼ lb lean rump steak, cut into 2.5 cm (1 inch) cubes
30–45 ml / 2–3 tbsp plain flour (optional)
salt and pepper

Grease a 1.1 litre / 2 pint pudding basin and have a pudding cloth ready for tying around it. Bring a large saucepan of water to the boil, for cooking the pudding.

Stir the suet and 2.5 ml / ½ tsp salt into the flour. When the ingredients are well-mixed, gradually stir in the milk. The mixture should bind together without being sticky. Use three-quarters of the pastry to line the basin, easing it in and making sure that it overlaps the rim of the basin by about 1 cm / ½ inch.

Cut the kidneys in half then discard their white cores and dice the halves. Layer the steak and kidney in the pastry-lined basin, seasoning each layer well and sprinkling the plain flour over the layers if you want the cooking juices to be thickened. Pour in enough cold water to three-quarters fill the basin.

Roll out the remaining pastry to cover the pudding. Dampen the edge of the pastry lining and place the lid on top. Pinch the pastry edges together to seal them well, then dampen the top edge and fold the overhanging pastry neatly on to the top of the pudding, pressing it in place.

Rinse the pudding cloth in very hot water – as hot as your hands can stand – then wring it out tightly. Open the cloth out on a clean surface or board and dredge it well with flour. Place the pudding basin in the middle of the cloth and tie both sets of opposing corners together over the middle of the pudding. Tie a piece of string through the knots in the cloth if the ends are too short to allow you to lower the pudding into the saucepan. Lower the pudding into the pan and bring the water back to the boil.

Boil the pudding for 4 hours, keeping the water bubbling steadily, but not too rapidly. Top up the water with fresh boiling water from the kettle as necessary to keep the pudding covered.

Use a spoon handle to pull up the string or cloth ends and lift the pudding from the pan. Open the cloth and stand the pudding on a plate or shallow dish or surround it with a clean napkin. Cut a round of pastry from the middle of the pudding to prevent it from bursting and serve it at once, cutting portions out of the basin.

If you prefer to turn the pudding out before serving it, loosen the pastry around the rim carefully with a heatproof plastic spatula, then invert the pudding on a shallow dish, leaving the pudding basin in place while you carry the dish to the table. Lift off the basin at the last minute or the pudding may collapse.

SERVES FOUR TO SIX

CORNISH PASTIES

FILLING
1 large or 2 small potatoes
1 small turnip
1 onion, chopped
300 g / 11 oz lean chuck steak, finely diced
salt and pepper

PASTRY
500 g / 18 oz plain flour
5 ml / 1 tsp salt
150 g / 5 oz lard
60 ml / 4 tbsp shredded suet
flour for rolling out
beaten egg for glazing

Set the oven at 230ºC / 450ºF / gas 8. To make the pastry, sift the flour and salt into a bowl. Rub in the lard, then mix in the suet. Moisten with enough cold water to make a stiff dough. Roll out on a lightly-floured surface and cut into eight 16 cm / 6½ inch rounds.

To make the filling, dice the potatoes and turnip, then mix with the onion and add salt and pepper to taste. Add the meat and 30 ml / 2 tbsp water, and mix well. Divide between the pastry rounds, placing a line of mixture across the centre of each round.

Dampen the edges of each pastry round. Lift them to meet over the filling. Pinch together to seal, then flute the edges. Make small slits in both sides of each pasty near the top. Place the pasties on a baking sheet and brush with egg. Bake for 10 minutes, then lower the oven temperature to 180ºC / 350ºF / gas 4. Continue baking for a further 45 minutes, or until the meat is tender when pierced by a thin, heated skewer through the top of a pasty.

MAKES EIGHT

Salads
& Vegetables

*A wide variety of dishes suited to all
occasions; whether a salad for
lunch, a vibrant side dish
or a main meal.*

FENNEL AND CUCUMBER SALAD

½ large cucumber, diced
6 radishes, sliced
1 fennel bulb, sliced
1 garlic clove, crushed
5 ml / 1 tsp chopped mint
2 eggs, hard-boiled and quartered, to garnish

DRESSING
30 ml / 2 tbsp olive oil
15 ml / 1 tbsp lemon juice
salt and pepper

Combine the cucumber, radishes, fennel and garlic in a salad bowl. Sprinkle with the mint. Make the dressing by shaking the ingredients together in a tightly-closed screw-top jar. Pour over the salad, toss lightly and serve with the hard-boiled egg garnish.

SERVES SIX

GRAPEFRUIT AND CHICORY SALAD

3 grapefuit
3 small heads of chicory
50 g / 2 oz seedless raisins
15 ml / 1 tbsp grapefruit juice
45 ml / 3 tbsp oil
2.5 ml / ½ tsp French mustard
salt and pepper
mustard and cress to garnish

Cut the grapefruit in half. Cut the fruit into segments and put them in a bowl. Remove all the pulp and pith from the grapefruit shells; stand the shells upside down on absorbent kitchen paper to drain.

Shred the chicory, reserving some neat rounds for the garnish, and add to the grapefruit segments with all the remaining ingredients except the garnish. Toss the mixture lightly together, then pile back into the grapefruit shells. Garnish with the cress and reserved chicory and serve at once.

SERVES SIX

STRAWBERRY AND TOMATO SALAD

450 g / 1 lb firm tomatoes, peeled
salt
pinch of paprika
15 ml / 1 tbsp lemon juice
350 g / 12 oz firm strawberries, hulled and quartered
30 ml / 2 tbsp salad oil

GARNISH
a few whole strawberries
a cucumber, thinly sliced

Cut the tomatoes in half and remove the seeds and pulp, reserving these for use in another recipe. Cut the tomato flesh into thin slices, place in a bowl and add salt and paprika to taste., Sprinkle with lemon juice; set aside.

Just before serving, add the strawberries and transfer the mixture to a serving platter or dish. Drizzle with the oil and garnish with the whole strawberries and cucumber slices.

SERVES SIX

COLESLAW

Coleslaw looks marvellous in a natural cabbage bowl.
Use a sharp knife to cut out the centre of a Savoy cabbage, using the
cut portion for the coleslaw. Rinse the cabbage bowl under cold water,
shake off excess moisture and dry between the leaves with absorbent kitchen
paper. Trim the base of the cabbage bowl so that it stands neatly.

450 g / 1 lb firm white or Savoy cabbage, finely shredded
100 g / 4 oz carrots, coarsely grated
2 celery sticks, thinly sliced
½ small green pepper, seeded and thinly sliced
150 ml / ¼ pint mayonnaise or plain yoghurt
lemon juice
salt and pepper

Mix all the ingredients in a salad bowl, adding enough lemon juice to give the mayonnaise or yoghurt a tangy taste. Chill before serving.

SERVES FOUR

VARIATION

• **Fruit and Nut Slaw** Core and dice, but do not peel, 1 red-skinned eating apple. Toss in 15 ml / 1 tbsp lemon juice, then add to the slaw with 25 g / 1 oz seedless raisins or sultanas and 25 g / 1 oz chopped walnuts, almonds or hazelnuts.

DRESSED CUCUMBER

1 cucumber, peeled
salt and pepper
45 ml / 3 tbsp salad oil
60 ml / 4 tbsp vinegar

Slice the cucumber very thinly and place it in a dish. Season the cucumber and sprinkle the oil and vinegar over the slices. Turn the slices in the dressing and serve the salad immediately. Snipped chives and chopped dill, fennel, tarragon or parsley can be sprinkled over the salad.

SERVES FOUR

POTATO SALAD

10–12 waxy potatoes
60 ml / 4 tbsp tarragon, cider or white wine vinegar
90 ml / 6 tbsp salad oil
15 ml / 1 tbsp finely chopped parsley
salt and pepper

Boil the potatoes in their skins, in salted water, for about 20 minutes or until just tender. Then drain and peel them, removing the skin as thinly as possible. Cover the potatoes and set them aside to cool.

Whisk a little seasoning with the vinegar, then whisk in the oil and parsley. Cut the potatoes into slices, about 1 cm / ½ inch thick, and layer them in a serving bowl, sprinkling each layer with some of the dressing. Pour the remaining dressing over the top to ensure all the potato slices are coated.

Cover the dish and set the salad aside for 2–3 hours so that the dressing flavours the potatoes well before the salad is served.

SERVES SIX

SPINACH AND BACON SALAD

450 g / 1 lb fresh young spinach
150 g / 5 oz button mushrooms, thinly sliced
1 small onion, thinly sliced
15 ml / 1 tbsp oil
6 rindless streaky bacon rashers, cut into strips
75 ml / 5 tbsp French dressing

Remove the stalks from the spinach, wash the leaves well in cold water, then dry thoroughly on absorbent kitchen paper. If time permits, put the leaves in a polythene bag and chill for 1 hour.

Tear the spinach into large pieces and put in a salad bowl with the mushroom and the onion.

Heat the oil in a small frying pan and fry the bacon until crisp. Meanwhile, toss the salad vegetables with the French dressing. Pour in the hot bacon and fat, toss lightly to mix and serve at once.

SERVES FOUR

MRS BEETON'S TIP

If preferred, the bacon may be grilled
until crisp and crumbled into the
salad just before serving.

CHICKEN AND CELERY SALAD

1 large lettuce, separated into leaves
1 celery heart
350 g / 12 oz cooked chicken, cut into serving pieces
10 ml / 2 tsp tarragon or white wine vinegar
salt and pepper
150 ml / ¼ pint mayonnaise

GARNISH
lettuce leaves
2 hard-boiled eggs, sliced or chopped
stoned black olives and / or gherkin strips

Wash the lettuce leaves and dry them thoroughly. Shred the outer leaves with the celery. Put in a bowl with the chicken and the vinegar. Toss lightly and add salt and pepper to taste.

Spoon the chicken mixture into a bowl or on to a platter. Coast with the mayonnaise. Garnish with lettuce leaves, sliced or chopped egg and olives and / or gherkin strips.

SERVES SIX

VARIATION

For a substantial, meal-in-one salad, toss in some cooked pasta shapes or cooked rice.

BROAD BEANS WITH CREAM SAUCE

250 ml / 8 fl oz Chicken Stock (page 229)
15 ml / 1 tbsp chopped fresh herbs (parsley, thyme, sage, savory)
1 kg / 2¼ lb broad beans, shelled
1 egg yolk
150 ml / ¼ pint single cream
salt and pepper

Combine the stock and herbs in a saucepan. Bring to the boil, add the beans and cook for 5–15 minutes until tender. Lower the heat to a bare simmer. Beat the egg yolk with the cream in a small bowl. Add 30 ml / 2 tbsp of the hot stock and mix well, then pour the contents of the bowl into the pan. Heat gently, stirring all the time, until the sauce thickens slightly. Do not allow the mixture to boil or it will curdle. Add salt and pepper to taste and serve.

SERVES FOUR

COURGETTES WITH DILL

A simple dish to go with fish.

25 g / 1 oz butter
grated rind of ½ lemon
8 small courgettes, trimmed and sliced
45 ml / 3 tbsp chopped fresh dill
squeeze of lemon juice
salt and pepper

Melt the butter in a large frying pan. Add the lemon rind and cook for a few seconds, then add the courgettes. Cook over medium to high heat for 2–3 minutes, add salt and pepper, and dill. Toss in a little lemon juice and serve.

SERVES FOUR

CAULIFLOWER CHEESE

**1 firm cauliflower
30 ml / 2 tbsp butter
60 ml / 4 tbsp plain flour
200 ml / 7 fl oz milk
125 g / 4½ oz Cheddar cheese, grated
pinch of dry mustard
pinch of cayenne pepper
25 g / 1 oz dried white breadcrumbs
salt and pepper**

Bring a saucepan of salted water to the boil, add the cauliflower, cover the pan and cook gently for 20–30 minutes until tender. Drain well, reserving 175 ml / 6 fl oz of the cooking water. Leave the cauliflower head whole or cut carefully into florets. Place in a warmed ovenproof dish, cover with greased greaseproof paper and keep hot.

Set the oven at 220°C / 425°F / gas 7 or preheat the grill. Melt the butter in a saucepan, stir in the flour and cook for 1 minute. Gradually add the milk and reserved cooking water, stirring all the time until the sauce boils and thickens. Remove from the heat and stir in 100 g / 4 oz of the cheese, stirring until it melts into the sauce. Add the mustard and cayenne, with salt and pepper to taste.

Pour the sauce over the cauliflower. Mix the remaining cheese with the breadcrumbs and sprinkle them on top. Brown the topping for 7–10 minutes in the oven or under the grill. Serve at once.

SERVES FOUR

CARROTS WITH CIDER

This traditional way of cooking carrots was originally known as the 'conservation method' because it preserved as many of the nutrients as possible.

75 g / 3 oz butter
675 g / 1½ lb young carrots, trimmed and scraped
60 ml / 4 tbsp double cream
125 ml / 4 fl oz dry cider
few drops of lemon juice
salt and pepper

Melt 25 g / 1 oz of the butter in a heavy-bottomed saucepan. Add the carrots and cook over very gentle heat for 10 minutes, shaking the pan frequently so that the carrots do not stick to the base. Pour over 100 ml / 3½ fl oz boiling water, with salt to taste. Cover the pan and simmer the carrots for about 10 minutes more or until tender. Drain, reserving the liquid for use in soup or stock.

Melt the remaining butter in the clean pan. Gradually stir in the cream and cider. Add the lemon juice and salt and pepper to taste. Stir in the carrots, cover the pan and cook gently for 10 minutes more. Serve at once.

SERVES SIX

GLAZED CARROTS

50 g / 2 oz butter
575 g / 1¼ lb young carrots, scraped but left whole
3 sugar cubes, crushed
1.25 ml / ¼ tsp salt
Beef Stock (see method) (page 228)
15 ml / 1 tbsp chopped parsley to garnish

Melt the butter in a saucepan. Add the carrots, sugar and salt. Pour in enough stock to half cover the carrots. Cook over gentle heat, without covering the pan, for 15–20 minutes or until the carrots are tender. Shake the pan occasionally to prevent sticking.

Using a slotted spoon, transfer the carrots to a bowl and keep hot. Boil the stock rapidly in the pan until it is reduced to a rich glaze. Return the carrots to the pan, two or three at a time, turning them in the glaze until thoroughly coated. Place on a heated serving dish, garnish with parsley and serve at once.

SERVES SIX

FENNEL WITH LEEKS

4 fennel bulbs, trimmed and halved
juice of ½ lemon
knob of butter or 30 ml / 2 tbsp olive oil
4 leeks, sliced
1 bay leaf
2 fresh thyme sprigs
150 ml / ¼ pint Chicken (page 229) or Vegetable Stock (page 232)
45 ml / 3 tbsp dry sherry (optional)
salt and pepper

Set the oven at 180°C / 350°F / gas 4. As soon as the fennel is prepared, sprinkle the lemon juice over the cut bulbs. Heat the butter or oil in a frying pan and sauté the leeks for 2 minutes to soften them slightly. Add the pieces of fennel to the pan, pushing the leeks to one side. Turn the pieces of fennel in the fat for a minute or so, then tip the contents of the pan into an ovenproof casserole.

Add the bay leaf and thyme to the vegetables and sprinkle in salt and pepper to taste. Pour the stock and sherry (if used) over the fennel and cover the dish. Bake for 1–1¼ hours, turning the fennel mixture over twice, until tender. Taste for seasoning, remove the bay leaf and serve.

SERVES FOUR

BUTTERED LEEKS

50 g / 2 oz butter
675 g / 1½ lb leeks, trimmed, sliced and washed
15 ml / 1 tbsp lemon juice
salt and pepper
30 ml / 2 tbsp single cream (optional)

Melt the butter in a heavy-bottomed saucepan. Add the leeks and lemon juice, with salt and pepper to taste. Cover the pan and cook the leeks over very gentle heat for about 30 minutes or until very tender. Shake the pan from time to time to prevent the leeks from sticking to the base. Serve in the cooking liquid. Stir in the cream when serving, if liked.

SERVES FOUR

MRS BEETON'S TIP

Leeks can be very gritty. The easiest way to wash them is to trim the roots and tough green leaves, slit them lengthways to the centre, and hold them under cold running water to flush out the grit.

EXCELLENT BAKED TOMATOES

8–10 large, firm, ripe tomatoes
salt and pepper
50 g / 2 oz fresh white breadcrumbs
50 g / 2 oz melted butter

Set the oven to 200°C / 400°F / gas 6. Peel the tomatoes and cut out their stalks, then cut them neatly into thick slices. Lay the tomato slices in an ovenproof dish, overlapping them neatly, and season them to taste.

Sprinkle the breadcrumbs over the tomatoes and trickle the butter evenly over the top. Bake the tomatoes for 20–30 minutes, until the breadcrumbs are lightly browned. Serve at once.

SERVES FOUR

SPINACH WITH CREAM

1 kg / 2¼ lb spinach
50 g / 2 oz butter
pinch of sugar
grated nutmeg
90 ml / 6 tbsp single cream
salt and pepper

Trim the stalks of the spinach leaves and wash them well. Shake off excess water, then pack the wet leaves into a large saucepan and cover it tightly. Cook the spinach over a moderate to high heat, shaking the pan often at first and adjusting the heat to avoid burning the leaves. The heat should be high to start, then reduced as the pan heats up and the spinach begins to cook. After 3–5 minutes, the spinach will be greatly reduced and tender. Drain it well in a colander or sieve.

Squeeze excess water from handfuls of spinach and chop the bundles – the easiest way to do this is to cut them in half or quarters lengthways, then shred them while still holding the spinach firmly together.

Melt the butter and stir in the spinach. Add seasoning, the sugar and nutmeg. Stir over gentle heat for a minute or so, until the spinach is hot, then stir in the cream and heat it through without allowing it to boil. Serve at once.

SERVES FOUR

BRUSSELS SPROUTS WITH CHESTNUTS

This is a classic accompaniment to the Christmas turkey. The slightly sweet flavour of the chestnuts is the perfect foil for the Brussels sprouts.

225 g / 8 oz chestnuts, shelled
(see Mrs Beeton's Tip, below)
1 kg / 2¼ lb Brussels sprouts
75 g / 3 oz cooked ham, finely chopped
60 ml / 4 tbsp single cream
salt and pepper

Set the oven at 180°C / 350°F / gas 4. Place the cleaned nuts in a saucepan, just cover with water and bring to the boil. Cover the pan, lower the heat, and simmer for about 20 minutes or until the nuts are tender. Drain, then cut each chestnut into quarters.

Trim the sprouts, pulling off any damaged leaves. Using a sharp knife, cut a cross in the base of each. Cook the sprouts in a saucepan of salted boiling water for 5–10 minutes until just tender. Drain well.

Combine the sprouts, chestnuts and ham in a small casserole. Stir in the cream and season with salt and pepper. Cover and bake for 15 minutes.

SERVES SIX

MRS BEETON'S TIP

Shelling chestnuts is made a lot easier by using the microwave. Make a slit in the shell of each nut, then rinse them thoroughly but do not dry them. Put the damp nuts in a bowl, cover loosely and cook on High for 5 minutes. When cool enough to handle, remove the shells.

RED CABBAGE WITH APPLES

45 ml / 3 tbsp oil
1 onion, finely chopped
1 garlic clove, crushed
900 g / 2 lb red cabbage, finely shredded
2 large cooking apples
15 ml / 1 tbsp soft light brown sugar or golden syrup
juice of ½ lemon
30 ml / 2 tbsp red wine vinegar
salt and pepper
15 ml / 1 tbsp caraway seeds (optional)

Heat the oil in a large saucepan, add the onion and garlic and fry gently for 5 minutes. Add the cabbage. Peel, core and slice the apples and add them to the pan with the sugar or syrup. Cook over very gentle heat for 10 minutes, shaking the pan frequently.

Add the lemon juice and vinegar, with salt and pepper to taste. Stir in the caraway seeds, if used. Cover and simmer gently for 1–1½ hours, stirring occasionally and adding a little water if the mixture appears dry. Check the seasoning before serving.

SERVES SIX

BAKED STUFFED MARROW

butter for greasing
1 marrow
1 small onion, finely chopped or grated
225 g / 8 oz minced beef
100 g / 4 oz pork sausagemeat or 100 g / 4 oz extra minced beef
25 g / 1 oz fresh white breadcrumbs
15 ml / 1 tbsp chopped parsley
15 ml / 1 tbsp snipped chives
5 ml / 1 tsp Worcestershire sauce
salt and pepper
1 egg, beaten

SAUCE
25 g / 1 oz butter
25 g / 1 oz plain flour
300 ml / ½ pint milk, stock or mixture (see method)
75–100 g / 3–4 oz Cheddar cheese, grated
pinch of dry mustard

Generously grease a large, shallow casserole. Set the oven at 180°C / 350°F / gas 4. Halve the marrow lengthways and scoop out the seeds. Lay the halves side by side in the prepared dish. Put the onion into a bowl with the beef, sausagemeat, if used, breadcrumbs, parsley, chives, Worcestershire sauce and salt and pepper. Mix well. Bind with beaten egg, avoiding making it too moist.

Divide the stuffing between each marrow half. Cover and bake for 1 hour. Strain off most of the liquid in the casserole. Meanwhile make the sauce.

Melt the butter in a saucepan. Stir in the flour and cook over low heat for 2–3 minutes, without colouring. Over very low heat, gradually add the liquid (the casserole juices may be used), stirring constantly. Bring to the boil, stirring, then lower the heat and simmer for 1–2 minutes until smooth and thickened. Add the cheese, mustard and salt and pepper to taste. Pour the cheese sauce over the marrow and bake, uncovered, for a further 20 minutes, until the sauce topping is golden brown.

SERVES FOUR TO SIX

MUSHROOMS IN CREAM SAUCE

50 g / 2 oz butter
450 g / 1 lb small button mushrooms
10 ml / 2 tsp arrowroot
125 ml / 4 fl oz Chicken (page 229) or Vegetable Stock (page 232)
15 ml / 1 tbsp lemon juice
30 ml / 2 tbsp double cream
salt and pepper
30 ml / 2 tbsp chopped parsley

Melt the butter in large frying pan, add the mushrooms and fry over gentle heat without browning for 10 minutes.

Put the arrowroot in a small bowl. Stir in 30 ml / 2 tbsp of the stock until smooth. Add the remaining stock to the mushrooms and bring to the boil. Lower the heat and simmer gently for 15 minutes, stirring occasionally. Stir in the arrowroot, bring to the boil, stirring, then remove the pan from the heat.

Stir in the lemon juice and cream, with salt and pepper to taste. Serve sprinkled with parsley.

SERVES FOUR TO SIX

PANFRIED ONION AND APPLE

40 g / 1½ oz butter
350 g / 12 oz onions, sliced in rings
450 g / 1 lb cooking apples
10 ml / 2 tsp caster sugar
salt and pepper

Melt the butter in a heavy-bottomed frying pan. Add the onions and fry gently. Peel, core and slice the apples into the pan. Mix lightly to coat the apples in the melted butter. Sprinkle the sugar over the top, cover and simmer for 30 minutes or until the onions and apples are tender. Add salt and pepper to taste.

SERVES FOUR

GLAZED ONIONS

Glazed onions make a tasty accompaniment to grilled steak, baked ham or bacon chops. They are often used as a garnish.

400 g / 14 oz button onions
Chicken Stock (see method) (page 229)
15 ml / 1 tbsp soft light brown sugar
25 g / 1 oz butter
pinch of grated nutmeg
salt and pepper

Skin the onions and put them in a single layer in a large saucepan. Add just enough stock to cover. Bring to a simmering point and cook for 15–20 minutes until the onions are just tender, adding a small amount of extra stock if necessary.

By the time the onions are cooked, the stock should have reduced almost to a glaze. Remove from the heat and stir in the remaining ingredients. Turn the onions over with a spoon so that the added ingredients mix well and the onions are coated in the mixture.

Return the pan to the heat until the onions become golden and glazed. Serve at once, with the remaining syrupy glaze.

SERVES FOUR

VARIATION

• **Citrus Glazed Onions** Melt 25 g / 1 oz butter in a frying pan. Add 400 g / 14 oz button onions. Sprinkle with 15 ml / 1 tbsp soft light brown sugar. Add salt and pepper to taste and fry, turning the onions occasionally until golden brown. Stir in 150 ml / ¼ pint orange juice and 10 ml / 2 tsp lemon juice. Cover and simmer for 15 minutes.

CREAMED ONIONS

butter for greasing
1 kg / 2¼ lb small onions, peeled but left whole
100 ml / 3½ fl oz double cream
White Sauce (page 233) made using 300 ml / ½ pint milk
grated nutmeg
25 g / 1 oz butter
50 g / 2 oz dried white breadcrumbs
30 ml / 2 tbsp chopped parsley
salt and pepper

Grease a 1 litre / 1¾ pint casserole. Set the oven at l60ºC / 325ºF / gas 3. Bring a saucepan of water to the boil. Add the onions and cook for 10–15 minutes until just tender. Drain well.

Add the double cream to the White Sauce and reheat gently without boiling. Stir in the nutmeg with salt and pepper to taste, add the onions and mix lightly.

Spoon the mixture into the prepared casserole. Top with the breadcrumbs and dot with the butter. Bake for 20 minutes. Serve hot, sprinkled with the parsley.

SERVES SIX TO EIGHT

TURNIPS IN WHITE SAUCE

*If you have dismissed turnips as only fit for soups and
casseroles, try this recipe and discover how superb they are as
a side dish for roast and grilled meats, and for splendid main
dishes such as Beef Wellington.*

**8 small turnips
50 g / 2 oz butter
1 small onion, finely chopped
1 small carrot or ½ medium carrot, finely diced
strip of pared lemon rind
45 ml / 3 tbsp plain flour
300 ml / ½ pint milk
pinch of ground mace
pinch of sugar
salt and pepper**

Cook the turnips in a saucepan of boiling salted water for about 20 minutes,
until they are tender.

Meanwhile, melt half the butter in a small saucepan and cook the onion, carrot
and lemon rind, if used, for about 10 minutes, or until the onion has softened
but not browned. Stir in the flour, then gradually pour in the milk and bring the
sauce to the boil, stirring continuously. Reduce the heat and simmer the sauce
for about 3 minutes. Discard the lemon rind and season the sauce to taste,
adding a pinch of ground mace and sugar. Beat in the remaining butter.

Drain the turnips and turn them into a serving dish. Coat the turnips with the
sauce and serve them at once.

SERVES FOUR

BRAISED CELERY

1 head of celery, trimmed
150 ml / ¼ pint White Stock (page 230) or Chicken Stock (page 229)
25 g / 1 oz butter
15 ml / 1 tbsp plain flour
pinch of ground mace
grated nutmeg
30 ml / 2 tbsp double cream
salt and pepper

Cut the celery into 10 cm / 4 inch lengths and place in a saucepan. Add the stock and seasoning. Heat the stock until it simmers, then cover the pan tightly and braise the celery for about 30 minutes, or until it is tender.

Cream the butter with the flour to a smooth paste. Use a slotted spoon to transfer the celery to a warmed serving dish. Whisk lumps of the butter and flour into the simmering stock and continue whisking until the sauce boils and thickens. Add the mace and just a little nutmeg, then stir in the cream and heat the sauce gently without allowing it to boil. Taste the sauce for seasoning before pouring it over the celery.

SERVES FOUR

MRS BEETON'S TIP

This is a very plain recipe. Braised celery is often
flavoured by sautéing a finely chopped small onion
and diced small carrot in a little butter before
adding the celery and stock. A bay leaf and a sprig
of thyme can be added with the liquid.

BAKED JACKET POTATOES

4 large, even-sized baking potatoes
oil for brushing (optional)
butter or flavoured butter, to serve

Set the oven at 200°C / 400°F / gas 6. Scrub the potatoes, dry them with absorbent kitchen paper and pierce the skin several times with a skewer. If you like soft jackets, brush the potatoes all over with oil.

Bake the potatoes directly on the oven shelf for 1–1½ hours. Test by pressing gently with the fingers. To serve, cut a cross in the top of each potato with a sharp knife. Squeeze the sides of the potato so that the top opens up. Add a pat of plain or flavoured butter and serve.

SERVES FOUR

TOPPINGS

The easy option. Cut the potatoes almost but not quite in half and open out. Top with any of the mixtures suggested below.

- **Sausage and Chutney** Mix hot or cold sliced cooked sausage with diced eating apple, chopped spring onions and a little of your favourite chutney.
- **Egg Mayonnaise** Mash hard-boiled eggs with a little mayonnaise or plain yogurt. Add 5 ml / 1 tsp tomato ketchup or tomato purée and some snipped chives.
- **Sardine** Mash canned sardines in tomato sauce and mix with diced cucumber. Serve with shredded lettuce.
- **Cheese Soufflé** Combine 100 g / 4 oz grated Cheddar cheese and 1 beaten egg. Cut potatoes in half, pile some of the mixture on each half and grill until topping puffs up and turns golden brown.
- **Peas and Bacon** Combine 100 g / 4 oz cooked petits pois and 3 crumbled grilled rindless bacon rashers. Top with a knob of butter.
- **Broccoli and Asparagus** Mix 175 g / 6 oz cooked broccoli and 100 g / 4 oz drained canned asparagus tips. Stir in 150 ml / ¼ pint soured cream, with salt and pepper to taste.

MICROWAVE COOKING TIMES ON HIGH
(600–650 WATT OVENS)

Large potatoes (350 g / 12 oz)

1 potato	*8 minutes*
2 potatoes	*15 minutes*
4 potatoes	*27 minutes*

Medium potatoes (150 g / 5 oz)

1 potato	*4 minutes*
2 potatoes	*5–6 minutes*
4 potatoes	*10 minutes*
6 potatoes	*18–19 minutes*

FILLINGS

Make a meal of baked jacket potatoes by cutting them in half, scooping out the centres and mashing them with selected ingredients. Pile the fillings back into the potato shells and heat through, if necessary, in a 180°C / 350°F / gas 4 oven for about 20 minutes. Alternatively, reheat in the microwave oven or under a moderate grill.

- **Cheese and Ham** Mash the potato. Grate in 100 g / 4 oz Cheddar cheese, add 50 g / 2 oz chopped ham (use trimmings for economy) and mix with 25 g / 1 oz softened butter. Replace in oven until golden.
- **Kipper** Mash the potato with 75 g / 3 oz flaked cooked kipper. Add 1 chopped hard-boiled egg, with salt and pepper to taste. Thin with a little milk, if necessary. Reheat.
- **Frankfurter** Mash the potato with butter. For each potato, add 2 heated chopped frankfurters and 15 ml / 1 tbsp tomato relish. Add chopped parsley.

SCALLOPED POTATOES WITH ONIONS

butter for greasing
675 g / 1½ lb potatoes, peeled and cut into 5-mm / ¼-inch slices
450 g / 1 lb onions, sliced in rings
125 ml / 4 fl oz milk or cream
20 ml / 4 tsp butter
salt and pepper

Grease a baking dish. Set the oven at 190°C / 375°F / gas 5. Layer the potatoes and onions in the prepared dish, sprinkling salt and pepper between the layers and ending with potatoes. Pour the milk or cream over the top. Dot the surface with butter and cover with foil or a lid. Bake for 1½ hours, removing the cover for the last 20–30 minutes of the cooking time to allow the potatoes on the top to brown.

SERVES FOUR TO SIX

ROAST POTATOES

6 large potatoes, peeled and quartered
120 ml / 8 tbsp vegetable or olive oil, goose or duck fat
or other fat reserved for roasting
pinch of salt

Place the potatoes in a large saucepan and just cover with cold water. Bring to the boil then boil, uncovered, for 5 minutes.

Meanwhile, switch the oven to 220°C / 425°F / gas mark 7 and place the oil or fat in a large roasting tin towards the top of the oven to heat thoroughly. Drain the potatoes thoroughly (reserving the water for gravy, stock or soup). Return them to the pan in batches and shake vigorously to soften the edges, or you can scratch them with a fork.

Take the tin from the oven and add the potatoes. Turn them quickly in the oil then cook at the top of the oven for 50–60 minutes, turning once halfway through cooking until crisp and golden on the outside and soft in the centre. Drain and sprinkle with salt. Serve as soon as possible.

SERVES FOUR

ROAST PARSNIPS

Look for firm, unblemished parsnips. Allow ½ large parsnip per person. To prepare them, peel, then cut them in half, in chunks or slices.

To roast parsnips arrange them around a joint of meat or in a separate dish and brush with fat. Allow about 45 minutes–1¼ hours at 180–190°C / 350–375°F / gas 4–5, until tender and golden.

Try drizzling the roasting parsnips with runny honey 10 minutes before the end of cooking time.

MRS BEETON'S TIP

Prepare the parsnips a day ahead and store in an airtight bag in the fridge until ready to use.

PEASE PUDDING

575 g / 1¼ lb split peas, soaked overnight in cold water to cover
1 small onion, peeled but left whole
1 bouquet garni
50 g / 2 oz butter, cut into small pieces
2 eggs, beaten
salt and pepper

Drain the peas, put them in a saucepan and add cold water to cover. Add the onion, the bouquet garni and salt and pepper to taste. Bring to the boil, skim off any scum on the surface of the liquid, then reduce the heat to very low and simmer the peas for 2–2½ hours or until tender. Drain the peas thoroughly. Press them through a sieve or purée in a blender or food processor. Add the pieces of butter with the beaten eggs. Beat well. Spoon the mixture into a floured pudding cloth and tie tightly. Suspend the bag in a large saucepan of boiling salted water and simmer gently for 1 hour. Remove from the pan, take the pudding out of the cloth and serve very hot.

SERVES SIX

MRS BEETON'S TIP

Modern cooks, unfamiliar with pudding cloths, can bake this nutritious pudding in a greased casserole. It will need about 30 minutes to cook in an oven preheated to 180°C / 350°F / gas 4.

ASPARAGUS PUDDING

225 g / 8 oz asparagus
45 ml / 3 tbsp plain flour
4 eggs
50 g / 2 oz cooked ham, finely chopped
50 g / 2 oz hot melted butter, plus extra for greasing the dish
300 ml / ½ pint milk
salt and pepper

Grease a 900 ml / 1½ pint soufflé dish or similar container suitable for steaming the pudding. Prepare a large saucepan of boiling water topped with a steamer. Cut a piece of double-thick greaseproof paper and another of foil, each large enough to cover the pudding.

Trim the asparagus, steam or boil the spears until nearly tender, then drain and slice them. Mix the flour with seasoning, then add the eggs, ham, half the melted butter and a little of the milk. Gradually beat the ingredients together until smooth, then beat in the remaining milk to make a smooth batter.

Stir the asparagus into the batter, then turn it into the dish. Cover the dish with the paper and foil, tying the cover securely around the rim to prevent steam from entering. Steam the pudding for 1½ hours, or until set. The time may vary according to the shape of the container. Turn out the pudding on to a warmed serving dish and pour the remaining melted butter around it. Serve the pudding at once.

SERVES FOUR

MRS BEETON'S TIP

Mrs Beeton suggested that this asparagus pudding should be served as a side dish. However, it makes an excellent light lunch or supper. Individual puddings (cooked in small basins or individual soufflé dishes) make an appetizing starter.

WINTER VEGETABLE CASSEROLE

*This simple casserole can be simmered very slowly
on the hob, if preferred.*

50 g / 2 oz butter
30 ml / 2 tbsp oil
2 onions, sliced
1 garlic clove, crushed (optional)
2 leeks, trimmed, sliced and washed
225 g / 8 oz swede, cubed
100 g / 4 oz turnip, cubed
3 carrots, sliced
100 g / 4 oz mushrooms, sliced
100 g / 4 oz pearl barley, washed
5 ml / 1 tsp dried thyme
1 bay leaf
salt and pepper
450 ml / ¾ pint Vegetable Stock (page 232)
30 ml / 2 tbsp chopped parsley to garnish

Set the oven to 180°C / 350°F / gas 4. Melt the butter in the oil in a large flame-proof casserole. Add the onions, garlic, leeks, swede, turnip and carrots and fry for about 10 minutes, stirring frequently.

Stir in the mushrooms, barley, thyme and bay leaf, with plenty of salt and pepper. Pour in the stock. Cover the casserole and transfer it to the oven. Bake for 1–1½ hours until all the vegetables are cooked and the barley is tender. Fluff up the grains with a fork, sprinkle the parsley over the top and serve at once.

SERVES FOUR

Pastry, Pancakes & Bread

*Pastry for sweet and savoury dishes,
dumplings to top bubbling
casseroles, crumpets for
teatime, and more.*

SHORT CRUST PASTRY

225 g / 8 oz plain flour
2.5 ml / ½ tsp salt
100 g / 4 oz margarine (or half butter, half lard)
flour for rolling out

Sift the flour and salt into a bowl, then rub on the margarine until the mixture resembles fine breadcrumbs. Add enough cold water to make a stiff dough.

Press the dough together with your fingertips. If time permits, wrap in grease-proof paper and rest in the refrigerator for 30 minutes. To use, roll out on a lightly-floured surface.

MAKES ABOUT 225 g / 8 oz

VARIATION

• **Wholemeal Short Crust Pastry** Although wholemeal flour may be used on its own, this does tend to create a rather chewy pastry. Using 100 g / 4 oz each of plain and wholemeal flour gives a very satisfactory result.

FLAKY PASTRY

Flaky pastry does not have as many layers as puff pastry.
It contains less fat to flour and the dough is rolled and folded fewer times.

225 g / 8 oz plain flour
1.25 ml / ¼ tsp salt
175 g / 6 oz butter or 75 g / 3 oz each butter and lard, chilled
5 ml / 1 tsp lemon juice
flour for rolling out

Sift the flour and salt into a bowl. If using butter and lard, mix them together roughly. Rub in a quarter of the fat, keeping the remaining fat chilled. Stir in the lemon juice and enough cold water to mix the ingredients to a soft dough. The mixture should take about 125 ml / 4 fl oz water but this should be added by the spoonful to avoid making the dough too wet.

On a lightly-floured surface, roll out the dough into an oblong measuring about 25 x 15 cm / 10 x 6 inches. Mark the dough into thirds. Cut the fat into 3 equal portions. Dot one portion of fat over the top two-thirds of the dough, in neat lumps.

Fold the bottom thirds of the dough up over the middle portion, then fold the top third down so that the lumps of fat are enclosed completely. Press the edges of the dough together with the rolling pin. Give the dough a quarter turn in a clockwise direction, then roll out as before.

Repeat the process of dotting the dough with fat, folding and rolling it, twice more. Chill the dough briefly between each rolling. Finally, fold and roll the pastry once more, without any fat, then chill again before using it as required.

MAKES ABOUT 450 g / 1 lb

PUFF PASTRY

225 g / 8 oz plain flour
1.25 ml / ¼ tsp salt
225 g / 8 oz butter, chilled
5 ml / 1 tsp lemon juice
flour for rolling out

Sift the flour and salt into a bowl. Rub in 50 g / 2 oz of the butter. Add the lemon juice and enough cold water to mix the ingredients to a smooth, fairly soft dough. The mixture should take about 125 ml / 4 fl oz water but this must be added by the spoonful to avoid making the dough too wet. Wrap the dough in cling film and chill briefly.

Shape the remaining butter into a rectangle measuring about 10 x 7.5 cm / 4 x 3 inches, then chill again. On a lightly-floured surface, roll out the dough into an oblong measuring about 25 x 15 cm / 10 x 6 inches, or slightly smaller. Place the butter in the middle of the dough, then fold the bottom third over it and fold the top third down to enclose the butter completely.

Press the edges of the dough together with the rolling pin. Give the dough a quarter turn in a clockwise direction. Roll out the dough into an oblong as before, fold it again, the wrap in cling film. Chill for 30 minutes. Roll and fold the pastry 6 times in all, chilling well each time. To remember the number of rollings, mark dents in the dough with your fingertips.

After the process of rolling and folding is complete, chill the pastry again before using it as required.

MAKES ABOUT 450 g / 1 lb

ROUGH PUFF PASTRY

*A slightly easier version of puff pastry; all the fat must be well
chilled for success. For best results, chill the bowl of flour too;
always make sure your hands are very cold by holding them
under cold running water before handling the dough.*

**225 g / 8 oz plain flour
1.25 ml / ¼ tsp salt
175 g / 6 oz butter, cut in chunks and chilled
5 ml / 1 tsp lemon juice
flour for rolling out**

Sift the flour and salt into a bowl. Add the butter and mix in lightly using a
round-bladed knife. Mix in the lemon juice and enough ice-cold water to make
a soft dough. The mixture should take about 125 ml / 4 fl oz (or very slightly
more) but add the water a spoonful at a time to avoid making the dough too wet.
The dough should be soft and very lumpy.

On a lightly-floured surface roll out the dough into an oblong, keeping the
corners square. Mark the oblong of dough into thirds, then fold and roll it as for
Flaky Pastry (page 147). Repeat the process four times in all, chilling the dough
between each rolling or as necessary.

The rolled dough should be smooth. Wrap it in cling film and chill well before
rolling it out to use as required.

MAKES ABOUT 450 g / 1 lb

HOT WATER CRUST PASTRY

This pastry is used for pork, veal and ham, and raised game pies.
It must be moulded while still warm (see page 111).

200 g / 7 oz plain flour
2.5 ml / ½ tsp salt
75 g / 3 oz lard
100 ml / 3½ fl oz milk or water

Sift the flour and salt into a warm bowl and make a well in the centre. Keep the bowl in a warm place.

Meanwhile, heat the lard and milk or water until boiling. Add the hot mixture to the flour, mixing well with a wooden spoon until the pastry is cool enough to knead with the hands. Knead thoroughly and mould as required.

Bake at 220°C / 425°F / gas 7 until the pastry is set, then reduce the oven temperature to 180°C / 350°F / gas 4 until fully baked.

MAKES 350 g / 12 oz

PANCAKES

Pancakes are much too good to be reserved exclusively for
Shrove Tuesday. Simple, versatile, and always popular,
they lend themselves to a wide range of fillings.

100 g / 4 oz plain flour
1.25 ml / ¼ tsp salt
1 egg, beaten
250 ml / 8 fl oz milk, or half milk and half water
oil for frying

Make the batter. Sift the flour and salt into a bowl, make a well in the centre and add the beaten egg. Stir in half the milk (or all the milk, if using a mixture of milk and water), gradually working the flour down from the sides.

Beat vigorously until the mixture is smooth and bubbly, then stir in the rest of the milk (or the water). Pour into a jug. The mixture may be left to stand at this stage, in which case it should be covered and stored in the refrigerator.

Heat a little oil in a clean 18 cm / 7 inch pancake pan. Pour off any excess oil, leaving the pan covered with a thin film of grease. Stir the batter and pour about 30–45 ml / 2–3 tbsp into the pan. There should be just enough to thinly cover the base. Tilt and rotate the pan so that the batter runs over the surface evenly.

Cook over moderate heat for about 1 minute until the pancake is set and golden brown underneath. Make sure the pancake is loose by shaking the pan, then either toss it or turn it with a palette knife or fish slice. Cook the second side for about 30 seconds or until golden.

Slide the pancake out on to a warmed plate. Serve at once, with a suitable filling or sauce, or keep warm over simmering water or in a very low oven while making more pancakes in the same way. Add more oil to the pan when necessary.

MAKES EIGHT

VARIATIONS

- **Rich Pancakes** Add 15 g / ½ oz cooled melted butter or 15 ml / 1 tbsp oil to the batter with 1 egg yolk. Alternatively, enrich the batter by adding 1 whole egg.
- **Cream Pancakes** Use 150 ml / ¼ pint milk and 50 ml / 2 fl oz single cream instead of 250 ml / 8 fl oz milk. Add 2 eggs and 25 g / 1 oz cooled melted butter, then stir in 15 ml / 1 tbsp brandy with caster sugar to taste. The mixture should only just coat the back of a spoon as the pancakes should be very thin.

SUET PUDDING

This plain pudding to serve with roast meat may be cooked in
a basin if preferred. Slices of cooked pudding may be added to
the roasting tin around a joint of meat for 2–5 minutes before serving.
Traditionally, the slices of pudding would have been served before
the meat to fill up a hungry family.

butter for greasing
350 g / 12 oz plain flour
10 ml / 2 tsp baking powder
2.5 ml / ½ tsp salt
150 g / 5 oz shredded suet
about 150 ml / ¼ pint milk
meat juices or melted butter to serve

Grease a large piece of greaseproof paper and lay it on a large sheet of foil. Sift the flour, baking powder and salt into a mixing bowl. Stir in the suet, then add enough milk to make a soft, but not sticky, dough.

Gently knead the dough into an oblong shape measuring about 25 cm / 10 inches long. Place it on the greaseproof paper. Fold the paper edges together several times, then seal the foil in the same way. Keep the wrapping loose to allow room for the pudding to rise. Twist or fold the ends of the paper and foil to seal them.

Bring a large saucepan or deep roasting tin of water to the boil and add the pudding. Cook for 3 hours, topping up with the water and fresh boiling water as necessary. If using a roasting tin, tent foil over the top of it and seal it on the rim to keep in the steam, and top up the water frequently.

To serve, open the package and slice the pudding. Arrange the slices on a heated serving plate and trickle over meat juices or melted butter. Serve promptly.

SERVES SIX TO EIGHT

DUMPLINGS

**100 g / 4 oz self-raising flour
50 g / 2 oz shredded beef suet
salt and pepper**

Mix the flour and suet in a bowl. Add salt and pepper to taste and bind with enough cold water to make a soft, smooth dough. With floured hands, divide the dough into 16 portions; roll into balls. Drop into simmering salted water, stock, soup or stew, lower the heat and simmer for 15–20 minutes. Serve with the liquid or with boiled meat, stew or vegetables.

MAKES ABOUT SIXTEEN

VARIATION

• **Herb Dumplings** Add 25 g / 1 oz grated onion and 5 ml / 1 tsp chopped fresh herbs to the flour and suet.

CRUMPETS

200 g / 7 oz strong white flour
2.5 ml / ½ tsp salt
2.5 ml / ½ tsp sugar
100 ml / 3½ fl oz milk
10 ml / 2 tsp dried yeast
pinch of bicarbonate of soda
fat for frying

Sift the flour, salt and sugar into a large bowl. Place the milk in a saucepan, add 125 ml / 4 fl oz water and warm gently. The mixture should be just hand-hot. Pour the mixture into a small bowl, sprinkle the dried yeast on top and leave for 10–15 minutes or until frothy.

Add the yeast liquid to the flour and beat to a smooth batter. Cover the bowl with a large lightly oiled polythene bag and leave in a warm place for about 45 minutes or until the batter has doubled in bulk.

Dissolve the bicarbonate of soda in 15 ml / 1 tbsp warm water; beat into the batter. Cover and leave to rise again for 20 minutes.

Heat a griddle or heavy-bottomed frying pan over medium heat, then grease it when hot. Grease metal crumpet rings, poaching rings or large plain biscuit cutters about 7.5 cm / 3 inches in diameter. Place the rings on the hot griddle, pour a spoonful of batter into each to cover the base thinly and cook until the top is set and the bubbles have burst.

Remove the rings and turn the crumpets over. Cook the other side for 2–3 minutes only, until firm but barely coloured. Cool the crumpets on a wire rack. Serve toasted, with butter.

MAKES TEN TO TWELVE

IRISH SODA BREAD

butter or oil for greasing
575 g / 1¼ lb plain flour
5 ml / 1 tsp bicarbonate of soda
5 ml / 1 tsp salt
5 ml / 1 tsp cream of tartar (if using fresh milk)
300 ml / ½ pint buttermilk or soured milk or fresh milk
flour for dusting

Grease a baking sheet. Set the oven at 190–200°C / 375–400°F / gas 5–6. Mix all the dry ingredients in a bowl, then make a well in the centre. Add enough milk to make a fairly slack dough, pouring it in almost all at once, not spoonful by spoonful. Mix with a wooden spoon, lightly and quickly.

With floured hands, place the mixture on a lightly-floured surface and flatten the dough into a round about 2.5 cm / 1 inch thick. Turn on to the prepared baking sheet. Make a large cross in the surface with a floured knife to make it heat through evenly.

Bake for about 40 minutes. Pierce the centre with a thin skewer to test for readiness; it should come out clean. Wrap the loaf in a clean tea-towel to keep it soft until required.

MAKES ONE 750 g / 1¾ lb LOAF

GRANARY BREAD

oil for greasing
800 g / 1¾ lb granary flour
10 ml / 2 tsp salt
10 ml / 2 tsp molasses
25 g / 1 oz fresh yeast or 15 ml / 1 tbsp dried yeast
10 ml / 2 tsp corn oil
flour for kneading
15 ml / 1 tbsp cracked wheat

Grease two 23 x 13 x 7.5 cm / 9 x 5 x 3 inch loaf tins. Mix the flour and salt in a large bowl. Measure 500 ml / 17 fl oz lukewarm water. Stir in the molasses.

Blend the fresh yeast to a thin paste with a little of the warm water and molasses. Set aside in a warm place until frothy – about 5 minutes. Alternatively, sprinkle dried yeast over all the warm water and molasses and set aside until frothy, then stir well. Add the yeast liquid, remaining liquid and the oil to the flour and mix to a soft dough. Turn onto a floured surface and knead for about 4 minutes or until the dough is smooth, elastic and no longer sticky. Return to the bowl and cover with cling film. Leave in a warm place until doubled in bulk – this will take about 2 hours or longer.

Knead the dough again until firm. Cut into two equal portions and form each into a loaf shape. Place the dough in the prepared loaf tins, brush the surface with salted water and sprinkle with the cracked wheat. Place the tins in a large, lightly oiled polythene bag. Leave in a warm place for 45 minutes or until the dough has doubled in bulk. Set the oven to 230°C / 450°F / gas 8.

Bake for 30–40 minutes, until the loaves are browned and crisp, and sound hollow when tapped on the bottom.

MAKES TWO 800 g / 1¾ lb LOAVES

Puddings & Desserts

*The British love their puddings. Here you'll find
nursery favourites, traditional steamed
and party puddings, sophisticated
desserts and healthier
alternatives.*

TRADITIONAL APPLE PIE

675 g / 1½ lb cooking apples
100 g / 4 oz sugar
6 cloves
caster sugar for dredging

SHORT CRUST PASTRY
350 g / 12 oz plain flour
4 ml / ¾ tsp salt
175 g / 6 oz margarine (or half butter, half lard)
flour for rolling out

Set the oven at 200°C / 400°F / gas 6. To make the pastry, sift the flour and salt into a bowl, then rub in the margarine until the mixture resembles fine breadcrumbs. Add enough cold water to make a stiff dough. Press the dough together with your fingertips.

Roll out the pastry on a lightly-floured surface and use just over half to line a 750 ml / 1¼ pint pie dish. Peel, core and slice the apples. Place half in the pastry-lined dish, then add the sugar and cloves. Pile the remaining apples on top, cover with the remaining pastry and seal the edges. Brush the pastry with cold water and dredge with caster sugar.

Bake for 20 minutes, then lower the oven temperature to 180°C / 350°F / gas 4 and bake for 20 minutes more. The pastry should be golden brown. Dredge with more caster sugar and serve hot or cold.

SERVES SIX

VARIATIONS

- **Apricot Pie** Use two 375 g / 15 oz cans apricots, drained, instead of apples. Omit the sugar and cloves.
- **Blackberry and Apple Pie** Use half blackberries and half apples and replace the cloves with 2.5 ml / ½ tsp grated lemon rind.

- **Damson Pie** Use damsons instead of apples and increase the sugar to 150 g / 5 oz and omit the cloves.
- **Gooseberry Pie** Use cleaned, topped and tailed gooseberries instead of apples. Omit the cloves.
- **Redcurrant and Raspberry Pie** This is a winning combination. Use 450 / 1 lb redcurrants and 225 g / 8 oz raspberries instead of apples. Reduce the sugar to 30 ml / 2 tbsp and omit the cloves.
- **Rhubarb Pie** Use rhubarb cut into 2 cm / ¾ inch lengths instead of apples. Increase the sugar to 150 g / 5 oz.

PASTRY HORNS

Puff Pastry (page 148), made using 100 g / 4 oz flour
flour for rolling out
beaten egg and milk for glazing

Roll out the pastry 5 mm / ¼ inch thick on a lightly-floured surface, then cut into strips 35 cm / 14 inches long and 2 cm / ¾ inch wide. Moisten the strips with cold water.

Wind each strip around a cornet mould, working from the point upward, keeping the moistened surface on the outside. Lay the horns on a dampened baking sheet, with the final overlap of the pastry strip underneath. Leave in a cool place for 1 hour.

Set the oven at 220°C / 425°F / gas 7. Brush the horns with beaten egg and milk. Bake for 10–15 minutes or until golden brown. Remove the moulds and return the horns to the oven for 5 minutes. Cool completely on a wire rack. When cold, fill the horns with a sweet or savoury filling.

MAKES EIGHT

MINCE PIES

Festive mince pies can also be made using Flaky (page 147),
Rough Puff (page 149) or Puff Pastry (page 148) with mouthwatering results.
If using any of these pastries you will require 200 g / 7 oz flour.

350 g / 12 oz Mincemeat (page 224)
25 g / 1 oz icing or caster sugar for dredging

SHORT CRUST PASTRY
300 g / 10 oz plain flour
5 ml / 1 tsp salt
150 g / 5 oz margarine (or half butter, half lard)
flour for rolling out

Set the oven at 200°C / 400°F / gas 6. To make the pastry, sift the flour and salt into a bowl, then rub in the margarine until the mixture resembles fine bread-crumbs. Add enough cold water to make a stiff dough. Press the dough together with your fingertips.

Roll out the pastry on a lightly-floured surface and use just over half of it to line twelve 7.5 cm / 3 inch patty tins. Cut out 12 lids from the rest of the pastry. If liked, make holly leaf decorations from the pastry trimmings.

Place a spoonful of mincemeat in each pastry case. Dampen the edges of the cases and cover with the pastry lids. Seal the edges well. Brush the tops with water and add any pastry decorations. Dredge with the sugar. Make 2 small cuts in the top of each pie. Bake for 15–20 minutes or until golden brown.

MAKES TWELVE

TREACLE TART

An old favourite which is today as popular as ever.
Try it with cornflakes instead of breadcrumbs for a tasty change.

45 ml / 3 tbsp golden syrup
50 g / 2 oz soft white breadcrumbs
5 ml / 1 tsp lemon juice

SHORT CRUST PASTRY
150 g / 5 oz plain flour
2.5 ml / ½ tsp salt
65 g / 2½ oz margarine (or half butter, half lard)
flour for rolling out

Set the oven at 200ºC / 400ºF / gas 6. To make the pastry, sift the flour and salt into a bowl, then rub in the margarine until the mixture resembles fine breadcrumbs. Add enough cold water to make a stiff dough. Press the dough together with your fingertips.

Roll out the pastry on a lightly-floured surface and use just over three-quarters of it to line a 20 cm / 8 inch pie plate, reserving the rest for a lattice topping.

Melt the syrup in a saucepan. Stir in the breadcrumbs and lemon juice, then pour the mixture into the prepared pastry case.

Roll out the reserved pastry to a rectangle and cut into 1 cm / ½ inch strips. Arrange in a lattice on top of the tart. Bake for about 30 minutes.

SERVES SIX

VARIATION

• **Treacle Jelly Tart** Make as above, but omit the breadcrumbs and add 1 beaten egg to the syrup. Bake in a 180ºC / 350ºF / gas 4 oven until golden brown. When cold, the filling sets like jelly.

CUSTARD TARTLETS

1 egg
15 ml / 1 tbsp caster sugar
125 ml / 4 fl oz milk
pinch of grated nutmeg

SWEET SHORT CRUST PASTRY
100 g / 4 oz plain flour
1.25 ml / ¼ tsp salt
50 g / 2 oz margarine (or half butter, half lard)
5 ml / 1 tsp caster sugar
flour for rolling out

Set the oven at 180°C / 350°F / gas 4. To make the pastry, sift the flour and salt into a bowl, then rub in the margarine until the mixture resembles fine breadcrumbs. Stir in the caster sugar. Add enough cold water to make a stiff dough. Press the dough together with your fingertips. Roll out and use to line twelve 7.5 cm / 3 inch patty tins.

Beat the egg lightly in a bowl and add the sugar. Warm the milk in a saucepan, then pour it onto the egg. Strain the custard mixture into the pastry cases and sprinkle a little nutmeg on top of each.

Bake for about 30 minutes, until the custard is firm and set. Leave to cool before removing from the tins.

MAKES TWELVE

VARIATION

- **Custard Meringue Tartlets** Make as above, but omit the nutmeg and bake for 15 minutes only. Lower the oven temperature to 140°C / 275°F / gas 1. Whisk 2 egg whites in a clean, grease-free bowl until stiff. Fold in 75 g / 3 oz caster sugar. Pile the meringue on to the tartlets. Bake for about 30 minutes.

ALMOND AND APRICOT TARTLETS

10 ml / 2 tsp apricot jam
50 g / 2 oz butter or margarine
50 g / 2 oz sugar
1 egg
15 ml / 1 tbsp plain cake crumbs
15 ml / 1 tbsp ground almonds
3 drops almond essence
10 ml / 2 tsp nibbed almonds
15 ml / 1 tbsp Apricot Glaze (page 189)
10 ml / 2 tsp chopped angelica

SHORT CRUST PASTRY
100 g / 4 oz plain flour
1.25 ml / ¼ tsp salt
50 g / 2 oz margarine (or half butter, half lard)
flour for rolling out

Set the oven at 190°C / 375°F / gas 5. To make the pastry, sift the flour and salt into a bowl, then rub in the margarine until the mixture resembles fine bread-crumbs. Add enough cold water to make a stiff dough. Press the dough together lightly.

Roll out the pastry on a lightly-floured surface and use to line twelve 7.5 cm / 3 inch patty tins. Put a little apricot jam in each. In a bowl, cream the butter or margarine with the sugar until pale and fluffy. Gradually beat in the egg. Stir in the cake crumbs, ground almonds and almond essence. Half-fill each pastry case with the mixture and smooth the tops. Sprinkle the nibbed almonds on top.

Bake for 15 minutes or until firm to the touch. Leave the tartlets to cool. Warm the apricot glaze, brush it on top of the tartlets, then sprinkle with the chopped angelica.

MAKES TWELVE

MRS BEETON'S BAKEWELL PUDDING

strawberry or apricot jam
50 g / 2 oz butter
50 g / 2 oz caster sugar
1 egg
50 g / 2 oz ground almonds
50 g / 2 oz fine cake crumbs
few drops almond essence
icing sugar for dusting

SHORT CRUST PASTRY
100 g / 4 oz plain flour
1.25 ml / ¼ tsp salt
50 g / 2 oz margarine (or half butter, half lard)
flour for rolling out

Set the oven at 200°C / 400°F / gas 6. To make the pastry, sift the flour and salt into a bowl, then rub in the margarine until the mixture resembles fine breadcrumbs. Add enough cold water to make a stiff dough. Press the dough together lightly.

Roll out the pastry on a lightly-floured surface and use to line an 18 cm / 7 inch flan tin or ring placed on a baking sheet. Spread a good layer of jam over the pastry base.

In a mixing bowl, cream the butter with the sugar until pale and fluffy. Beat in the egg, then add the almonds, cake crumbs and essence. Beat until well mixed. Pour into the flan case, on top of the jam.

Bake for 30 minutes or until the centre of the pudding is firm. Sprinkle with icing sugar and serve hot or cold.

SERVES FOUR TO FIVE

VARIATIONS

- **Bakewell Tart** Make as above, but use raspberry jam and only 25 g / 1 oz bread or cake crumbs and 25 g / 1 oz ground almonds. Bake for 25 minutes.
- **Almond Tartlets** Line twelve 7.5 cm / 3 inch patty tins with the pastry. Replace the cake crumbs with an extra 50 g / 2 oz ground almonds and the almond essence with 2.5 ml / ½ tsp lemon juice. Bake for 12–18 minutes.
- **West Riding Pudding** Line a 500 ml / 17 oz dish with the pastry. Make as for Bakewell Pudding but substitute 75 g / 3 oz plain flour and 2.5 ml / ½ tsp baking powder for the cake crumbs and ground almonds. If the mixture seems stiff, add a little milk. Bake at 190°C / 375°F / gas 5 for 1 hour. Serve hot or cold.

MRS BEETON'S MANCHESTER PUDDING

250 ml / 8 fl oz milk
2 strips lemon rind
75 g / 3 oz fresh white breadcrumbs
2 whole eggs plus 2 egg yolks
50 g / 2 oz butter, softened
45 ml / 3 tbsp caster sugar
45 ml / 3 tbsp brandy
45–60 ml / 3–4 tbsp jam
extra caster sugar for sprinkling

PUFF PASTRY
150 g / 5 oz plain flour
1.25 ml / ¼ tsp salt
150 g / 5 oz butter
2.5 ml / ½ tsp lemon juice
flour for rolling out

Heat the milk in a saucepan with the lemon rind, then remove from the heat and leave to infuse for 30 minutes. Put the breadcrumbs in a bowl, strain the flavoured milk over them and return the mixture to the clean pan. Simmer for 2–3 minutes or until the crumbs have absorbed all the milk.

Beat the eggs and yolks until liquid, then stir into the breadcrumbs with the butter, sugar and brandy. Mix thoroughly; the butter should melt in the warm mixture. Cover the surface with dampened greaseproof paper and leave to cool.

Set the oven at 200°C / 400°F / gas 6. Make the pastry. Sift the flour and salt into a mixing bowl and rub in 50 g / 2 oz of the butter. Add the lemon juice and mix to a smooth dough with cold water.

Shape the remaining butter into a rectangle on greaseproof paper. Roll out the dough on a lightly-floured surface to a strip a little wider than the butter and rather more than twice its length. Place the butter on one half of the pastry, fold the other half over it, and press the edges together with the rolling pin. Leave it in a cool place for 15 minutes to allow the butter to harden.

Roll out the pastry into a long strip. Fold the bottom third up and the top third down, press the edges together with the rolling pin and turn the pastry so that the folded edges are on the right and left. Roll and fold again, cover and leave in a cool place for 15 minutes. Repeat this process until the pastry has been rolled out 6 times.

Line a 750 ml / 1¼ pint pie dish with the pastry. If liked, cut a strip out of the pastry trimmings to fit the rim of the pie dish. Dampen the rim of the lining and fit the extra strip. Wrap any remaining pastry and reserve in the refrigerator for another purpose.

Spread the jam over the base of the pastry. Spoon the cooled breadcrumb mixture into the pastry case and bake for 15 minutes, then lower the heat to 180°C / 350°F / gas 4 and cook for 45–60 minutes more. The pudding should be set in the centre. Leave to cool. Serve cold, sprinkled with caster sugar.

SERVES SIX

PLUM PUDDING

Christmas pudding became known as plum pudding
in Tudor times, when dried plums (prunes)
were the popular prime ingredient.

butter for greasing
100 g / 4 oz cooking apple
200 g / 7 oz dried figs, chopped
100 g / 4 oz currants
225 g / 8 oz seedless raisins
200 g / 7 oz blanched almonds, chopped
25 g / 1 oz shelled Brazil nuts, chopped
100 g / 4 oz pine kernels
175 g / 6 oz dried white breadcrumbs
5 ml / 1 tsp mixed spice
100 g / 4 oz soft light brown sugar
100 g / 4 oz cut mixed peel
pinch of salt
grated rind and juice of 1 lemon
100 g / 4 oz butter or margarine
100 g / 4 oz honey
3 eggs, beaten

Grease two 750-ml / 1¼-pint pudding basins. Prepare two steamers or three-quarter fill two saucepans with water. Each pan should hold one pudding.

Peel, core and chop the apple. Put it in a large mixing bowl with the dried fruits, nuts, breadcrumbs, spice, sugar, peel, salt and the lemon rind and juice.

Combine the butter and honey in a saucepan and warm gently until the butter has melted. Beat in the eggs.

Stir the liquid mixture into the dry ingredients and mix well. Spoon the mixture into the basins, cover with greased greaseproof paper and a floured cloth or foil. Secure with string.

Place the basins in the steamers or carefully lower them into the pans of boiling water. Cover the pans and lower the heat so that the water is kept at a steady simmer. Boil the puddings for 3 hours or steam for 3½–4 hours, topping up each pan with boiling water as required.

To store, cover each pudding with a clean dry cloth, wrap in greaseproof paper and store in a cool, dry place until required. To reheat, boil or steam each pudding for 1½–2 hours.

EACH PUDDING SERVES SIX

MRS BEETON'S TIP

Plum puddings are traditionally flamed when served. To do this, warm 30–45 ml / 2–3 tbsp brandy either in a metal soup ladle over a low flame or in a measuring jug in the microwave for 15 seconds on High. Ignite the brandy (if warmed in a ladle it may well ignite spontaneously) and carefully pour it over the hot pudding. Do not use holly to decorate the top of a pudding that is to be flamed.

BAKED BREAD AND BUTTER PUDDING

9 thin slices of bread and butter, crusts cut off
75 g / 3 oz currants
grated rind of 1 lemon
grated nutmeg
40–50 g / 1½–2 oz caster sugar, plus extra for sifting
4 eggs
900 ml / 1½ pints milk

Butter a large ovenproof dish. Cut the slices of bread and butter in half or into quarters, then layer them in the dish. Sprinkle each layer with a few currants, a little lemon rind and grated nutmeg, and caster sugar.

Beat the eggs with the milk, then strain the mixture through a sieve over the pudding. For best results, leave the pudding to stand for about 2 hours, so that the bread is well-soaked. At least allow the pudding to stand for 30 minutes.

Set the oven to 180°C / 350°F / gas 4. Bake the pudding for about 1 hour, until it has risen and is golden and set. Sift a little caster sugar over the top and serve the pudding freshly baked.

SERVES SIX

VARIATION

- **Rich Bread and Butter Pudding** The pudding will be much richer if single cream is used instead of milk. Replacing a third of the milk with cream enriches it slightly. An additional 2–4 egg yolks can be added and a little chopped candied peel layered with the currants. The custard mixture can be flavoured with a little natural vanilla essence – about 2.5 ml / ½ tsp or less if it is highly concentrated. There is no need to add lemon rind with the vanilla essence.

BAKED RICE PUDDING

1.1 litres / 2 pints milk
strip of pared lemon rind
100 g / 4 oz pudding rice
30 ml / 2 tbsp sugar
15 g / ½ oz butter
2.5 ml / ½ tsp grated nutmeg

Heat the milk with the lemon rind until almost boiling, then set it aside to cool. Set the oven to 160°C / 325°F / gas 3.

Place the rice in a sieve. Wash it under cold running water, then tip it into an ovenproof dish. Sprinkle the sugar over the rice and stir in the milk, discarding the lemon rind. Float the butter on the pudding and sprinkle the nutmeg on top. Bake the pudding for about 2 hours. Stir the pudding after 20 minutes' cooking and at intervals of about 20 minutes for the first hour, then leave it to develop a deep golden crust. Serve on its own or with a large dollop of a preserve such as strawberry or raspberry jam.

SERVES SIX

MRS BEETON'S TIP

Leftover rice pudding can be used to make various dessert treats. Creamy rice pudding is delicious when layered with fruits and chilled.
For an extra rich dessert, fold some whipped cream into the pudding and spoon it into ramekins or individual soufflé dishes that can safely be used under the grill. Top each pudding with a layer of soft brown sugar and chill, then caramelize under a hot grill before serving.

JUNKET

The temperature is important in the making of junket; if it is too
hot or too cold it will not set. Also it is important to use fresh milk.
Homogenised milk gives a very light set but UHT or sterilized milk
will not set. This is due to the processing causing slight changes to the
structure of the milk that prevents the rennet culture from working.

600 ml / 1 pint milk
15 ml / 1 tbsp sugar
few drops vanilla essence
5 ml / 1 tsp rennet essence (vegetarian rennet is available
from health food shops)
grated nutmeg or ground cinnamon

In a saucepan, warm the milk to blood-heat (about 37°C / 98°F) with the sugar and vanilla essence. Stir in the rennet essence.

Pour the mixture into 1 large or 4 small dishes. Cover and leave to stand in a warm place for about 1 hour or until set. Do not move the junket at this stage.

Sprinkle the junket with spices and serve cold but not chilled.

SERVES FOUR

VARIATIONS

- **Almond or Rum Junket** Instead of the vanilla essence, add 2.5 ml / ½ tsp almond or rum essence to the milk. Decorate with toasted almonds, if liked.
- **Lemon or Orange Junket** Infuse the pared rind of 1 lemon or orange in the milk. Using a few drops of food colouring, tint the junket pale yellow or orange. Do not use any other flavouring.
- **Rich Junket** Flavour in any of the ways given above. Run a layer of single cream, flavoured with brandy, if liked, over the top of the junket.

PEARS IN WINE

100 g / 4 oz sugar
30 ml / 2 tbsp redcurrant jelly
1.5 cm / ¾ inch cinnamon stick
4 large ripe cooking pears (about 450 g / 1 lb)
250 ml / 9 fl oz red wine
25 g / 1 oz flaked almonds

Combine the sugar, redcurrant jelly and cinnamon stick in a saucepan wide enough to hold all the pears upright so that they fit snugly and will not fall over. Add 250 ml / 9 fl oz water and heat gently, stirring constantly, until the sugar and jelly have dissolved.

Peel the pears, leaving the stalks in place. Carefully remove as much core as possible without breaking the fruit. Stand them upright in the pan, cover, and simmer gently for 15 minutes. Add the wine and cook, uncovered, for 15 minutes more. Remove them gently with a slotted spoon and arrange on a serving dish.

Remove the cinnamon stick from the pan and add the almonds. Boil the liquid remaining in the pan rapidly until it is reduced to a thin syrup. Pour the syrup over the pears and serve warm. This dessert can also be served cold. Pour the hot syrup over the pears, leave to cool, then chill before serving.

SERVES FOUR

MRS BEETON'S TRIFLE

*Plain whisked or creamed sponge cake, individual buns,
or Madeira cake are ideal for this trifle. Originally, Mrs Beeton
made her custard by using 8 eggs to thicken 600 ml / 1 pint milk,
cooking it slowly over hot water. Using cornflour and egg yolks is
more practical and it gives a creamier, less 'eggy' result.*

4 slices of plain cake or individual cakes
6 almond macaroons
12 ratafias
175 ml / 6 fl oz sherry
30–45 ml / 2–3 tbsp brandy
60–90 ml / 4–6 tbsp raspberry or strawberry jam
grated rind of 1 lemon
25 g / 1 oz flaked almonds
300 ml / ½ pint double cream
30 ml / 2 tbsp icing sugar
candied and crystallized fruit and peel to decorate

CUSTARD
25 g / 1 oz cornflour
25 g / 1 oz caster sugar
4 egg yolks
5 ml / 1 tsp vanilla essence
600 ml / 1 pint milk

Place the sponge cakes in a glass dish. Add the macaroons and ratafias, pressing them down gently. Pour about 50 ml / 2 fl oz of the sherry into a basin and set it aside, then pour the rest over the biscuits and cake. Sprinkle with the brandy. Warm the jam in a small saucepan, then pour it evenly over the trifle base, spreading it lightly. Top with the lemon rind and almonds.

For the custard, blend the cornflour, caster sugar, egg yolks and vanilla to a smooth cream with a little of the milk. Heat the remaining milk until hot. Pour some of the milk on the egg mixture, stirring, then replace the mixture in the saucepan with the rest of the milk. Bring to the boil, stirring constantly, and simmer for 3 minutes.

Pour the custard over the trifle base and cover the surface with a piece of dampened greaseproof paper. Set aside to cool.

Add the cream and icing sugar to the reserved sherry and whip until the mixture stands in soft peaks. Swirl the cream over the top of the trifle and chill. Decorate with pieces of candied and crystallized fruit and peel before serving.

SERVES SIX

CHERRIES JUBILEE

This famous dish was created for Queen Victoria's Diamond Jubilee.
It is often finished at the table, with the cherries and sauce kept warm in
a chafing dish and the kirsch ignited and added at the last moment.

50 g / 2 oz sugar
450 g / 1 lb dark red cherries, stoned
10 ml / 2 tsp arrowroot
60 ml / 4 tbsp kirsch

Put the sugar in a heavy-bottomed saucepan. Add 250 ml / 8 fl oz water. Heat gently, stirring, until the sugar has dissolved, then boil steadily without stirring for 3–4 minutes to make a syrup. Lower the heat, add the cherries and poach gently until tender. Using a slotted spoon, remove the cherries from the pan and set them aside on a plate to cool.

In a cup, mix the arrowroot with about 30 ml / 2 tbsp of the syrup to a thin paste. Stir back into the pan. Bring to the boil, stirring constantly, until the mixture thickens. Remove from the heat.

Pile the cherries in a heatproof serving bowl. Pour the sauce over them. Heat the kirsch in a small saucepan or ladle. Ignite it, pour it over the cherries and serve at once.

SERVES FOUR

GOOSEBERRY FOOL

When elderflowers are available, try adding 2 heads, well washed and tied in muslin, to the gooseberries while poaching. Discard the muslin bags when the gooseberries are cooked.

575 g / 1¼ lb gooseberries, topped and tailed
150 g / 5 oz caster sugar
300 ml / ½ pint whipping cream

Put the gooseberries in a heavy-bottomed saucepan. Stir in the sugar. Cover the pan and cook the gooseberries over gentle heat for 10–15 minutes until the skins are just beginning to crack. Leave to cool.

Purée the fruit in a blender or food processor, or rub through a sieve into a clean bowl.

In a separate bowl, whip the cream until it holds its shape. Fold the cream gently into the gooseberry purée. Spoon into a serving dish or six individual glasses. Chill before serving.

SERVES SIX

VARIATIONS

• If a fruit is suitable for puréeing, it will make a creamy fool. Try rhubarb, apricots, red- or blackcurrants, raspberries or blackberries. Sieve the purée if necessary.

MICROWAVE TIP

Combine the gooseberries and sugar in a deep 1.2 litre / 2 pint dish. Cover lightly and cook for 6 minutes on High. Proceed as in the above recipe.

BANANA CUSTARD

500 ml / 17 fl oz milk
3 eggs plus 2 yolks
25 g / 1 oz caster sugar
few drops of vanilla essence
3 bananas (about 400 g / 14 oz)

DECORATION
30 ml / 2 tbsp crushed butterscotch or
grated chocolate or toasted flaked almonds

In a saucepan, bring the milk to just below boiling point. Put the eggs and sugar into a bowl, mix well, then stir in the scalded milk and vanilla essence. Strain the custard mixture into a heavy-bottomed saucepan or a heatproof bowl placed over a saucepan of simmering water. Alternatively, use a double saucepan, but make sure the water does not touch the upper pan.

Cook the custard over very gentle heat for 15–25 minutes, stirring all the time with a wooden spoon, until the custard thickens to the consistency of single cream. Stir well around the sides as well as the base of the pan or bowl to prevent the formation of lumps, especially if using a double saucepan. Do not let the custard boil or it may curdle.

As soon as the custard thickens, pour it into a jug to stop further cooking. Peel and slice the bananas and stir them into the custard. Stand the jug in a bowl of hot water for 5 minutes to allow the flavours to blend. Spoon into a serving dish or individual dishes and decorate with butterscotch, grated chocolate or flaked almonds.

If the custard is to be served cold, pour it into a bowl and cover the surface with a piece of dampened greaseproof paper to prevent discoloration and a skin forming. When cold, pour into a serving dish and decorate as desired.

SERVES FOUR

SUMMER PUDDING

This delectable dessert started life with the cumbersome name
of Hydropathic Pudding. It was originally invented for spa patients
who were forbidden rich creams and pastries. Vary the fruit filling
if you wish – blackberries or bilberries make very good additions –
but keep the total quantity of fruit at about 1 kg / 2¼ lb.

150 g / 5 oz caster sugar
225 g / 8 oz blackcurrants or redcurrants,
stalks removed
225 g / 8 oz ripe red plums, halved and stoned
1 strip of lemon rind
225 g / 8 oz strawberries, hulled
225 g / 8 oz raspberries, hulled
8–10 slices of day-old white bread,
crusts removed

Put the sugar into a saucepan with 60 ml / 4 tbsp water. Heat gently, stirring, until the sugar has dissolved. Add the black- or redcurrants, plums and lemon rind and poach until tender.

Add the strawberries and raspberries to the saucepan and cook for 2 minutes. Remove from the heat and, using a slotted spoon, remove the lemon rind.

Cut a circle from 1 slice of bread to fit the base of a 1.25-litre / 2¼-pint pudding basin. Line the base and sides of the basin with bread, leaving no spaces. Pour in the stewed fruit, reserving about 45–60 ml / 3–4 tbsp of the juice in a jug. Top the stewed fruit filling with more bread slices. Cover with a plate or saucer that exactly fits inside the basin. Put a weight on top to press the pudding down firmly. Leave in a cool place for 5–8 hours, preferably overnight.

Turn out carefully on to a plate or shallow dish to serve. If there are any places on the bread shell where the juice from the fruit filling has not penetrated, drizzle a little of the reserved fruit juice over. Serve with whipped cream or plain yogurt.

SERVES SIX

CRANACHAN

125 g / 4½ oz coarse oatmeal
400 ml / 14 fl oz double cream
50 g / 2 oz caster sugar
15 ml / 1 tbsp rum
150 g / 5 oz fresh raspberries

Toast the oatmeal under a low grill until lightly browned. Set aside to cool.

In a bowl, whip the cream until stiff. Stir in the toasted oatmeal and flavour with the sugar and rum.

Hull the raspberries. Stir them into the cream or layer with the Cranachan mixture, reserving 4 perfect fruit for decoration, if liked. Serve in 4 individual glass dishes.

SERVES FOUR

LEMON DELICIOUS PUDDING

*This pudding has a light spongy top
with lemon sauce underneath.*

butter for greasing
3 eggs, separated
75 g / 3 oz caster sugar
200 ml / 7 fl oz milk
15 ml / 1 tbsp self-raising flour, sifted
grated rind and juice of 2 large lemons
pinch of salt
15 ml / 1 tbsp icing sugar

Grease a deep 1-litre / 1¾-pint ovenproof dish. Set the oven at 180°C / 350°F / gas 4.

In a mixing bowl, beat the egg yolks together with the caster sugar until light, pale and creamy. Whisk the milk, flour, rind and lemon juice into the egg yolks. In a clean, grease-free bowl, whisk the egg whites with the salt, adding the icing sugar gradually. Continue to whisk until stiff but not dry. Fold into the lemon mixture.

Pour the mixture into the prepared dish and stand the dish in a roasting tin. Add hot water to come halfway up the sides of the dish. Bake for 1 hour.

SERVES FOUR

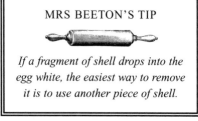

MRS BEETON'S TIP

*If a fragment of shell drops into the
egg white, the easiest way to remove
it is to use another piece of shell.*

Cakes

*Scones for tea, plain cakes, occasional cakes
and the recipes you need to decorate them
– your guests will be delighted
with the results.*

CLASSIC MADEIRA CAKE

butter for greasing
150 g / 5 oz butter or margarine
150 g / 5 oz caster sugar
4 eggs, beaten
200 g / 7 oz plain flour
10 ml / 2 tsp baking powder
pinch of salt
grated rind of 1 lemon
caster sugar for dredging
1 thin slice of candied glacé citron peel

Line and grease a 15 cm / 6 inch round cake tin. Set the oven at 180°C / 350°F / gas 4.

In a mixing bowl, cream the butter or margarine with the sugar until light and fluffy. Gradually add the eggs, beating well after each addition. Sift the flour, baking powder and salt together into a second bowl, then fold into the creamed mixture. Stir in the lemon rind and mix well. Spoon into the prepared tin. Dredge the top with caster sugar.

Bake for 20 minutes, then lay the slice of peel on top. Bake for a further 45–50 minutes or until cooked through and firm to the touch. Cool on a wire rack.

MAKES ONE 15 cm / 6 inch CAKE

VICTORIA SANDWICH CAKE

The original Victoria Sandwich was oblong, filled with jam or marmalade and cut into fingers or sandwiches. Now, the basic mixture is used with many different flavourings and fillings and is served as a single, round cake. For a softer-centred cake, bake the mixture in a 20 cm / 8 inch round cake tin, then split and fill. All loose crumbs must be brushed off before filling. Keep the filling fairly firm – if it is too moist, it will seep into the cake.

butter for greasing
150 g / 5 oz butter or margarine
150 g / 5 oz caster sugar
3 eggs, beaten
150 g / 5 oz self-raising flour or plain flour
5 ml / 1 tsp baking powder
pinch of salt
raspberry or other jam for filling
caster sugar for dredging

Line and grease two 18 cm / 7 inch sandwich tins. Set the oven at 180°C / 350°F / gas 4.

In a mixing bowl cream the butter or margarine with the sugar until light and fluffy. Add the eggs gradually, beating well after each addition. Sift the flour, salt and baking powder, if used, into a bowl. Stir into the creamed mixture, lightly but thoroughly, until evenly mixed.

Divide between the tins and bake for 25–30 minutes. Cool on a wire rack, then sandwich together with jam. Sprinkle the top with caster sugar or spread with Glacé Icing (page 197).

MAKES ONE 18 cm / 7 inch CAKE

ONE-STAGE VICTORIA SANDWICH

butter for greasing
150 g / 5 oz self-raising flour
pinch of salt
150 g / 5 oz soft margarine
150 g / 5 oz caster sugar
3 eggs

Line and grease two 18 cm / 7 inch sandwich tins. Set the oven at 180°C / 350°F / gas 4.

Put all the ingredients in a mixing bowl and stir. Beat until smooth, allowing 2–3 minutes by hand or 1–1½ minutes with an electric mixer.

Divide the mixture evenly between the tins; level each surface. Bake for 25–30 minutes. Cool on a wire rack, then fill and top as desired.

MAKES ONE 18 cm / 7 inch CAKE

FLAVOURINGS AND FILLINGS FOR VICTORIA SANDWICH CAKES

- **Chocolate Sandwich Cake** Substitute 60 ml / 4 tbsp of cocoa for an equal quantity of the flour. Sift the cocoa with the flour and continue as in the main recipe. Sandwich the cooled cakes together with chocolate spread and sift a little icing sugar over the top of the chocolate cake.
- **Cinnamon and Apple Sandwich Cake** Add 10 ml / 2 tsp of ground cinnamon to the flour. Continue as in the main recipe. Peel, core and slice a large cooking apple, then cook it with a little sugar until it is reduced to a pulp. Press the pulp through a sieve, return it to the saucepan and add 10 ml / 2 tsp of cornflour blended with 30 ml / 2 tbsp of milk. Bring to the boil, stirring, and cook until thickened. Sweeten the purée to taste, then leave it to cool. Gradually fold in 50 ml / 2 fl oz of whipped double cream, then use this apple cream to sandwich the cooled cakes together.

- **Coffee Sandwich Cake** Dissolve 30 ml / 2 tbsp of instant coffee in 30 ml / 2 tbsp boiling water and leave to cool. Fold this into the mixture last. Whip 150 ml / ¼ pint double cream with 5 ml / 1 tsp of instant coffee dissolved in 15 ml / 1 tbsp of boiling water and 30 ml / 2 tbsp of icing sugar. Sandwich the cooled cakes with this coffee cream.
- **Ginger Sandwich Cake** The combination of ground ginger and lemon rind makes a delicious cake. Add the grated rind of 1 lemon to the fat and sugar. Sift 15 ml / 1 tbsp of ground ginger with the flour. Prepare and bake the cake as in the main recipe. When cool, sandwich the layers with ginger marmalade.
- **Harlequin Sandwich Cake** Make the cake mixture as in the main recipe, then put half in one sandwich tin. Add pink food colouring to the second portion of mixture, making it a fairly strong colour. Put the second portion in the other sandwich tin and bake the cake. When cool, cut both cakes into rings: cut a 5 cm / 2 inch circle from the middle of each cake, then cut a 10 cm / 4 inch circle around it. Either use plain pastry cutters or cut out circles of paper and use a pointed knife to cut around them. You should have three rings of each cake. Carefully put the rings of cake together alternating the colours to make two layers. Sandwich the layers together with raspberry jam. Spread warmed raspberry jam over the top of the cake and sift icing sugar over it. Alternatively, fill the cake with whipped cream and swirl more whipped cream over the top. When slices are cut the pattern will show.
- **Lemon Sandwich Cake** Add the grated rind of 1 large lemon to the fat and sugar. Continue as in the main recipe, then sandwich the cooled cakes together with lemon curd.
- **Mocha Sandwich Cake** Substitute 30 ml / 2 tbsp of cocoa for an equal quantity of flour and sift it with the flour. Prepare the mixture as in the main recipe. Dissolve 10 ml / 2 tsp of instant coffee in 15 ml / 1 tbsp of boiling water and add it to the mixture. Sandwich the cooled cakes together with chocolate spread.
- **Orange Sandwich Cake** Add the grated rind of 1 large orange to the fat and sugar, then continue as in the main recipe. Sandwich the cooled cakes together with orange marmalade.

ONE-STAGE FRUIT CAKE

butter for greasing
225 g / 8 oz self-raising flour
5 ml / 1 tsp mixed spice (optional)
100 g / 4 oz soft margarine
100 g / 4 oz glacé cherries, chopped
100 g / 4 oz currants
75 g / 3 oz sultanas
25 g / 1 oz cut mixed peel
100 g / 4 oz soft light brown sugar
2 eggs
75 ml / 3 fl oz milk

Line and grease an 18cm / 7 inch round cake tin. Set the oven at 180°C / 350°F / gas 4. Mix the flour and spice, if used.

Put all the ingredients in a bowl, stir, then beat until smooth, allowing 2–3 minutes by hand or 1–1½ minutes with an electric mixer. Spoon the mixture into the prepared tin and bake for 2 hours. Cool on a wire rack.

MAKES ONE 18 cm / 7 inch CAKE

CHRISTMAS CAKE

butter for greasing
200 g / 7 oz plain flour
1.25 ml / ¼ tsp salt
5–10 ml / 1–2 tsp mixed spice
200 g / 7 oz butter
200 g / 7 oz caster sugar
6 eggs, beaten
30–60 ml / 2–4 tbsp brandy or sherry
100 g / 4 oz glacé cherries, chopped
50 g / 2 oz preserved ginger, chopped
50 g / 2 oz walnuts, chopped
200 g / 7 oz currants
200 g / 7 oz sultanas
150 g / 5 oz seedless raisins
75 g / 3 oz cut mixed peel

COATING AND ICING
Almond Paste (page 190)
Royal Icing (page 188)

Line and grease a 20 cm / 8 inch round cake tin. Use doubled greaseproof paper. Set the oven at 160°C / 325°F / gas 3.

Stir the flour, salt and spice into a bowl. In a mixing bowl, cream the butter and sugar together until light and fluffy. Gradually beat in the eggs and the brandy or sherry, adding a little flour if the mixture starts to curdle. Add the cherries, ginger and walnuts. Stir in the dried fruit, peel and flour mixture. Spoon into the prepared tin and make a slight hollow in the centre.

Bake for 45 minutes then reduce the oven temperature to 150°C / 300°F / gas 2 and bake for a further hour. Reduce the temperature still further to 140°C / 275°F / gas 1, and continue cooking for 45–60 minutes until cooked though and firm to the touch. Cool in the tin. Cover the cake with almond paste and decorate with royal icing.

MAKES ONE 20 cm / 8 inch CAKE

ROYAL ICING

Royal icing is used for special celebration cakes, especially for wedding cakes, because the icing has sufficient strength when it sets hard to hold the tiers. The icing cannot be applied directly to the cake because it would drag the crumbs and discolour badly, so rich fruit cakes are usually covered with a layer of almond paste or marzipan before the royal icing is applied.

2 egg whites
450 g / 1 lb icing sugar, sifted

It is vital to ensure that the bowl is clean and free from grease. Use a wooden spoon kept solely for the purpose and do not be tempted to skimp on the beating – insufficient beating will produce an off-white icing with a heavy, sticky texture.

Place the egg whites in a bowl and break them up with a fork. Gradually beat in about two-thirds of the icing sugar with a wooden spoon and continue beating for about 15 minutes until the icing is pure white and forms soft peaks. Add the remaining icing sugar, if necessary, to attain this texture. Cover the bowl with cling film and place a dampened tea-towel on top. Place the bowl inside a polythene bag if storing overnight or for longer.

Before use, lightly beat the icing to burst any air bubbles that have risen to the surface. Adjust the consistency for flat icing or piping.

SUFFICIENT TO COAT THE TOP AND SIDES
OF ONE 20 cm / 8 inch CAKE

ROYAL ICING QUANTITIES

Quick guide to quantities required to cover cakes (sufficient for 3 coats):

ROUND	ROYAL ICING	ROUND	ROYAL ICING
15 cm / 6 inch	575 g / 1¼ lb	25 cm / 10 inch	1 kg / 2¼ lb
18 cm / 7 inch	675 g / 1½ lb	28 cm / 11 inch	1.25 kg / 2¾ lb
20 cm / 8 inch	800 g / 1¾ lb	30 cm / 12 inch	1.4 kg / 3 lb
23 cm / 9 inch	900 g / 2 lb		

SQUARE	ROYAL ICING	SQUARE	ROYAL ICING
15 cm / 6 inch	675 g / 1½ lb	25 cm / 10 inch	1.25 kg / 2¾ lb
18 cm / 7 inch	800 g / 1¾ lb	28 cm / 11 inch	1.4 kg / 3 lb
20 cm / 8 inch	900 g / 2 lb	30 cm / 12 inch	1.5 kg / 3¼ lb
23 cm / 9 inch	1 kg / 2¼ lb		

APRICOT GLAZE

Brush this glaze over a cake before applying the marzipan.
Any yellow jam or marmalade may be used.

225 g / 8 oz apricot jam

Warm the jam with 30 ml / 2 tbsp water in a small saucepan over a low heat until the jam has melted. Sieve the mixture and return the glaze to the clean pan. Bring slowly to the boil allow to cool slightly before use.

SUFFICIENT TO COAT THE TOP AND SIDES
OF ONE 20 cm / 8 inch CAKE

ALMOND PASTE AND MARZIPAN

Either almond paste or marzipan may be used to cover a Battenburg cake, to fill a Simnel cake or as a base for royal icing on a Christmas or wedding cake. Both almond paste and marzipan provide a flat, even surface over which icing will flow in a smooth glossy sheet, and as a bonus, will prevent crumbs from the cake spoiling the appearance of the icing. Marzipan resembles almond paste, but is smoother and more malleable. It is easier to use than almond paste when making moulded decorations or petits fours.

ALMOND PASTE

This recipe makes a pale, creamy yellow-coloured paste that can be used to cover and decorate cakes, as well as for a base coat before applying icing.

225 g / 8 oz ground almonds
100 g / 4 oz caster sugar
100 g / 4 oz icing sugar
5 ml / 1 tsp lemon juice
few drops of almond essence
1 egg, beaten

Using a coarse sieve, sift the almonds, caster sugar and icing sugar into a mixing bowl. Add the lemon juice, almond essence and sufficient egg to bind the ingredients together. Knead lightly with the fingertips until smooth.

Wrap in cling film and overwrap in foil or a plastic bag to prevent the paste drying out. Store in a cool place until required.

MAKES ABOUT 450 g / 1 lb

MARZIPAN

1 egg
1 egg white
200 g / 7 oz icing sugar, sifted
200 g / 7 oz ground almonds
5 ml / 1 tsp lemon juice
few drops of almond essence

Whisk the egg, egg white and icing sugar in a heatproof bowl over hot water until thick and creamy. Add the ground almonds with the lemon juice and almond essence and mix well. Work in more lemon juice, if necessary. When cool enough to handle, knead lightly until smooth. Use as for almond paste.

MAKES ABOUT 400 g / 14 oz

TWELFTH NIGHT CAKE

*The tradition of the Twelfth Night Cake goes back to the days
of the early Christian Church and beyond. In the Middle Ages,
whoever found the bean in his cake became the 'Lord of Misrule' or
'King' for the festivities of Twelfth Night, with the finder of the pea
as his 'Queen'. Finding the bean was thought to bring luck. The
tradition survived until near the end of the nineteenth century.*

margarine for greasing
150 g / 5 oz margarine
75 g / 3 oz soft dark brown sugar
3 eggs
300 g / 11 oz plain flour
60 ml / 4 tbsp milk
5 ml / 1 tsp bicarbonate of soda
30 ml / 2 tbsp golden syrup
2.5 ml / ½ tsp mixed spice
2.5 ml / ½ tsp ground cinnamon
pinch of salt
50 g / 2 oz currants
100 g / 4 oz sultanas
100 g / 4 oz cut mixed peel
1 dried bean and 1 large dried whole pea (see above)

Line and grease a 15 cm / 6 inch round cake tin. Set the oven at 180°C / 350°F / gas 4.

In a mixing bowl, cream the margarine and sugar until light and fluffy. Beat in the eggs, one at a time, adding a little flour with each. Warm the milk, add the bicarbonate of soda and stir until dissolved. Add the syrup.

Mix the spices and salt with the remaining flour in a bowl. Add this to the creamed mixture alternately with the flavoured milk. Lightly stir the dried fruit and peel. Spoon half the cake mixture into the prepared tin, lay the bean and pea in the centre, then cover with the rest of the cake mixture. Bake for about 2 hours. Cool on a wire rack.

MAKES ONE 15 cm / 6 inch CAKE

BLACK BUN

A rich cake, encased in pastry, from the Highlands of Scotland,
served either on Twelfth Night (traditionally) or at Hogmanay
to celebrate the new year.

400 g / 14 oz plain flour
100 g / 4 oz blanched whole almonds, roughly chopped
675 g / 1½ lb muscatel raisins, seeded
675 g / 1½ lb currants
100 g / 4 oz cut mixed peel
200 g / 7 oz caster sugar
30 ml / 2 tbsp ground ginger
30 ml / 2 tbsp ground cinnamon
30 ml / 2 tbsp mixed spice
2.5 ml / ½ tsp freshly ground black pepper
10 ml / 2 tsp bicarbonate of soda
5 ml / 1 tsp cream of tartar
350 ml / 12 fl oz milk
15 ml / 1 tbsp brandy

PASTRY
450 g / 1 lb plain flour
225 g / 8 oz butter
5 ml / 1 tsp baking powder
flour for rolling out
beaten egg for glazing

Sift the flour into a large bowl. Add the almonds, fried fruit, peel, sugar and spices and mix well. Stir in the bicarbonate of soda and the cream of tartar, then moisten with the milk and brandy. Set the oven at 200°C / 400°F / gas 6.

Make the pastry. Put the flour into a mixing bowl. Rub in the butter until the mixture resembles fine breadcrumbs, then add the baking powder. Stir in enough water (about 125 ml / 4 fl oz) to form a stiff dough. Leave the dough to rest for a few minutes, then roll out on a lightly-floured surface to a thickness of about 5 mm / ¼ inch. Using three-quarters of the pastry, line a 23 cm / 9 inch round cake tin (about 10 cm / 4 inches deep), leaving a border around the edges for overlap. Roll out the remaining pastry for the lid.

Fill the pastry-lined tin with the cake mixture, and turn the edges of the pastry over it. Moisten the edges with water, put on the lid and seal. Decorate the pastry with any trimmings, prick with a fork all over the top and brush with egg.

Bake for 1 hour, then lower the oven temperature to 160°C / 325°F / gas 3, cover the top of the bun loosely with paper or foil and continue baking for 2 hours more.

Leave the bun to cool in the tin for 20 minutes, then remove it from the tin and cool completely. Keep for 1 month in an airtight tin before using.

MAKES ONE 23 cm / 9 inch CAKE

DUNDEE CAKE

butter for greasing
200 g / 7 oz plain flour
2.5 ml / ½ tsp baking powder
1.25 ml / ¼ tsp salt
150 g / 5 oz butter
150 g / 5 oz caster sugar
4 eggs, beaten
100 g / 4 oz glacé cherries, quartered
150 g / 5 oz currants
150 g / 5 oz sultanas
100 g / 4 oz seedless raisins
50 g / 2 oz cut mixed peel
50 g / 2 oz ground almonds
grated rind of 1 lemon
50 g / 2 oz blanched split almonds

Line and grease an 18 cm / 7 inch ground cake tin. Set the oven at 180°C / 350°F / gas 4. Sift the flour, baking powder and salt into a bowl. In a mixing bowl, cream the butter and sugar together well, and beat in the eggs. Fold the flour mixture, cherries, dried fruit, peel and ground almonds into the creamed mixture. Add the lemon rind and mix well.

Spoon into the prepared tin and make a slight hollow in the centre. Bake for 20 minutes, by which time the hollow should have filled in. Arrange the split almonds on top.

Return the cake to the oven, bake for a further 40–50 minutes, then reduce the temperature to 160°C / 325°F / gas 3 and bake for 1 hour more. Cool on a wire rack.

MAKES ONE 18 cm / 7 inch CAKE

WESTMORLAND PARKIN

This makes a dense, dark parkin with excellent keeping qualities.

butter for greasing
200 g / 7 oz butter or clarified dripping
450 g / 1 lb black treacle
450 g / 1 lb fine oatmeal
200 g / 7 oz plain flour
5 ml / 1 tsp ground ginger
2.5 ml / ½ tsp salt
10 ml / 2 tsp baking powder
200 g / 7 oz demerara sugar
100 ml / 3½ fl oz milk
5 ml / 1 tsp bicarbonate of soda

Line and grease two 20 cm / 8 inch square tins. Set the oven at 160°C / 325°F / gas 3.

Heat the butter or dripping and treacle gently in a saucepan, stirring until the fat has melted. Mix all the dry ingredients, except the bicarbonate of soda, in a mixing bowl and make a well in the centre.

Warm the milk in a saucepan over a low heat till hand-hot. Stir in the bicarbonate of soda until dissolved. Pour into the dry ingredients and mix well. Stir in the melted butter and treacle.

Spoon the mixture into the prepared tins and bake for about 1¼ hours or until cooked through and firm to the touch. Cool in the tins, then cut into squares.

MAKES TWO 20 cm / 8 inch CAKES
(ABOUT 32 SQUARES)

SIMNEL CAKE

butter for greasing
200 g / 7 oz plain flour
2.5 ml / ½ tsp baking powder
1.25 ml / ¼ tsp salt
150 g / 5 oz butter
150 g / 5 oz caster sugar
4 eggs
100 g / 4 oz glacé cherries, halved
150 g / 5 oz currants
150 g / 5 oz sultanas
100 g / 4 oz seedless raisins
50 g / 2 oz cut mixed peel
50 g / 2 oz ground almonds
grated rind of 1 lemon

DECORATION
double quantity Almond Paste (page 190) or
450 ml / 1 lb Marzipan (page 190)
30 ml / 2 tbsp smooth apricot jam (see method)
1 egg, beaten
Glacé Icing (page 197) made using 50 g / 2 oz icing sugar
Easter cake decorations

Line and grease a 18 cm / 7 inch cake tin. Set the oven at 180°C / 350°F / gas 4.

Sift the flour, baking powder and salt into a bowl. In a mixing bowl, cream the butter and sugar together well and beat in the eggs, adding a little of the flour mixture if necessary. Fold the flour mixture, cherries, dried fruit, peel and ground almonds into the creamed mixture. Add the lemon rind and mix well.

Spoon half the mixture into the prepared tin. Cut off one third of the almond paste and roll it to a pancake about 1 cm / ½ inch thick and slightly smaller than the circumference of the tin. Place it gently on top of the cake mixture and spoon them remaining cake mixture on top.

Bake for 1 hour, then reduce the oven temperature to 160°C / 325°F / gas 3 and bake for 1½ hours more. Cool in the tin, then turn out on a wire rack.

Warm, then sieve the apricot jam. When the cake is cold, divide the remaining almond paste in half. Roll one half to a round of a slightly smaller diameter than the top of the cake. Brush the top of the cake with apricot jam and press the almond paste lightly on to it. Trim the edge neatly.

Make 11 small balls with the remaining paste and place them around the edge of the cake. Brush the balls with the beaten egg and brown under the grill. Pour the Glacé Icing into the centre of the cake and decorate with chickens and Easter eggs.

MAKES ONE 18 cm / 7 inch CAKE

GLACÉ ICING

This simple icing is quickly prepared and is ideal for topping a plain sponge cake or a batch of small cakes. Make the icing just before it is to be used and keep any extra decorations to the minimum.

**100 g / 4 oz icing sugar, sifted
food colouring (optional)**

Place the icing sugar in a bowl. Using a wooden spoon, gradually stir in sufficient water (about 15 ml / 1 tbsp) to create icing with a consistency that thickly coats the back of the spoon. Take care not to add too much liquid or the icing will be too runny. At first the icing will seem quite stiff, but it slackens rapidly as the icing sugar absorbs the water. Stir in 1–2 drops of food colouring, if required.

**SUFFICIENT TO COVER THE TOP
OF ONE 18 cm / 7 inch CAKE**

BATTENBURG CAKE

butter for greasing
100 g / 4 oz self-raising flour
pinch of salt
100 g / 4 oz butter or margarine
100 g / 4 oz caster sugar
2 eggs
pink food colouring
Apricot Glaze (page 189)
200 g / 7 oz Almond Paste (page 190)

Line and grease a 23 x 18 cm / 9 x 7 inch Battenburg tin, which has a metal divider down the centre; or use a 23 x 18 cm / 9 x 7 inch tin and cut double greaseproof paper to separate the mixture into 2 parts. Set the oven at 190°C / 375°F / gas 5. Mix the flour and salt in a bowl.

In a mixing bowl, cream the butter or margarine and sugar together until light and fluffy. Add the eggs, one at time, with a little flour. Stir in, then beat well. Stir in the remaining flour lightly but thoroughly.

Place half the mixture in one half of the tin. Tint the remaining mixture pink, and place it in the other half of the tin. Smoothe both mixtures away from the centre towards the outside of the tin.

Bake for 25–30 minutes. Leave the cakes in the tin for a few minutes, then transfer them to a wire rack and peel off the paper. Leave to cool completely.

To finish the Battenburg, cut each slab of cake lengthways into 3 strips. Trim off any crisp edges and rounded surfaces so that all 6 strips are neat and of the same size. Arrange 3 strips with 1 pink strip in the middle. Where the cakes touch, brush with the glaze and press together lightly. Make up the other layer in the same way, using 2 pink with 1 plain strip in the middle. Brush glaze over the top of the base layer and place the second layer on top.

Roll out the almond paste thinly into a rectangle the same length as the strips and wide enough to wrap around them. Brush it with glaze and place the cake in the centre. Wrap the paste around the cake and press the edges together lightly. Turn so that the join is underneath; trim the ends. Mark the top of the paste with the back of a knife to make a criss-cross pattern.

MAKES ONE 23 x 18 cm / 9 x 7 inch CAKE

OLD ENGLISH CIDER CAKE

butter for greasing
225 g / 8 oz plain flour
7.5 ml / 1½ tsp grated nutmeg
1.25 ml / ¼ tsp ground cinnamon
5 ml / 1 tsp baking powder
pinch of salt
100 g / 4 oz butter or margarine
100 g / 4 oz caster sugar
2 eggs
125 ml / 4 fl oz dry still cider

Line and lightly grease a shallow 20 cm / 8 inch square cake tin. Set the oven at 180°C / 350°F / gas 4.

Sift the flour into a bowl with the spices, baking powder and salt. Cream the butter or margarine with the sugar until light and fluffy, then beat in the eggs. Beat half the flour mixture into the creamed mixture. Beat in half the cider. Repeat using the remaining flour and cider.

Spoon the mixture into the prepared tin and bake for 50–55 minutes until the cake is cooked through and firm to the touch. Cool the cake on a wire rack.

MAKES ONE 20 cm / 8 inch CAKE

PATTERDALE PEPPER CAKE

Store this traditional British cake for at least a week before cutting.

butter for greasing
450 g / 1 lb self-raising flour
15 ml / 1 tbsp ground ginger
1.25 ml / ¼ tsp ground cloves
2.5 ml / ½ tsp freshly ground black pepper
100 g / 4 oz butter
200 g / 7 oz caster sugar
100 g / 4 oz seedless raisins
100 g / 4 oz currants
25 g / 1 oz golden syrup, warmed
2 large eggs, lightly beaten
125 ml / 4 fl oz skimmed milk

Line and grease a deep 18 cm / 7 inch square cake tin or a somewhat shallower 20 cm / 8 inch cake tin.

Set the oven at 160°C / 325°F / gas 3. Sift the flour, spices and black pepper into a mixing bowl. Rub in the butter until the mixture resembles fine bread-crumbs. Stir in the sugar, and add the fruit and peel. Make a well in the flour mixture, pour in the syrup, eggs and milk, and beat lightly.

Spoon the mixture into the prepared tin and bake for 2½ hours or until cooked through and firm to the touch. Cool on a wire rack.

MAKES ONE 18 cm / 7 inch CAKE

SHEARING CAKE

In Welsh this simple cake is known as 'Cacen Gneifio' and traditionally it was prepared to serve with tea for all the farm workers who gathered to help on days when the sheep were sheared and dipped.

butter for greasing
400 g / 14 oz plain flour
pinch of salt
10 ml / 2 tsp baking powder
200 g / 7 oz butter
225 g / 8 oz soft light brown sugar
grated rind of ½ lemon
20 ml / 4 tsp caraway seeds
5 ml / 1 tsp grated nutmeg or to taste
2 eggs
200 ml / 7 fl oz milk

Line and grease a 20 cm / 8 inch round cake tin. Set the oven at 180°C / 350°F / gas 4.

Sift the flour, salt and baking powder into a mixing bowl. Rub in the butter until the mixture resembles breadcrumbs, then stir in the sugar, lemon rind and spices.

In a second bowl, beat the eggs lightly with the milk, then stir the liquid gradually into the dry ingredients.

Spoon the mixture into the prepared tin and back for 1½ hours or until cooked through and firm to the touch, covering the surface with a piece of greased paper or foil if it browns too quickly. Cool for 10 minutes in the tin, then invert on a wire rack to cool completely.

MAKES ONE 20 cm / 8 inch CAKE

SEED CAKE

butter for greasing
200 g / 7 oz plain flour
1.25 ml / ¼ tsp salt
2.5 ml / ½ tsp baking powder
15 ml / 1 tbsp caraway seeds
150 g / 5 oz butter or margarine
150 g / 5 oz caster sugar
4 eggs, beaten
15 ml / 1 tbsp milk (optional)

Line and grease a 15 cm / 6 inch cake tin. Set the oven at 180°C / 350°F / gas 4. Sift the flour, salt and baking powder into a bowl. Stir in the caraway seeds and mix well. Set aside.

Place the butter or margarine in a mixing bowl and beat until very soft. Add the sugar and cream together until light and fluffy. Add the beaten eggs gradually, beating well after each addition. If the mixture shows signs of curdling, add a little of the flour mixture.

Fold in the dry ingredients lightly but thoroughly, adding the milk if too stiff.

Spoon into the prepared tin, smooth the surface and make a slight hollow in the centre. Bake for 30 minutes, then reduce the oven temperature to 160°C / 325°F / gas 3 and bake for a further 50 minutes until firm to the touch. Cool the cake on a wire rack.

MAKES ONE 15 cm / 6 inch CAKE

GUY FAWKES GINGERBREAD

*Make this gingerbread at least a week before eating
and store in an airtight tin. It is best eaten sliced and spread
lightly with butter. An excellent treat for November 5th!*

**butter for greasing
200 g / 7 oz plain flour
1.25 ml / ¼ tsp salt
15 ml / 1 tsp ground ginger
50 g / 2 oz soft light brown sugar
50 g / 2 oz butter or margarine
100 g / 4 oz black treacle
75 ml / 5 tbsp milk
5 ml / 1 tsp bicarbonate of soda
1 egg, beaten**

Line and grease an 18 cm / 7 inch square tin or a 23 x 13 x 7.5 cm / 9 x 5 x 3 inch loaf tin. Set the oven at 180°C / 350°F / gas 4.

Sift the flour, salt and ginger into a mixing bowl. Add the sugar. Heat the butter or margarine, treacle, and most of the milk gently in a saucepan until the fat has melted.

In a second saucepan, warm the remaining milk and stir in the bicarbonate of soda until dissolved. Pour the melted mixture into the dry ingredients. Add the beaten egg with the milk and soda mixture and beat well.

Pour into the prepared tin and bake for 20 minutes. Reduce the oven temperature to 150°C / 300°F / gas 2 and bake for a further 30–40 minutes until cooked through and firm to the touch.

**MAKES ONE 18 cm / 7 inch SQUARE CAKE
OR ONE 23 x 13 x 7.5 cm / 9 x 5 x 3 inch LOAF**

PLAIN SCONES

butter for greasing
225 g / 8 oz self-raising flour
2.5 ml / ½ tsp salt
25–50 g / 1–2 oz butter or margarine
125–150 ml / 4–5 fl oz milk
flour for kneading
milk or beaten egg to glaze (optional)

Grease a baking sheet. Set the oven at 220°C / 425°F / gas 7. Sift the flour and salt into a large bowl. Rub in the butter or margarine, then mix to a soft dough with the milk, using a round-bladed knife. Knead very lightly on a floured surface until smooth.

Roll or pat out the dough to about 1 cm / ½ inch thick and cut into rounds, using a 6 cm / 2½ inch cutter. (Alternatively, divide into two equal portions and roll each piece into a round 1–2 cm / ½–¾ inch thick. Mark each round into six wedges.) Re-roll the trimmings and re-cut.

Place the scones on the prepared baking sheet. Brush the tops with milk or beaten egg, if liked. Bake for 10–12 minutes. Cool on a wire rack.

MAKES TWELVE

OTHER RAISING AGENTS

Scones can be made using plain flour with raising agents: for 225 g / 8 oz plain flour, use 5 ml / 1 tsp bicarbonate of soda and 10 ml / 2 tsp cream of tartar. Or use 20 ml / 4 tsp baking powder as the raising agent.

A VARIETY OF SCONE DOUGHS

- **Cheese Scones** Add 75 g / 3 oz grated cheese to the dry ingredients before mixing in the milk. Cut into finger shapes or squares.
- **Cheese Whirls** Add 75 g / 3 oz grated cheese to the dry ingredients. Roll out the dough into a rectangle. Sprinkle with another 50 g / 2 oz grated

cheese, then roll up the dough like a Swiss roll. Cut into 1 cm / ½ inch slices and lay them flat on greased baking sheets. Brush with milk or egg and bake as in the basic recipe.

- **Savoury Herb Scones** Add 50 g / 2 oz diced cooked ham, 30 ml / 2 tbsp grated Parmesan cheese and 5 ml / 1 tsp dried mixed herbs to the dry ingredients before mixing in the milk.
- **Fruit Scones** Add 50 g / 2 oz caster sugar and 50 g / 2 oz currants, sultanas or other dried fruit to the basic recipe.
- **Griddle Scones** Add 50 g / 2 oz sultanas to the basic recipe. Roll out to 1 cm / ½ inch thick, then cut into 6 cm / 2½ inch rounds. Cook on a moderately hot, lightly-floured griddle or heavy frying pan for 3 minutes or until the scones are golden brown underneath and the edges are dry. Turn over and cook for about another 2 minutes until golden brown on both sides. Cool in a linen tea-towel or similar cloth.
- **Inverary Muffins** Use only 75 ml / 3 fl oz buttermilk or soured milk to make the dough, and add 25 g / 1 oz caster sugar and 1 egg. Roll out 1 cm / ½ inch thick, and cut into 7.5 cm / 3 inch rounds. Cook on a griddle or heavy frying pan.
- **Nut Scones** Add 50 g / 2 oz chopped nuts to the basic recipe.
- **Syrup or Treacle Scones** Add 20 ml / 4 tsp soft light brown sugar, 2.5 ml / ½ tsp ground cinnamon or ginger, 2.5 ml / ½ tsp mixed spice and 15 ml / 1 tbsp warmed golden syrup or black treacle to the basic recipe. Add the syrup or treacle with the milk.
- **Potato Scones** Use 100 g / 4 oz flour and 100 g / 4 oz sieved cooked mashed potato. Reduce the milk to 65 ml / 2½ fl oz.

MRS BEETON'S TIP

Soured milk or buttermilk used instead of milk makes delicious scones. They are best made with plain flour plus 5 ml / 1 tsp bicarbonate of soda and 5 ml / 1 tsp cream of tartar. Scones may be used to make cobblers, both savoury and sweet. For a savoury cobbler, overlap savoury scones on a meat or vegetable casserole.

- **Rich Scones** Add 25 g / 1 oz sugar to the mixed dry ingredients for the basic recipe. Instead of mixing with milk alone, use 1 beaten egg with enough milk to make 125 ml / 4 fl oz.
- **Wholemeal Scones** Use half wholemeal flour and half plain white flour to make the scone dough.
- **Scones Made with Oil** Use 45 ml / 3 tbsp olive oil or corn oil instead of the fat in the basic recipe. Reduce the milk to 75 ml / 3 fl oz and add 1 egg.

HONEY BUNS

butter for greasing (optional)
200 g / 7 oz self-raising flour
pinch of salt
75 g / 3 oz butter or margarine
25 g / 1 oz caster sugar
1 egg
30 ml / 2 tbsp liquid honey
30 ml / 2 tbsp milk

Grease 18–20 bun tins or arrange an equivalent number of paper cake cases on baking sheets. Set the oven at 190°C / 375°F / gas 5.

Sift the flour and salt into a mixing bowl. Rub in the butter margarine until the mixture resembles fine breadcrumbs. Stir in the sugar.

Put the egg into a jug and add the honey and milk. Mix well. Add the liquid to the dry ingredients and beat until smooth.

Divide the mixture between the prepared bun tins or paper cases. Bake for 15–20 minutes or until well risen and cooked through. Cool on a wire rack.

MAKES EIGHTEEN TO TWENTY

LINCOLNSHIRE PLUM BREAD

Prunes give a delightfully rich taste to this bread.

butter for greasing
100 g / 4 oz prunes
100 g / 4 oz butter
100 g / 4 oz soft light brown sugar
2.5 ml / ½ tsp ground mixed spice
2.5 ml / ½ tsp ground cinnamon
2.5 ml / ½ tsp gravy browning (optional)
2 eggs, lightly beaten
15 ml / 1 tbsp brandy
100 g / 4 oz sultanas
100 g / 4 oz currants
175 g / 6 oz self-raising flour
pinch of salt

Soak the prunes overnight in cold water. Next day, grease and line a 23 x 13 x 75 cm / 9 x 5 x 3 inch loaf tin. Set the oven at 140°C / 275°F / gas 1. Drain the prunes well and pat dry. Remove the stones and chop the prunes finely.

Cream the butter and sugar in a bowl until light and fluffy. Beat in the spices and gravy browning, if used. Mix the eggs with the brandy, then beat into the creamed mixture. Toss the chopped prunes and other dried fruit in a little of the flour. Mix the rest of the flour with the salt. Fold it into the creamed mixture, then fold in all the dried fruit. Turn the mixture into the prepared tin and level the top.

Bake for 3 hours. Cool in the tin. When cold, turn out and store in an airtight tin.

MAKES ABOUT TWELVE SLICES

SALLY LUNNS

*Sally Lunn was a cake seller in Bath during the 18th century
and her cake, or bun, became very famous.*

**butter for greasing
400 g / 14 oz strong white flour
5 ml / 1 tsp salt
50 g / 2 oz butter
150 ml / ¼ pint milk
15 g / ½ oz fresh yeast or 10 ml / 2 tsp dried yeast
2.5 ml / ½ tsp sugar
1 egg
15 ml / 1 tbsp caster sugar for glazing**

Grease two 15 cm / 6 inch round cake tins. Sift the flour and salt into a large bowl. Rub in the butter. Warm the milk until lukewarm.

Blend the fresh yeast to a thin paste with the sugar and warm milk. Set aside in a warm place until frothy – about 5 minutes. Alternatively, sprinkle dried yeast over the warm milk and set aside until frothy, then stir well.

Beat the egg into the yeast liquid and stir into the flour mixture to form a very soft dough. Beat well. Pour the mixture into the prepared cake tins.

Place the tins in a large, lightly oiled polythene bag. Leave in a warm place until the dough has doubled in bulk – this will take 2 hours, or longer. Set the oven at 220°C / 425°F / gas 7.

Bake for 20–25 minutes, until golden brown. To make the glaze, boil together 15 ml / 1 tbsp water and the sugar until syrupy. Brush the hot glaze over the top of the Sally Lunns.

To serve, split each Sally Lunn crossways, into three rounds and toast each piece on both sides. Butter thickly or fill with clotted cream, re-form the cake, and cut into slices or wedges.

MAKES TWO 15 cm / 6 inch SALLY LUNNS

Biscuits

Sweet and savoury biscuits including such British classics as shortbread, digestives and flapjacks.

SHORTBREAD

Shortbread should be handled as lightly – and as little – as possible; if the dough is worked too much, it will toughen. Wooden moulds, carved with an appropriate motif such as a thistle, are sometimes used for this Scottish speciality, but it is easier to shape the dough by hand.

butter for greasing
100 g / 4 oz plain flour
1.25 ml / ¼ tsp salt
50 g / 2 oz rice flour, ground rice or semolina
50 g / 2 oz caster sugar
100 g / 4 oz butter

Invert a baking sheet, then grease the surface now uppermost. Set the oven at 180°C / 350°F / gas 4.

Mix all the ingredients in a mixing bowl. Rub in the butter until the mixture binds together to a dough. Shape into a large round about 1 cm / ¼ inch thick. Pinch up the edges to decorate. Place on the prepared baking sheet, and prick with a fork. Bake for 40–45 minutes. Cut into wedges while still warm.

MAKES EIGHT WEDGES

VARIATIONS

- **Shortbread Biscuits** Roll out the dough on a lightly-floured surface to a thickness of just under 1 cm / ¼ inch. Cut into rounds with a 5–6 cm / 2–2½ inch cutter. Place on 1–2 greased baking sheets, allowing room for spreading. Prick the surface of each biscuit in several places with a fork. Bake for 15–20 minutes. Leave to stand for a few minutes, then cool on a wire rack.
- **Original Scotch Shortbread** Omit the salt and rice flour, and use 225 g / 8 oz plain flour. Reduce the sugar to 25 g / 1 oz. Add 10 ml / 2 tsp caraway seeds. Top the shortbread round with strips of candied peel.

DOVER BISCUITS

butter for greasing
200 g / 7 oz plain flour
1.25 ml / ¼ tsp salt
2.5 ml / ½ tsp ground cinnamon
50 g / 2 oz currants
100–150 g / 4–5 oz butter or margarine
100–150 g / 4–5 oz caster sugar
1 egg, separated
flour for rolling out
caster sugar for topping

Thoroughly grease two or three baking sheets. Set the oven at 180°C / 350°F / gas 4. Mix the flour, salt and cinnamon in a bowl, then add the currants and stir to coat thoroughly.

In a mixing bowl, beat the butter or margarine until soft, add the sugar and continue to beat until light and fluffy. Beat in the egg yolk, reserving the white. Fold in the flour mixture, first using a knife and then the fingers.

Knead the biscuit dough lightly on a floured surface, then roll out to a thickness of 5 mm / ¼ inch. Cut into rounds with a 6 cm / 2½ inch cutter. Re-roll and re-cut any trimmings.

Place the biscuits on the prepared baking sheets, pricking the top of each in several places. Bake for 10 minutes, then remove from the oven and add the topping: brush the biscuits with beaten egg white and sprinkle with caster sugar. Return to the oven and bake for a further 5 minutes. Leave to stand for 5 minutes, then cool on a wire rack.

MAKES TWENTY-SIX TO THIRTY

JIM-JAMS

butter or margarine for greasing
150 g / 5 oz plain flour
50 g / 2 oz ground almonds
1.25 ml / ¼ tsp salt
100 g / 4 oz butter or margarine
100 g / 4 oz caster sugar
1 egg yolk
flour for rolling
strawberry jam for filling
sifted icing sugar for dredging

Thoroughly grease two or three baking sheets. Set the oven to 180°C / 350°F / gas 4. Mix the flour, ground almonds and salt in a bowl.

In a mixing bowl, beat the butter or margarine until soft, add the sugar and continue to beat until light and fluffy. Beat in the egg yolk. Fold in the flour mixture, first using a knife and then the fingers.

Knead the biscuit dough lightly on a floured surface, then roll out to a thickness of 5 mm / ¼ inch. Cut the dough into rounds with a 6 cm / 2½ inch cutter. Re-roll and re-cut trimmings.

Place the biscuits on the prepared baking sheets, pricking the top of each in several places. Bake for 12–15 minutes, until golden. Leave to stand for 5 minutes, then cool on a wire rack.

When quite cold, sandwich the biscuits together in pairs with strawberry jam and dredge with icing sugar, if liked.

MAKES TWENTY-SIX TO THIRTY

DIGESTIVE BISCUITS

butter for greasing
75 g / 3 oz wholemeal flour
25 g / 1 oz plain white flour
25 g / 1 oz fine or medium oatmeal
2.5 ml / ½ tsp baking powder
1.25 ml / ¼ tsp salt
15 ml / 1 tbsp soft light brown sugar
50 g / 2 oz butter or margarine
30 ml / 2 tbsp milk
flour for rolling out

Grease a baking sheet. Set the oven at 180°C / 350°F / gas 4. Mix all the dry ingredients in a mixing bowl, sifting the sugar if it is lumpy. Rub in the butter or margarine until the mixture binds together and mix to a pliable dough with the milk.

Knead the biscuits dough lightly on a floured board and roll out to a thickness of just under 5 mm / ¼ inch. Cut into rounds with a 6 cm / 2 ½ inch round cutter, place on the prepared baking sheet and prick with a fork. Bake for 15 minutes or until golden brown. Leave to stand for a few minutes, then cool on a wire rack.

MAKES ABOUT TWELVE

GINGER SNAPS

margarine for greasing
200 g / 7 oz self-raising flour
pinch of salt
5 ml / 1 tsp ground ginger
100 g / 4 oz soft light brown sugar
75 g / 3 oz margarine
100 g / 4 oz golden syrup
1 egg, beaten

Thoroughly grease several baking sheets. Set the oven at 160°C / 325°F / gas 3. Sift together the flour, salt and ginger. Stir in the sugar. Melt the margarine with the syrup in a large heavy-bottomed saucepan. When the fat has melted, add the dry ingredients and beaten egg and beat until smooth and thick.

Using 2 teaspoons, place rounds of the mixture on to the prepared baking sheets, allowing plenty of room for spreading. Bake for 15 minutes. Leave to stand for a few minutes, then cool on a wire rack.

MAKES ABOUT FIFTY-SIX

BOURBON BISCUITS

oil for greasing
50 g / 2 oz butter or margarine
50 g / 2 oz caster sugar
15 ml / 1 tbsp golden syrup
100 g / 4 oz plain flour
15 g / ½ oz cocoa
2.5 ml / ½ tsp bicarbonate of soda
flour for rolling out

FILLING
50 g / 2 oz butter or margarine
75 g / 3 oz icing sugar, sifted
15 ml / 1 tbsp cocoa
5 ml / 1 tsp coffee essence or
2.5 ml / ½ tsp instant coffee dissolved in
5 ml / 1 tsp boiling water and cooled

Line and grease a baking sheet. Set the oven to 160°C / 325°F / gas 3.

In a mixing bowl, cream the butter or margarine with the sugar very thoroughly; beat in the syrup. Sift the flour, cocoa and bicarbonate of soda into a second bowl, mix well, then work into the creamed mixture to make a stiff dough. Knead well, and roll out on a lightly floured surface into an oblong strip about 23 x 13 cm / 9 x 5 inches and 5 mm / ¼ inch thick. Cut in half to form two rectangles about 6 cm / 2½ inches wide. Place on the prepared baking sheet and bake for 15–20 minutes. Cut into equal sized fingers while still warm. Cool on wire rack.

Prepare the filling. In a bowl, beat the butter or margarine until soft, then add the sugar, cocoa, and coffee. Beat until smooth. Sandwich the cooled fingers in pairs with the filling.

MAKES FOURTEEN TO SIXTEEN

MELTING MOMENTS

butter or margarine for greasing
100 g / 4 oz margarine or half margarine and half blended white
vegetable fat
75 g / 3 oz caster suagr
30 ml / 2 tbsp beaten egg
125 g / 4½ oz self-raising flour
pinch of salt
rolled oats for coating
4–5 glacé cherries, quartered

Grease two baking sheets. Set the oven to 180°C / 350°F / gas 4.

In a mixing bowl, cream the margarine or mixed fats and sugar until pale and fluffy. Add the egg with a little flour and beat again. Stir in the remaining flour with the salt, mix well, then shape the mixture into 16–20 balls with the hands.

Place the rolled oats on a sheet of greaseproof paper and toss the balls in them to coat them evenly all over. Space the balls on the prepared baking sheets. Place a small piece of glacé cherry in the centre of each.

Bake for about 20 minutes until pale golden brown. Leave to stand for a few minutes on the baking sheets, then cool on a wire rack.

MAKES SIXTEEN TO TWENTY

VARIATION

- **Custard Treats** Substitute 40 g / 1½ oz of the flour with custard powder for a deliciously creamy biscuit with a rich buttery colour. Omit the rolled oats coating.

FLAPJACKS

margarine for greasing
175 g / 6 oz margarine
100 g / 4 oz soft light brown sugar
30 ml / 2 tbsp golden syrup
175 g / 6 oz rolled oats

Grease a 28 x 18 cm / 11 x 7 inch baking tin. Set the oven at 160°C / 325°F / gas 3. Melt the margarine in a large saucepan. Add the sugar and syrup, and warm gently. Do not boil. Remove from the heat and stir in the oats.

Press into the prepared tin, then bake for 25 minutes or until firm. Cut into fingers while still warm and leave in the tin to cool.

MAKES ABOUT TWENTY

VARIATIONS

- **Sultana Flapjacks** Add 50 g / 2 oz sultanas to the basic mixture, stirring them in with the oats.
- **Sesame Flapjacks** Sesame seeds contribute their own, distinctive flavour to this traditional recipe. Press the flapjack mixture into the tin, then sprinkle a layer of sesame seeds over the top and press them down well with the back of a spoon. Do not use roasted sesame seeds.
- **Honey Flapjacks** Use clear honey instead of golden syrup; continue as in the main recipe.

ALMOND MACAROONS

butter for greasing
2 egg whites
150 g / 5 oz caster sugar
100 g / 4 oz ground almonds
10 ml / 2 tsp ground rice
split almonds or halved glacé cherries

Grease two baking sheets and cover with rice paper. Set the oven at 160°C / 325°F / gas 3.

In a clean dry bowl, whisk the egg whites until frothy but not stiff enough to form peaks. Stir in the sugar, ground almonds, and ground rice. Beat with a wooden spoon until thick and white.

Put small spoonfuls of the mixture 5 cm / 2 inches apart on the prepared baking sheets or pipe them on. Place a split almond or halved glacé cherry on each macaroon and bake for 20 minutes or until pale fawn in colour. Cool slightly on the baking sheets, then finish cooling on wire racks.

MAKES SIXTEEN TO TWENTY

VARIATION

- **Ratafias** Ratafias are used in trifles, to decorate desserts, and as petits fours. Follow the recipe above, but reduce the size of the biscuits so that when cooked they are only 2 cm / ¾ inch in diameter. Omit the split almond or glacé cherry topping.

BRANDY SNAPS

These traditional treats make a popular addition to a buffet table or may be served as a tempting dessert. Fill them at the last moment with fresh whipped cream.

margarine for greasing
50 g / 2 oz plain flour
5 ml / 1 tsp ground ginger
50 g / 2 oz margarine
50 g / 2 oz soft dark brown sugar
30 ml / 2 tbsp golden syrup
10 ml / 2 tsp grated lemon rind
5 ml / 1 tsp lemon juice

Grease two or three 25 x 20 cm / 10 x 8 inch baking sheets. Also grease the handles of several wooden spoons, standing them upside down in a jar until required. Set the oven at 180°C / 350°F / gas 4.

Sift the flour and ginger into a bowl. Melt the margarine in a saucepan. Add the sugar and syrup and warm gently, but do not allow to become hot. Remove from the heat and add the sifted ingredients with the lemon rind and juice. Mix well.

Put spoonfuls of the mixture on the prepared baking sheets spacing well apart to allow for spreading. Do not put more than 6 spoonfuls on a baking sheet. Bake for 8–10 minutes.

Remove from the oven and leave to cool for a few seconds until the edges begin to firm. Lift one of the biscuits with a palette knife and roll loosely around the greased handle of one of the wooden spoons. Allow to cool before removing biscuits. Alternatively, make brandy snap cups by moulding the mixture in greased patty tins or over oranges.

MAKES FOURTEEN TO EIGHTEEN

RUSKS

*This is an old Suffolk recipe for simple, dry biscuits which are
made from a yeasted bread dough. The original recipe used
fresh yeast but this version takes advantage of easy-blend yeast.
The sugar may be omitted if preferred.*

butter for greasing
225 g / 8 oz strong plain flour
15 g / ½ oz easy-blend dried yeast
25 g / 1 oz sugar
2.5 ml / ½ tsp salt
25 g / 1 oz butter
75 ml / 3 fl oz milk
1 egg, beaten
flour for kneading

Grease a large baking sheet. Set the oven at 220°C / 425°F / gas 7.

Place the flour, yeast, sugar and salt in a mixing bowl. Stir the ingredients
together, then make a well in the middle. In a small saucepan, heat the butter
and milk together very gently until the butter has melted, then remove the pan
from the heat and leave to cool until warm.

Pour the milk mixture into the well in the dry ingredients, add the beaten egg
and stir well. Gradually stir in the flour mixture to make a firm dough. Turn the
dough out on to a lightly-floured surface and knead thoroughly until smooth
and elastic. The dough should be kneaded for about 10 minutes.

Place the dough in a clean, lightly-floured bowl and cover it with a clean cloth.
Set the dough to rise in a warm place until it had doubled in bulk. This may take
up to 1½ hours.

Lightly knead the dough again, then divide it into six portions. Shape each
portion of dough into an oblong roll measuring about 13 cm / 5 inches in length.
Place the rolls on the baking sheet and bake them for about 15–20 minutes, or
until they are evenly golden.

Remove the rolls from the oven and reduce the temperature to 180°C / 350°F / gas 4. Using a clean tea-towel to protect your hand, split each roll in half lengthways to make a slim rusk. Return them to the baking sheet, cut side uppermost, and cook for a further 30–40 minutes, or until they are crisp and lightly browned on the cut side. The rusks are ready when they are quite dry.

Leave the rusks to cool on a wire rack, then transfer them to an airtight container.

MAKES TWELVE

OATCAKES

fat for greasing
50 g / 2 oz bacon fat or dripping
100 g / 4 oz medium oatmeal
1.25 ml / ¼ tsp salt
1.25 ml / ¼ tsp bicarbonate of soda
fine oatmeal for rolling out

Grease two baking sheets. Set the oven at 160°F / 325°F / gas 3.

Melt the bacon fat or dripping in a large saucepan. Remove from the heat and stir in the dry ingredients, then add enough boiling water to make a stiff dough.

When cool enough to handle, knead the dough thoroughly, then roll out on a surface dusted with fine oatmeal, to a thickness of 5 mm / ¼ inch. Cut into wedge-shaped pieces and transfer to the prepared baking sheets. Bake for 20–30 minutes. Cool on a wire rack.

MAKES ABOUT SIXTEEN

CARAWAY CRACKERS

Originally, these simple biscuits were sweetened with
50 g / 2 oz caster sugar but the flavour of the caraway seeds makes
such an excellent savoury cracker that the sugar is omitted in this recipe.
However, you may like to try the old recipe and add the sugar
to the flour. If you are making the savoury crackers,
try using brown flour instead of white.

butter for greasing
50 g / 2 oz butter
225 g / 8 oz plain flour
30 ml / 2 tbsp caraway seeds
good pinch of salt
1 egg, beaten
milk for glazing

Grease two baking sheets. Set the oven at 180°C / 350°F / gas 4. Place the butter in a small bowl and beat it until it is very soft. Gradually beat in the flour, caraway seeds and salt until the ingredients are thoroughly mixed.

Add the beaten egg and mix well to make a firm dough. Knead the dough briefly on a floured surface, then roll it out thinly and cut out 5 cm / 2 inch circles.

Place the crackers on the baking sheets and brush them with a little milk, then bake them for about 12–15 minutes. Transfer the crackers to a wire rack to cool.

MAKES ABOUT THIRTY

Preserves, Stocks & Sauces

All sorts of good things, including mincemeat, lemon curd, stocks, gravy, and sauces to accompany meals and puddings.

EXCELLENT MINCEMEAT

3 large cooking apples, cored
3 large lemons
450 g / 1 lb raisins
450 g / 1 lb currants
450 g / 1 lb suet
900 g / 2 lb soft light brown sugar
25 g / 1 oz candied orange peel, chopped
25 g / 1 oz candied citron or lemon peel, chopped
30 ml / 2 tbsp orange marmalade
250 ml / 8 fl oz brandy

Set the oven at 200°C / 400°F / gas 6. Bake the apples in a covered ovenproof dish for 50–60 minutes, until they are thoroughly tender.

Grate the lemon rind and squeeze out their juice. Set both rind and juice aside. Chop the lemon shells and simmer them, in just enough water to cover, for about 1 hour or until the shells are soft enough to chop very finely. Drain, cool and chop the shells.

Scoop the apple flesh from the skins and mix it with the reserved lemon rind and juice, then stir in all the remaining ingredients, including the chopped lemon shells. Cover the bowl and leave the mincemeat to stand for 2 days, stirring occasionally.

Press the mincemeat down well into sterilized pots and cover them with airtight lids. Label the mincemeat and allow it to mature for at least 2 months.

MAKES ABOUT 4 kg / 9 lb

LEMON CURD

Lemon curd is not a true preserve but it keeps well in a refrigerator.
Use very fresh eggs bought from a reputable source.

2 lemons
225 g / 8 oz granulated sugar
75 g / 3 oz butter, cut into dice
3 eggs

Wash, dry and grate the lemons. Squeeze out the juice and put it with the sugar in the top of a double saucepan or heatproof bowl set over boiling water. Stir occasionally until the sugar has dissolved. Remove from the heat and stir in the butter. Leave to cool.

Beat the eggs lightly in a bowl. Pour the cooled lemon mixture over them, mix well, then strain the mixture back into the pan or bowl. Place over gentle heat, stirring frequently until the mixture thickens enough to coat the back of a wooden spoon lightly. Pour into warmed clean jars. Cover with waxed paper discs. Put on lids and label when cold. Leave for 24 hours to thicken. Store in the refrigerator. Use within 2–3 weeks.

MAKES ABOUT 450 g / 1 lb

VARIATION

- **Orange Curd** Substitute 2 oranges and add the juice of 1 lemon. Use only 50 g / 2 oz butter, melting it in the double saucepan or bowl before adding the rind, juices and sugar.

CUSTARD SAUCE

This is a classic, thin custard.

500 ml / 17 fl oz milk
2.5 ml / ½ tsp natural vanilla essence, to taste
6 egg yolks
25–50 g / 1–2 oz caster sugar

Warm the milk with the vanilla. In a heatproof bowl, beat the egg yolks with the sugar until creamy. Add the warm milk to the egg mixture. Stand the bowl over a pan of hot, not simmering water, and stir the custard for 20–30 minutes, until it thickens slightly to coat the back of a spoon. Take care not to let the water boil or overcook the custard or it will curdle. Serve hot or cold.

MAKES ABOUT 500 ml / 17 fl oz

CUSTARD SAUCE (SIMPLE)

Cornflour stabilizes this custard, which is boiled.
It is far thicker than a custard sauce which is made with yolks alone.

30 ml / 2 tbsp cornflour
30 ml / 2 tbsp caster sugar
600 ml / 1 pint milk
2.5 ml / ½ tsp natural vanilla essence

Mix the cornflour and sugar to a smooth paste with a little of the milk. Heat the rest of the milk, then stir it into the cornflour. Return the mixture to the pan, bring to the boil, lower the heat and simmer for 1–2 minutes, stirring all the time. Stir in the vanilla and egg yolks, then immediately take the pan off the heat. Taste the custard for sweetness and flavouring. Serve at once.

MAKES ABOUT 750 ml / 1¼ PINTS

RICH STRONG STOCK

This recipe makes a large quantity of stock which freezes well for future use. Although the quantities may be reduced, a large volume of liquid is required to cover marrow bones. It is more practical to invest in a large stockpot or saucepan and to boil a large quantity occasionally than to reduce the weight of ingredients in proportion to water to make a weaker meat stock.

675 g / 1½ lb shin of beef on the bone
675 g / 1½ lb knuckle of veal on the bone, or other stewing veal
450 g / 1 lb beef marrow bones
1 chicken drumstick or poultry trimmings
1 onion, sliced
1 carrot, quartered
100 g / 4 oz gammon or bacon, diced
1 small turnip, roughly chopped
2 celery sticks, quartered
2 open cup mushrooms, quartered
1 tomato, quartered
1 bouquet garni
4 white peppercorns
2 cloves
1 blade of mace

Set the oven at 200°C / 400°F / gas 6. Put the bones in a roasting tin and roast for about 2 hours until browned. Transfer the bones to a large saucepan. Pour off the fat from the tin, add some boiling water and stir to scrape all the sediment off the tin. Then add to the bones in the pan. Add the onion and carrot.

Add about 5.6 litres / 10 pints water to cover the bones generously. Bring to the boil, skim the surface, then lower the heat and add the remaining ingredients. Simmer for about 5 hours. Cool, then strain. Skim off surface fat. Season and use as required.

MAKES ABOUT 5.6 LITRES / 10 PINTS

BEEF STOCK

This is a simple recipe which gives a reasonably flavourful stock.

a little beef dripping or lard
1 kg / 2¼ lb shin of beef, stewing or braising beef, in one piece
2 large onions, sliced
2 large carrots
4 celery sticks
1 bouquet garni
1 blade of mace
12 black peppercorns
salt

Set the oven to 230°C / 450°F / gas 8. Use the dripping or lard to lightly grease a heavy-bottomed, flameproof casserole which can be placed in the oven. Place the beef in the casserole and roast it, uncovered, for 20 minutes. Turn the meat over and continue roasting for a further 20 minutes, by which time it should be well sealed and lightly browned outside.

Remove the meat from the casserole, add the onions, carrots and celery, then replace the meat on top. Pour 300 ml / ½ pint water over the vegetables around the meat. Place the casserole on the hob and bring the liquid to simmering point. Add the bouquet garni, mace and peppercorns, then cover the casserole tightly. Simmer the ingredients over very low heat for 15 minutes.

Pour 600 ml / 1 pint water into the casserole. Add salt to taste. Heat until simmering, cover and simmer gently for 30 minutes. Add 1.4 litres / 2½ pints extra water in two or three batches, simmering for 15 minutes between each addition. Each time water is added, the cooking juices from the pan should be stirred in. When all the water has been added, bring the water to simmering point and cover the pan tightly. Cook the stock over very low heat, so the liquid barely simmers, for about 4 hours.

When the meat is completely tender and the stock has a good flavour, remove the pan from the heat. Leave the meat to cool in the stock for 2–3 hours. Remove the meat and strain the stock. Skim any fat from the surface.

MAKES ABOUT 2.25 LITRES / 4 PINTS

MRS BEETON'S TIP

The best stock is made from meat on the bone. The stock can be left unsalted, allowing the seasoning to be added according to the requirements of the dish in which the stock is used; however, if the stock is salted, the cooked piece of beef will have more flavour and can be minced or finely chopped for making rissoles or similar dishes.

CHICKEN STOCK

4 chicken drumsticks or 1 meaty chicken carcass
1 small onion, sliced
1 carrot, roughly chopped
1 celery stick, sliced
1 bouquet garni
5 ml / 1 tsp white peppercorns

Break or chop the carcass into manageable pieces. Put it in a large saucepan with 1.75 litres / 3 pints cold water. Bring to the boil; skim the surface. Add the remaining ingredients, lower the heat and simmer for 3–4 hours. Cool quickly, then strain. Skim off surface fat. Season and use as required.

MAKES ABOUT 1.4 LITRES / 2½ PINTS

VARIATIONS

- **Rich Chicken Stock** Use drumsticks and roast them at 200°C / 400°F / gas 6 for 40 minutes. Drain off the fat. Continue as above, adding 225 g / 8 oz cubed belly pork with the chicken.
- **Game Stock** Use the carcasses of 1 or 2 game birds such as pheasant or grouse, with the giblets, instead of the chicken.

CLARIFYING STOCK

Scald a saucepan (not aluminium), a piece of muslin, a metal sieve and a whisk. Pour the strained stock into the pan. Lightly whisk 2 egg whites and crush the shells from 2 eggs; add to the stock. Heat slowly to simmering point, whisking to form a thick white crust. Stop whisking, allow the stock to rise in the pan, then turn the heat off just before it boils. Repeat twice more. Line the sieve with the muslin and place it over a clean bowl. Strain the stock through the muslin. Try not to break the crust which acts as a filter.

PRESSURE COOKER TIP

Meat and poultry stocks, made with raw or cooked meat and bones, can be prepared in the pressure cooker in approximately 40 minutes at 15 1b pressure. Follow the manufacturer's recommendations regarding the maximum quantity of ingredients and liquid for the pan; failing this, make a concentrated stock by reducing the volume of water to ensure that the pan is no more than half to two-thirds full. Add extra water and simmer briefly in the open pan after the pressure has been reduced.

WHITE STOCK

**1.4 kg / 3 lb knuckle of veal on the bone, or other
stewing veal
2 chicken drumsticks or poultry trimmings
1 onion, sliced
1 carrot, quartered
2 celery sticks, quartered
2 open cup mushrooms, quartered
1 bouquet garni
4 white peppercorns
1 blade of mace**

Put the bones in a large saucepan. Add 900 ml / 1½ pints water. Bring to the boil, skim the surface, then add the remaining ingredients. Lower the heat and simmer for 30 minutes. Add a further 900 m1 / 1½ pints water and simmer for about 3 hours more. Cool quickly, then strain. Skim off surface fat. Season and use as required.

MAKES ABOUT 1.5 LITRES / 2¾ PINTS

FISH STOCK

Do not overcook fish stock or its flavour will be dull or even bitter.

25 g / 1 oz butter
1 onion sliced
2 carrots, sliced
fish trimmings without gills or
350 g / 12 oz white fish fillet, in chunks
strip of pared lemon rind
1 bouquet garni
salt and pepper

Melt the butter in a large saucepan. Fry the onion, carrots, and fish trimmings in the butter for 10 minutes. If using fish fillet, fry the vegetables for 5 minutes, then add the fillet and cook for a further 5 minutes.

Add the strip of lemon rind and the bouquet garni, with 1.1 litres / 2 pints water. Stir in a little salt and pepper and bring the stock to the boil. Reduce the heat, cover than pan and simmer the stock for 30 minutes. Strain the stock through a muslin-lined sieve or coffee filter paper.

MAKES ABOUT 1 LITRE / 1¾ PINTS

VEGETABLE STOCK

*Vary the vegetables according to the market selection
and your personal taste.*

**2 onions, sliced
2 leeks, trimmed, sliced and washed
1 small turnip, chopped
4 celery sticks, sliced
2 tomatoes, chopped
1 bouquet garni
6 black peppercorns
2 cloves
a few lettuce leaves
a few spinach leaves
a few watercress sprigs
2.5 ml / ½ tsp yeast extract (optional)
salt**

Put the root vegetables, celery, tomatoes, herbs and spices in a large saucepan.
Add 2 litres / 3½ pints water. Bring to the boil, lower the heat and simmer for
1 hour.

Add the lettuce, spinach and watercress and simmer for 1 hour more. Stir in the
yeast extract, if using, and add salt to taste.

MAKES ABOUT 1.75 LITRES / 3 PINTS

WHITE SAUCE

This makes a thick, coating sauce

50 g / 2 oz butter
50 g / 2 oz plain flour
600 ml / 1 pint milk, stock or a mixture
salt and pepper

Melt the butter in a saucepan. Stir in the flour and cook over low heat for 2–3 minutes, without browning. With the heat on the lowest setting, gradually add the liquid, stirring constantly. If lumps begin to form, stop pouring in liquid and stir the sauce vigorously, then continue pouring in the liquid when smooth. Increase the heat to moderate and cook the sauce, stirring, until it boils and thickens. Lower the heat and simmer for 1–2 minutes, beating briskly to give the sauce a gloss. Add salt and pepper to taste.

MAKES 600 ml / 1 PINT

VARIATION

• **Pouring Sauce** Follow the recipe above, but use only 40 g / 1½ oz each of butter and flour.

MRS BEETON'S TIP

White Sauce can be made by the all-in-one method. Simply combine the butter, flour and liquid in a saucepan and whisk over moderate heat until the mixture comes to the boil. Lower the heat and simmer for 3–4 minutes, whisking constantly until the sauce is thick, smooth and glossy. Add salt and pepper to taste.

GRAVY

**giblets, carcass bones or trimmings
from meat, poultry or game
1 bay leaf
1 thyme sprig
1 clove
6 black peppercorns
1 onion, sliced
pan juices from roasting (see Mrs Beeton's Tip)
25 g / 1 oz plain flour (optional)
salt and pepper**

Place the giblets, bones, carcass and / or trimmings (for example wing ends) in a saucepan. Pour in water to cover, then add the bay leaf, thyme, clove, peppercorns and onion. Bring to the boil and skim off any scum, then lower the heat, cover the pan and simmer for about 1 hour.

Strain the stock and measure it. You need about 600–750 ml / 1–1¼ pints to make gravy for up to six servings. If necessary, pour the stock back into the saucepan and boil until reduced.

Pour off most of the fat from the roasting tin, leaving a thin layer and all the cooking juices. Place the tin over moderate heat; add the flour if the gravy is to be thickened. Cook the flour, stirring all the time and scraping all the sediment off the tin, for about 3 minutes, until it is browned. If the gravy is not thickened, pour in about 300 ml / ½ pint of the stock and boil, stirring and scraping, until the sediment on the base of the tin is incorporated.

Slowly pour in the stock (or the remaining stock, if making thin gravy), stirring all the time. Bring to the boil and cook for 2–3 minutes to reduce the gravy and concentrate the flavour slightly. Taste and add more salt and pepper if required.

SERVES FOUR TO SIX

MRS BEETON'S TIP

The quality of the sediment on the base of the cooking tin determines the quality of the gravy. If the meat was well seasoned and roasted until well browned outside, the sediment should have a good colour and flavour. Any herbs (other than large stalks), onions or flavouring roasted under the meat should be left in the pan until the gravy is boiled, then strained out before serving.

GRAVY NOTES

• If making gravy for a meal other than a roast, for example to accompany sausages or toad-in-the-hole, use a little fat instead of the pan juices and brown the flour well over low to moderate heat. Meat dripping gives the best flavour but butter or other fat may be used.

• To make onion gravy, slowly brown 2 thinly sliced onions in the fat before adding the flour – this is excellent with grilled sausages or toad-in-the-hole.

• Gravy browning may be added if necessary; however, it can make the sauce look artificial and unpleasant. Pale gravy is perfectly acceptable, provided it has good flavour.

• Always taste gravy when cooked. It should be well seasoned. If it lacks flavour, or is rather dull, a dash of Worcestershire sauce, Mushroom Ketchup (page 239) or about 5–15 ml / 1–3 tsp tomato purée may be whisked in.

• Gravy may be enriched by adding up to half wine instead of stock.

• Add 60 ml / 4 tbsp port or sherry, and 15 ml / 1 tbsp redcurrant jelly to make a rich gravy for duck, game, lamb, pork or venison.

• Add 2 chopped pickled walnuts and 15 ml / 1 tbsp walnut oil to the pan juices to make a delicious walnut gravy.

• Use vegetable stock to make vegetable gravy. Cook a finely diced carrot and 2 thinly sliced onions in butter or margarine instead of using meat juices. Add 1.25 ml / ¼ tsp ground mace and 30 ml / 2 tbsp chopped parsley.

• Add 100 g / 4 oz thinly sliced mushrooms to the pan juices to make a mushroom gravy. The sauce may be further enriched by adding a little Mushroom Ketchup (page 239) .

BREAD SAUCE

600 ml / 1 pint milk
1 large onion studded with 6 cloves
1 blade of mace
4 peppercorns
1 allspice berry
1 bay leaf
100 g / 4 oz fine fresh white breadcrumbs
15 ml / 1 tbsp butter
salt and pepper
freshly grated nutmeg
30 ml / 2 tbsp single cream (optional)

Put the milk in a small saucepan with the studded onion, mace, peppercorns, allspice and bay leaf. Bring very slowly to boiling point, then remove from the heat, cover the pan and set it aside for 30 minutes.

Strain the flavoured milk into a heatproof bowl, pressing the onion against the sides of the strainer to extract as much of the liquid as possible. Stir in the breadcrumbs and butter, with salt, pepper and nutmeg to taste.

Set the bowl over simmering water and cook for 20 minutes, stirring occasionally until thick and creamy. Stir in the cream, if using, just before serving.

MAKES ABOUT 250 ml / 8 fl oz

MICROWAVE TIP

There is no need to infuse the onion in the milk if the sauce is to be made in the microwave. Simply put the clove-studded onion in a deep bowl, cover and cook on High for 2 minutes. Add the spices, bay leaf and milk, cover loosely and cook on High for 6–6½ minutes. Stir in the remaining ingredients, except the cream, and cook for 2 minutes more. Remove the studded onion, whole spices and bay leaf. Whisk the sauce, adding the cream if liked.

CHRISTOPHER NORTH'S SAUCE

Serve this potent sauce as a relish with roast beef, veal or game,
or use it to pep up gravies and other sauces.

175 ml / 6 fl oz port
30 ml / 2 tbsp Worcestershire sauce
10 ml / 2 tsp Mushroom Ketchup (page 239)
10 ml / 2 tsp caster sugar
15 ml / 1 tbsp lemon juice
1.25 ml / ¼ tsp cayenne pepper
2.5 ml / ½ tsp salt

Mix all the ingredients together in the top of a double saucepan or a heatproof bowl set over simmering water. Heat gently, without boiling. Serve at once or cool quickly and refrigerate in a closed jar until required.

MAKES ABOUT 250 ml / 8 fl oz

APPLE SAUCE

450 g / 1 lb apples
4 cloves
15 g / ½ oz butter
rind and juice of ½ lemon
sugar (see method)

Peel, core and slice the apples. Put them in a saucepan with 30 ml / 2 tbsp water, add the cloves, butter and lemon rind. Cover and cook over low heat until the apple is reduced to a pulp. Remove the cloves. Beat until smooth, rub through a sieve or process in a blender or food processor. Return the sauce to the clean pan, stir in the lemon juice and add sugar to taste. Reheat gently, stirring until the sugar has dissolved. Serve hot or cold.

MAKES ABOUT 350 ml / 12 fl oz

BROWN APPLE SAUCE

In Mrs Beeton's day, this tangy, apple-flavoured gravy was frequently served as an accompaniment to roast pork or goose. It is also suitable for grilled pork chops or gammon steaks.

350 g / 12 oz Bramley apples
300 ml / ½ pint Gravy (page 234), made with poultry or
pork cooking juices
45 ml / 3 tbsp sugar
salt and pepper
cayenne pepper

Quarter, peel, core and slice the apples. Put them in a saucepan with the gravy. Bring to the boil, reduce the heat and cover the pan. Simmer for 10–15 minutes until the apple is reduced to a pulp. Beat the pulp into the gravy until smooth. Add the sugar with salt, pepper and cayenne to taste. Serve hot.

MAKES ABOUT 600 ml / 1 pint

MINT SAUCE

60 ml / 4 tbsp chopped mint
30 ml / 2 tbsp caster sugar
150 ml / ¼ pint vinegar

Mix the sugar and vinegar until the sugar has dissolved. It is easier to dissolve the sugar if it is first mixed with 45 ml / 3 tbsp freshly boiled water before the mint is added, and this also makes the sauce taste less harsh if malt vinegar is used. Wine vinegar or cider vinegar can be used if preferred. Cider makes a mild sauce which is especially good with lamb.

MAKES ABOUT 150 ml / ¼ pint

MUSHROOM KETCHUP

Taken directly from Mrs Beeton's first edition recipe, this ketchup must be sterilized when bottled to ensure that it keeps safely. However, a more practical and safer alternative is to freeze the ketchup in small quantities. The exact yield depends on the mushrooms.

600 ml / 8 pints open mushrooms
100 g / 4 oz salt

FLAVOURING INGREDIENTS
(see method)
cayenne pepper
allspice
blades of mace
brandy

The mushrooms should be clean and dry. Layer them in a large bowl, sprinkling each layer with salt. Cover and leave in a cool place for 4 hours. Break the mushrooms into small pieces using your fingers, not a knife. Press them down well in the bowl and cover closely. Leave the mushrooms to stand for 3 days, mashing them at least twice a day to extract their liquor and stirring well.

Measure the volume of mushrooms and liquor at the end of the salting process, then pour both into a large, heatproof bowl. To every 1.1 litres / 2 pints, add 7 g / ¼ oz cayenne pepper, 15 g / ½ oz each of ground allspice and ginger, and 2 blades of mace, pounded to a powder. Stir well, then stand the bowl over a saucepan of boiling water and boil for 30 minutes stirring occasionally. Pour the mushrooms into one or more clean jugs, cover and leave to cool overnight.

Pour off the ketchup carefully, leaving all the sediment behind. Do not squeeze the mushrooms. Add a little brandy (a few drops to every 600 ml / 1 pint), then decant the ketchup into suitable bottles. Cover, sterilize at 88°C / 190°F for 30 minutes and seal immediately. Cool, then check the seal before storing the ketchup to ensure the bottles are airtight.

BENTON SAUCE

Fresh horseradish is very useful. Not only is it the basis of an excellent sauce to serve with roast beef, but it also adds piquancy to seafood cocktail sauces and dips. In Mrs Beeton's day, a little horseradish was also added to apple sauce, to be served with pork or beef.

30 ml / 2 tbsp freshly grated horseradish
10 ml / 2 tsp prepared mustard
10 ml / 2 tsp caster sugar
125 ml 4 fl oz malt vinegar

Pound the horseradish with the mustard and sugar in a small bowl. Gradually add the vinegar, mixing well.

MAKES ABOUT 150 ml / ¼ pint

HORSERADISH SAUCE

60 ml / 4 tbsp grated horseradish
5 ml / 1 tsp caster sugar
5 ml / 1 tsp salt
2.5 ml / ½ tsp pepper
10 ml / 2 tsp prepared mustard
malt vinegar (see method)
45–60 ml / 3–4 tbsp single cream (optional)

Mix the horseradish, sugar, salt, pepper and mustard in a non-metallic bowl. Stir in enough vinegar to make a sauce with the consistency of cream. The flavour and appearance will be improved if the quantity of vinegar is reduced, and the single cream added.

MAKES ABOUT 150 ml / ¼ pint

TARTARE SAUCE

2 hard-boiled egg yolks
2 egg yolks
salt and pepper
15 ml / 1 tbsp white wine vinegar
300 ml / ½ pint oil (olive oil or a mixture of olive with
grapeseed or sunflower oil)
15 ml / 1 tbsp chopped capers
15 ml / 1 tbsp chopped gherkin
30 ml / 2 tbsp chopped parsley
15 ml / 1 tbsp snipped chives

Sieve the hard-boiled egg yolks into a bowl. Add one of the raw yolks and mix thoroughly, then work in the second raw yolk. Stir in salt and pepper to taste and mix to a paste with the vinegar.

Beating vigorously, gradually add the oil, drop by drop. When all the oil has been incorporated and the mixture is thick, stir in the capers, gherkin and herbs.

MAKES ABOUT 300 ml / ½ pint

Useful Weights and Measures

USING METRIC OR IMPERIAL MEASURES

Throughout the book, all weights and measures are given first in metric, then in imperial. For example 100 g / 4 oz, 150 ml/ ¼ pint or 15 ml / 1 tbsp.

When following any of the recipes use either metric or imperial – do not combine the two sets of measures as they are approximate equivalents, not interchangeable.

EQUIVALENT METRIC / IMPERIAL MEASURES

Weights The following chart lists some of the metric / imperial weights that are used in the recipes.

METRIC	IMPERIAL	METRIC	IMPERIAL
15 g	½ oz	375 g	13 oz
25 g	1 oz	400 g	14 oz
50 g	2 oz	425 g	15 oz
75 g	3 oz	450 g	1 lb
100 g	4 oz	575 g	1¼ lb
150 g	5 oz	675 g	1½ lb
175 g	6 oz	800 g	1¾ lb
200 g	7 oz	900 g	2 lb
225 g	8 oz	1 kg	2¼ lb
250 g	9 oz	1.4 kg	3 lb
275 g	10 oz	1.6 kg	3½ lb
300 g	11 oz	1.8 kg	4 lb
350 g	12 oz	2.25 kg	5 lb

Liquid Measures The following chart lists some metric / imperial equivalents for liquids. Millilitres (ml), litres and fluid ounces (fl oz) or pints are used throughout.

METRIC	IMPERIAL
50 ml	2 fl oz
125 ml	4 fl oz
150 ml	¼ pint
300 ml	½ pint
450 ml	¾ pint
600 ml	1 pint

Spoon Measures Both metric and imperial equivalents are given for all spoon measures, expressed as millilitres and teaspoons (tsp) or tablespoons (tbsp).

All spoon measures refer to British standard measuring spoons and the quantities given are always for level spoons.

Do not use ordinary kitchen cutlery instead of proper measuring spoons as they will hold quite different quantities.

METRIC	IMPERIAL
1.25 ml	¼ tsp
2.5 ml	½ tsp
5 ml	1 tsp
15 ml	1 tbsp

Length All linear measures are expressed in millimetres (mm), centimetres (cm) or metres (m) and inches or feet. The following list gives examples of typical conversions.

METRIC	IMPERIAL
5 mm	¼ inch
1 cm	½ inch
2.5 cm	1 inch
5 cm	2 inches
15 cm	6 inches
30 cm	12 inches (1 foot)

MICROWAVE INFORMATION

Occasional microwave hints and instructions are included for certain recipes, as appropriate. The information given is for microwave ovens rated at 650–700 watts.

The following terms have been used for the microwave settings: High, Medium, Defrost and Low. For each setting, the power input is as follows: High = 100% power, Medium = 50% power, Defrost = 30% power and Low = 20% power.

All microwave notes and timings are for guidance only: always read and follow the manufacturer's instructions for your particular appliance. Remember to avoid putting any metal in the microwave and never operate the microwave empty.

Be very careful when heating liquids in the microwave as they can 'superheat'; i.e. the liquid's surface looks still but underneath there can be boiling bubbles that explode when the container is moved.

OVEN TEMPERATURES

Whenever the oven is used, the required setting is given as three alternatives: degrees Celsius (°C), degrees Fahrenheit (°F) and gas.

The temperature settings given are for conventional ovens. If you have a fan oven, adjust the temperature according to the manufacturer's instructions.

°C	°F	GAS
110	225	¼
120	250	½
140	275	1
150	300	2
160	325	3
180	350	4
190	375	5
200	400	6
220	425	7
230	450	8
240	475	9

Index

245

ÉADAOIN

Éadaoin

Seacht Snaidhm na Seirce

Scéal Mór Grá na nGael
Tochmharc Étaíne

DIARMUID JOHNSON

LEABHAR
BREAC

An Chéad Eagrán 2020
© Diarmuid Johnson 2020

ISBN 978-1-909907-68-3

Clóchur, dearadh agus pictiúr clúdaigh: Caomhán Ó Scolaí
Clódóireacht: CL Print

Foras na Gaeilge
Tugann Foras na Gaeilge tacaíocht do Leabhar Breac

Leabhar Breac, Indreabhán, Co. na Gaillimhe.

Mé Éadaoin, is sean mo dhán,
Chéasas rí, charas leannán.

Na Príomh-Charachtair

An Daghda – dia mór de dhéithe Thuatha Dé Danann
Ealcmhar – seantiarna Bhrú na Bóinne
Aonghas – mac leis an Daghda agus le Bóinn
Bóinn – máthair Aonghasa, abhainn
Midhir – an tiarna i bhfearann an tsí i mBrí Léith
Eochaidh Aireamh – an chéad rí i dTeamhair; céile Éadaoine
Éadaoin – bean de shliocht éanlaith an tsí
Fuamnach – bandraoi, banchéile Mhidhir
Breasal – draoi, oide Fhuamnaí

Carachtair eile

Dairbre – an comhairleoir atá ag an rí Eochaidh Aireamh
Dianchéacht – ollamh leighis Thuatha Dé Danann
Miach agus Oirmiach – dís eile d'aos leighis Thuatha Dé
    Danann
Fear Bachaill – aoire
Fear Oide – oide mhacra na Mí
Ailill Mhaigh Inis – athair Éadaoine abhus i dtír na
    neamhbhuan
Gormlaith – máthair Éadaoine i gcomhair a hathbhreithe
Eadar Dubh – fear Ghormlatha
Fionnlámh – athair altramais na tríú gine
Casmhaol – máthair altramais na tríú gine
Eochaidh Feidhleach – an dara rí i dTeamhair; athair
    Chonaire Mhóir

CUID I

CAIBIDIL I

Brú na Bóinne

I

Mian a tharla don Daghda — cairdeas sliasta a dhéanamh le Bóinn, aithne chollaí a chur uirthi, comhrac na ngéag a dhéanamh léi, agus cumann an dá ghabhal. A mhian ba láidir, a aigne ba chráite, ba mhinic gan suan é, gan suan gan srann, óir bhí rún na drúise ag dordán ina chuisle agus ina chroí. Bhí bac air, ámh. Bac agus laincis: Ealcmhar Sean. Is é Ealcmhar a bhí i bhfeighil an Bhrú.

Ealcmhar! Cén mealladh amach ar chéile na Bóinne? Cén bréagadh chun bealaigh? Cén cuireadh chun coigríche? Cén gliceas, cén cleas, cén gníomh? Chuir an Daghda tochas ina ioscaid. Agus nuair a chuir, rith fuascailt na faidhbe leis. 'Cuairt na hÉireann!' ar sé in ard a mheigill, agus bhuail béim dá lorg agus dá lom-mhaide ar urlár agus ar fhaiche Uisnigh.

Ní cian dá éis sin, thug an Daghda a mhall-ruathar sáilmhór spadchéimiúil ó Uisneach Mí go bruach na Bóinne bitháille. Is san áit agus san ionad sin a labhair sé le hEalcmhar an Bhrú, agus nuair a labhair, is de bhriathra binne bána a bhéil a shíl sé an bréagadh agus an bogadh a dhéanamh.

'Tiarna chomh tiarnúil leatsa,' ar sé, 'flaith chomh flaithiúil leat, ruire chomh ríoga leat, nach mór is mithid dó dúichí na tíre a thaisteal agus a thaithí arís? Nach mór is mithid dó a chlú agus a cheannas a choigilt agus a chruinnchuimsiú arís ar fud Inse Fáil? Nach mór is mithid dó féachaint agus friotháil na hinse fraoch-chorcra seo a dhéanamh, idir chladaí agus chuanta, idir bhánta agus chruacha?'

'Umm....' arsa Ealcmhar go sean.

'Nach mithid don tiarna sin feasta gluaiseacht leis ar camchuairt,' arsa an Daghda, 'gluaiseacht leis d'fhonn deimhniú fearainn agus dearbhú flaithiúnais a dhéanamh — fearann agus flaithiúnas Inse Fódla?'

Is amhlaidh a tharla. Ghluais Ealcmhar leis. Agus nuair ba shiúlach dó i gcríocha aistreánacha iargúlta iomadúla na tíre, thug an Daghda luí na Bóinne air féin, shín lena taobh tais tláith, agus chuir an síol sa gclais go mór meirbh magairleach. Lig Bóinn a cnead aoibhnis. Arsa sí: 'Is óg an mac a gineadh i dtosach lae, mac a bhéarfar idir fuineadh gréine agus feascar na hoíche.'

Is ansin a chan an Daghda briocht draíochta agus tincheadail mhóra, briocht agus tincheadail a bhain

idir ocras agus íota d'Ealcmhar ar a chamchuairt dó.
Agus de bharr na mbriocht agus na dtincheadal sin, ba
luath le hEalcmhar imeacht ama agus aimsire. Má ba
luath ba líofa, má ba líofa ba luaimneach. Naoi lá agus
naoi n-oíche, dar leis, b'aon lá agus aon oíche amháin.
Naoi mí ba mhí. Naoi dtráth b'aon tráth amháin.

Nuair ab amhlaidh an scéal, chuir an Daghda
teimheal tromcheo ar an tír, teimheal tromcheo a cheil
grua agus gnúis na gréine, agus de bharr an teimhil
tromcheo sin, ba chian go liathadh an lae, ba chian go
léas agus go loinnir an léirsholais tar éis na lán-oíche.

Ealcmhar: bliain dó ar chamchuairt mhór na
hÉireann. Bliain gan filleadh ar Bhrú ná ar Bhóinn.
Agus ar fhilleadh dó i bhfoirceann a chuid siúil agus a
chuid seachráin, ba shlán an bhean dá galar clainne.
Rian den ghin, den toircheas ná den bhreith níor léir
ar a sciamh, ar a cneas, ná ar a dealbh dhílis féin.

Maidir le hAonghas Óg, thug an Daghda ar
altramas do Mhidhir é — Midhir Bhrí Léith, Midhir
an tsí — agus níl inseacht ná aithris ar an oiliúint a
cuireadh air go ceann naoi mbliana i ndiaidh imeachtaí
agus eachtraí an ama sin.

II

Teafa ab ainm don áit. Teafa iarthar Mí. É i gcóngar

an tsí i mBrí Léith. Má agus machaire ann. Agus trí chaogaid mac i mbun a gcuid cluichí ar an má sin: caoga i mbun báire, caoga i mbun bigireachta, caoga i mbun cleasa bior.

'Maith an báire sin,' arsa Fear Oide.

'Maith ón,' arsa Midhir.

'Cé is ceann báire orthu?'

'Mac Feabhail a shloinne. Triath a ainm.'

'Gael?'

'Fear Bolg. A athair is reachtaire i measc a chine féin.'

Lig an macra gáir. Sliotar eile curtha ag Triath mac Feabhail i líon an bháire.

Nuair ba chaite tráth sin na gcluichí, leag an macra uathu a gcuid bonsacha agus a gcranna báire, agus dhruid leo chuig an mboth foghlama chun feasa agus chun foircheadail. Fear Oide i lár an bhotha. Gach mac den mhacra ina shuí ar bhun crainn. Labhair Fear Oide.

'Eolas Inse Fáil!' ar sé.

Biorú na gcluas istigh, cluasa an mhacra.

'Trí mhá?' arsa an t-oide.

'Maigh Bhré, Maigh Cruachan, Maigh Life.

'Trí áth?'

'Áth Luain, Áth Coille, Áth Cliath.'

'Trí dhúiche gan bhóthar gan tóchar?'

'Bréifne, Boireann, Béara.'

Tar éis eolas Inse Fáil, tugadh seal ar an tomhas céille:

'An trí lán?' arsa an t-oide.

'Blaosc cnó, corn bó, ubh circe,' arsa an macra.

'Trí chrann feasa?'

'Dair, coll, caorthann.'

'Trí áilleacht ar aonach?'

'Bean chaomh, each luath, cú sheang.'

Ó tugadh seal ar an tomhas céille, chuathas le fios na héigse:

'Trí chúram file?' arsa an t-oide.

'Rosc, rann, agus riail.'

'Trí rún draoi?'

'Rúsc, luibh, toit.'

Ó canadh fios na héigse, chuathas seal le rún na cruinne:

'Trí áit, trí ghin?' arsa an t-oide.

'Broinn mná, úth bó, inneoin gabhann.'

'Trí ní gan chónaí?'

'Beach, tonn, lasair.'

D'eitil fáinleog isteach sa mboth, na faon-eití ag tobscuabadh an aeir.

D'fhéach Fear Oide an t-éan. Chas dual dá fhéasóg faoina mhéar.

'Trí ní nach féidir éalú orthu?' ar sé.

17

Is é Aonghas a labhair: 'Cuileog, eascann, agus scáth an éin.'

'Slán an focal,' arsa Fear Oide, 'scor go fóill!'

Húirte háirte! Ag fágáil bhoth na foghlama don mhacra, chuir Triath mac Feabhail cogar i gcluais Aonghasa Óig.

'Sliotar i mo dhorn,' ar sé, 'ciotóg nó deasóg?'

'Ní nós liomsa labhairt le clann na bhFear Bolg,' arsa Aonghas.

Chuir Triath a smut agus a smig san aer.

'Maidir leat féin,' ar sé, 'an mac nach fios cén chú a chac é!'

Gheit croí Aonghasa ina chléibh. 'Fios do bhriathar chugam!' ar sé.

Focal níor chan Triath, ach a dhá láimh ar a dhá chorróg go fonóideach.

Chas Aonghas Óg tuaifeal ar a sháil, agus thug barr na faiche air féin go dithneasach, a dhá shúil fuaite den talamh, a aigne chomh suaite le cleite fáin i gcuilithí na habhann, an meirbh-allas ag briseadh ar a éadainín agus ar a urla. Dar leis ariamh gur mhac le Midhir é, mac le Midhir agus oidhre fine agus fearainn ar an sí! Shiúil sé leis agus rún daingean ina chroí fios agus fáth an scéil a thabhairt chun follais gan feitheamh.

Faoi chrann fuinseoige a bhí Midhir. É i mbun fichille. Dhearc sé an mac chuige an cosán aníos go béalteann buartha. Tháinig Aonghas i leith.

'Céard is fáth do bhuartha, a mhic?'

Ba thúisce tocht ná scéal.

'Triath mac Feabhail a thug masla agus achasán dom,' ar sé ar tharraingt athanála dó.

D'imir Midhir beart fichille.

'Cén masla?'

Chrom Aonghas a cheann. Ba náir leis an nath.

'An mac nach fios cén chú a chac é.'

Focal níor chan Midhir, ach lig a shainosna.

'Cé hiad m'athair agus mo mháthair?' arsa Aonghas.

D'éirigh Midhir ina sheasamh gur fhéach an mac.

'Is mise t'athair altramais, ach is é an Daghda t'athair féin,' ar sé.

'An Daghda?'

'Is ea. Eisean is sine fios agus fearann in Éirinn.'

'Cé is máthair dom?'

'Bóinn.'

Cluineadh gártha an mhacra i mbun a gcluiche ar an má thíos.

'Is mian liom aithne a chur ar m'athair agus ar

mo mháthair,' arsa Aonghas, 'agus is náir liom mo cheilt anseo gan dearbhfhine.'

'Rachaimid go hUisneach amárach,' arsa Midhir.

III

Tigh an Daghda is in Uisneach a bhí. In Uisneach Mí, i gceartlár Inse Fódla. Ceithre dhoras ar an teach sin. Amharc ón teach ar cheithre harda na hÉireann. Siar: Áth Luain, Áth Eascrach, Áth Oirbeann. Soir: Máigh Bhré, Áth Cliath. Ó thuaidh: Teafa, an Bhréifne, Loch Éirne. Ó dheas: Sliabh Bladhma, Sí na mBan Fionn.

Amharc fós tigh an Daghda ar fhithis na gealaí. Amharc ar roth na gréine. Agus amharc ar dhís mharcach an tóchar aduaidh. Dhá each faoin dís mharcach sin. Dhá each ghlasdubha agus a n-eireaball fite ina dtrilseáin. Iad cluasdearg cruinnchrúbach, biorach broinnleathan, airgiúil aigeanta. Bhain an ghrian splanc as an torc tiarnúil órdhuilleach a bhí ina dhíon uchta agus urbhruinne ar an marcach ba mhó den dís.

Chuir an Daghda a dhá bhois ar bharr a mhaide mhóir mhaolmhullaigh, chuir an maide mór maolmhullaigh sin faoina smig smugairleach smearfhéasógach, agus dhearc uaidh an bealach soir go meigeall-smaointeach.

'Ní ag lorg céile fichille a tháinig tú, a Mhidhir?' arsa an Daghda nuair a ráinig an dís mharcach faiche Uisnigh.

'Céile fichille liom agam!' arsa Midhir.

D'fhéach an Daghda an mac óg go grinn.

'Cé ar díobh thú, a mhic?' ar sé.

Níor labhair Aonghas, ach thug cúlfhéachaint ar Mhidhir go cúthail aníos.

Ba ró-ait leis an mac óg an neach ollmhór aduain alt-ramhar éagruthach áibhéileach úllsúileach aosta a bhí roimhe.

'Téimis ar fhód ar leith,' arsa Midhir leis an Daghda de chogar.

Chuaigh.

Shuigh Aonghas idir dhá chleith de chleitheanna an tí. Morc mór tine i lár an urláir os a chomhair. Coire ar an tine sin agus leite á bruith ann. Dá mbeadh an macra mór ina theannta anois, arsa Aonghas leis féin, bhí áit suí ag trí naonúr díobh sa gcoire. Agus beathú trí naonúr eile sa leite.

Bhain Aonghas lán na súl as an áras ardfhairsing iltaobhach a bhí ina thimpeall. Bhí lorg mór cois dorais thiar. Lorg an Daghda. Airde naoi dtroithe ann. Tiús géag darach ann. Beirt tréanfhear ní bhainfeadh cor as. Chonaic an mac óg rud eile: luibheanna ag triomú faoi na frathacha. Dhá chuach uisce agus iad crochta ar dhá dhealg sleamhna seanadhmaid. Nead dreoilín i gceann den dá chuach uisce sin. An dreoilín níor léir, ach dordán beiche ba chlos sa bhfardhoras. Lig Aonghas méanfach. Bhí boladh leamh-mhilis na leitean ag cur ocrais air. Bhris sé greim den bháirín eornan a bhí faoina chrios aige. Chuir faoina fhiacail é. Bhí meirfean air. Do chodail.

'D'aithníos é,' arsa an Daghda.

Thug Midhir glaic eile den mhin coirce don each dubhghlas.

'Tá sé in aois a chéad ghaisce.'

'Ní iomchuí dó a bheith gan fearann,' arsa Midhir.

'Fearann?'

'Tá fios a ghinealaigh aige.'

Lig an Daghda cnead as a chliabhrach mór meirgeach aniar.

'Tá fearann agamsa dó ós mac liom é,' arsa sé.

'Cén fearann sin?'

'Fearann na Bóinne!' arsa an Daghda.

'Bóinn?'

'Fearann na Bóinne, an fearann agus an Brú.'

'Nach faoi Ealcmhar atá an Brú?' arsa Midhir.

'Is ea más ea.' D'fhuaraigh an t-agallamh beagán. Shín an Daghda a leabharghéag suas i mbolg an lae gur scuab an scamall de ghnúis na gréine. 'Ealcmhar a chur as an mBrú, sin rud is féidir!' ar sé.

'Fios do bhriathair uait,' arsa Midhir.

Don achainí sin níor thug an Daghda ach cluais bhodhar. Chuir sé tochas ina ioscaid.

'Sílim gur fear meala thú féin.'

'Fear meala?'

'Sáith beach atá agam,' arsa an Daghda, 'iad i gcrann ar fhaiche Uisnigh ó Bhealtaine. Is doiligh a rá cé leis iad. Do chomhairle?'

'Téimis á bhféachaint,' arsa Midhir.

Chuaigh.

Ag dul trasna na faiche fionnscothaí dóibh, lig an Daghda brúcht. Gur labhair.

'Téadh Aonghas go Brú na Bóinne Lá Samhna,' arsa sé. 'Is lá gan fuath gan fíoch an lá sin in Inis Fódla. Síothúil do chách an lá sin. Síothúil soilbhir. Ach tugadh an mac sleá agus sciath leis. Sleá agus sciath, agus claíomh cúig dhorn i dtruaill faoina chrios. Tugadh fós crann tabhaill agus urchair. Beidh Ealcmhar sa mBrú an lá sin. Gan de threalamh ná de ghléas gaisce aige ach gabhlóg coill. Gabhlóg de choll geal na seanbhliana. Beidh brat ar Ealcmhar. Dealg óir sa mbrat. Téadh Aonghas chuige.'

Sheas an Daghda faoi chrann mór beithe agus Midhir lena thaobh.

'Seo é crann na mbeach,' ar sé.

D'fhéach Midhir an crann. Beacha den tsáith ag dord-theacht agus ag dord-imeacht.

'Liom an crann. Ní liom an tsáith. Cé leis an mhil? Do chomhairle, a Mhidhir?'

'Nach leat an fhaiche seo?'

'Is liom.'

'Nach leat an crann?'

'Is liom.'

'Nach tú a d'aimsigh na beacha?'

'Is mé.'

'Is leat an mhil dá réir sin.'

'Cá bhfios duit?' arsa an Daghda.

Don achainí sin níor thug Midhir ach cluais bhodhar.

'Comhairle d'Aonghas uaitse i ndíbirt Ealcmhair ón mBrú,' ar sé.

Lig an Daghda osna.

'Lá Samhna i mBrú na Bóinne. Ealcmhar gan arm gan imdhíon. Bagraíodh Aonghas lámhach agus lánmhárú air. Iarrfaidh Ealcmhar aisce agus anacal. Éileamh Aonghasa? Ceannas an Bhrú go ceann lae agus oíche.

Thug an Daghda sracfhéachaint ar an gcrann.

'Agus dar leat gur liom féin an mhil?'

'Lá agus oíche?' arsa Midhir.

'Lá agus oíche,' arsa an Daghda, 'mar lá agus oíche ní chaifear go brách ach iad ag síorleanacht a chéile. Agus is ina laetha agus ina hoícheanta a chaitear an aimsir.'

'Atá go maith,' arsa Midhir.

Chas sé ar a ais i dtreo an árais.

'An mhil?' arsa an Daghda.

Thiontaigh Midhir.

'Fear a aimsíonn sáith beach i bhfogas gairm coiligh de dhoras a thí, is leis trian na meala. Más leis an fhaiche, is leis ar fad í. Sin é dlí na mbeach.'

IV

Caitheadh an bhliain go préamhach craobhach. Ídíodh macnas an tsamhraidh ré ar ré, agus ní raibh in éadan dian drithleach na gréine ach meathloinnir i log na spéire nuair a tharla an ní: teacht Aonghasa don Bhrú faoi Shamhain.

Aonghas Óg — an ceangal catha agus comhraic ar a chasfholt fáinneach gruaige. A ghaisce uime. Crann tabhaill faoina chrios. Léine ar a cholainn chaomh churata, ionar ar an léine, liúrach ar an ionar, scabal ar an liúrach go díonach dlúth anuas.

Iall ar osán, troith ar chosán, agus a réim roimhe go buacach bríomhar chun gabháil fearainn agus flaithiúnais de réir cheart fine agus sleachta.

Shroich sé an Brú. Isteach leis. B'shiúd roimhe san arduaimh airgiúil istigh tiarna agus triath na Bóinne. Ealcmhar Sean. É cloch-ársa cianchnámhach caoch. Gan samhail ag a fhéasóg ach crann draighin nó nead eala ar eanach. Folt a chinn ba luachair cois locha agus mionéin an chriathraigh ag neadú ann go gobach.

Brat ar Ealcmhar. Brat lín. Brat gan smál gan teimheal agus é ag sileadh leis óna dhá shlinneán síos. Gan arm gan éide ghaisce aige. Gan sciath gan sleá. Gan fleasc gan faobhar. Ach gabhlóg fionnchoill i ngreim deasóige aige. Thóg Ealcmhar a cheann.

'Cé hé an malrach beag óg sin?' ar sé de thrombhriathra stadacha a mheirgchanúna féin.

'Is mise Aonghas Óg mac an Daghda,' arsa an macghaiscíoch aonair, 'agus is ag éileamh an Bhrú seo dom féin atáim ag triall agus ag tadhall ort inniu. An Brú seo agus a bhfuil ann, an Brú seo agus a bhfuil uime.'

Shíl Ealcmhar éirí dá shuí, ach greamú bundúin den leic, sin é ba scéal dó.

'An Brú seo agus gach a ghabhann leis, sin é a éilímse ortsa, a Ealcmhair, óir is í an Bhóinn mo mháthair féin, agus is é brú mo mháthar atá dlite dom ina mhaoin agus ina mhacshlabhra.'

Ní túisce sin ráite ach ghléas Aonghas a chrann tabhaill go hathlámh agus go haibéil le hurchar a threascartha a theilgean faoi bhaithis lom leochaileach Ealcmhair.

'Fóill, a mhic!' arsa Ealcmhar an Bhrú. 'Fóill!'

Marcach go hUisneach an tslí mhór anoir! Moing agus fallaing ag déanamh easa ar an aer. Ceo anála ar bhéal an eich puthach pathach.

'Chugainn cloigeann agus ceithre chrúb,' arsa an Daghda leis an bpeata iora a bhí ar a ghuaille.

Scinn an t-iora chun crainn agus bladhm faoina eireaball.

Ní cian gur ráinig an marcach úrchnoc Uisnigh.

'Scéal ó Bhrú na Bóinne,' arsa an marcach, 'Aonghas Óg i seilbh an Bhrú. A chlaíomh nocht. Orlach ní ghéillfidh. A cheansú ní furast. A ghoin ní féidir. Olc an tuar. Achainí ó Ealcmhar: do chomhairle?'

Lig an Daghda síob-osna as seol mór a chléibh a chuir duilliúr críon na Samhna ag fiodrince agus ag faoilleáil ar fud na faiche. Thug an t-iora rua an poll agus an nead air féin.

'An ólfá braon den fhíor ón tobar?' ar sé leis an marcach.

D'ól. Agus an t-each.

'Scéal d'Ealcmhar!' arsa an Daghda.

Chuir an marcach goic ar a cheann.

'Is ina laetha agus ina hoícheanta a chaitear an aimsir.'

Suas leis an Daghda go fardhoras an tí, é ag mugailt agus ag meigeallach dó féin faoi naoscaid os cionn an rúitín a bhí á ghriogadh go mionmhór. Chas sé ar a sháil ar an tairseach.

'Chugaibh mé cois Bóinne amárach.'

B'íseal spéir os Brú na Bóinne. Lagsholas dúluachra ar an dúiche. Ealcmhar agus an Daghda ar bhéala na Brú — dhá mhullach mhaolmhóra i ndlúthchogar lena chéile.

'Is leis an mac óg an Brú?' arsa Ealcmhar.

'Is leis,' arsa an Daghda, 'Theith tú roimhe. Is mairg a thréigfeadh a bhuannacht.'

Briathar níor chan Ealcmhar Sean.

'Atá fearann eile agam duit,' arsa an Daghda.

'Umm?'

'Cleiteach.'

Ba chlos mallmhonabhar na seanabhann ala bheag ama go fóill. Rinne Ealcmhar cró snáthaide den tsúil chlé agus poll bró den tsúil dheas.

'Cleiteach?'

'Cleiteach gona thrí fhearann. Is subhach an áit. Meas ar chraobh duit, coirm bhuí duit, trí chaogaid óglach ag imirt ar an gcluiche-mhá sa ngleann duit. Do chlú slán, oineach i ndán. Cleiteach.'

'Cleiteach,' arsa Ealcmhar.

'Cleiteach!' arsa an Daghda.

Bhuail sé béim de bhun a loirg mhóir agus a lom-mhaide ar an bhfód faoi. Cág cág! D'éirigh ráig préachán de chrann faoi sceoin.

Ní cian dá éis sin a tógadh dún agus dea-chathair d'Ealcmhar i gCleiteach tamall siar ó Bhrú na Bóinne. A chónaí sa dún sin i ndiaidh na haimsire sin go haonarach sean gan bhuar gan bhard gan bhean.

Agus ag sin imeachtaí Aonghasa Óig mhic an Daghda go fóill, an ghin, an bhreith agus na mac-ghníomhartha, a uchtú agus oiliúint le Midhir, an t-imreas agus an iomarbhá le Triath mac Feabhail na bhFear Bolg, dúshlán agus dílonnú Ealcmhair, agus an teacht i réim agus i rath i mBrú úrársa na Bóinne.

An Tochmharc

I

Faoi Shamhain na hathbhliana, tháinig Midhir go Brú na Bóinne. Torc tiarnúil ar a bhráid. Síbhrat uaine uime. É caoinbhreac casfholt. Ba shoilbhir a theacht óir is leis ba mhian tuairisc a dhalta a chur, tuairisc a dhalta agus a ghlasmhic altramais.

Chonaic Midhir an Brú uaidh. Tulach in aice an Bhrú. Aonghas ina shuí ar an tulach sin agus an machaire ar a aghaidh amach. Trí chaogaid de mhacra na tíre ar an machaire sin ag cleachtadh a gcuid gcleas agus a gcuid cluichí. Buíon le báire, buíon le bigireacht, buíon le caitheamh na mbior. Rud eile a chonaic Midhir: Ealcmhar Sean i nDún Cleiteach siar. A dhá shúil amhail dhá ghealach ag lomstánadh go bocht santach thar an tseanabhainn bhaineann anall.

'Mochean do theacht, a oide liom!' arsa Aonghas ar fheiceáil Mhidhir dó an chonair aníos. Leath a ghean gáire ar a bhéal.

'Is maith do shuí, a dhalta,' arsa Midhir.

'Is maith ón.'

'Bliain duit i bhfearann an Bhrú....' arsa Midhir.

Rinneadh dhá leith dá bhriathar. Éamh ó mhachaire na gcluichí! Éamh, uaill agus allagar! Bhí bruth agus teaspach na himeartha ar bhuíon den mhacra, agus is borb baoth a bhí siad ag bearnú agus ag bascadh a chéile ar an má ar aghaidh an Bhrú. D'éirigh Aonghas ina sheasamh de ling agus de léim.

'Fóill!' arsa Midhir, 'rachad féin ag déanamh síotha agus athmhuintearais i measc na n-óg.'

Chuaigh sin. Ach ba thrua an ní. Theilg mac den mhacra bior coill uaidh d'urchar iomraill. Bhuail an bior Midhir faoin tsúil. Phreab an tsúil amach as a cheann. Í ar sliobarna go sleamhain lena ghrua agus lena leiceann. Gan ach féith amháin á ceangal leis an mogall. Le meachán na súile, bhris an fhéith. Rug Midhir greim doirn agus dearnan ar an tsúil sular sciorr sí go caoch col-easpach go lár agus go lántalamh. Thit socht ar an macra mór. Chúlaigh siad leo d'aon náirchúlú amháin. Aníos le Midhir ar feadh na conaire go ciorraithe cráite.

'Olc mo theacht anseo, óir an dúiche ab áil liom a féachaint ní follas dom í, agus mo dhúiche féin Brí Léith, filleadh uirthi feasta ní furast ná ní féidir!'

'Ní fíor!' arsa Aonghas. 'Cuirfear fios ar Dhian-chéacht, ós eisean is fearr leigheas agus liacht in Inis Fódla, agus is é a leigheasfas an éalaing agus an ainimh a cuireadh ort go míchinniúnach ar an machaire seo inniu.'

Chuaigh Midhir faoin mBrú go goll. Chuir Aonghas deifir agus dithneas le haimsiú Dhianchéachta.

Ní cian gur tháinig lia leighis agus ollamh íocshláinte Thuatha Dé Danann. Bhí seo de bhua aige: an tinneas a bhí i dteach, d'aithneodh sé an tinneas sin ar an deatach os cionn an tí. Bua eile dá chuid: an galar a bhí ag gabháil don cholainn, d'aithneodh sé an galar sin ar osnaíl agus ar éagaoin an othair. Bua eile fós: gach créacht agus lot b'inleigheasta dó ach snáth na hintinne a bheith gan snoí, smior na droma a bheith slán gan sileadh, agus an ceann gan teascadh den cholainn.

Bhí Miach agus Oirmiach i gcuideachta Dhianchéachta, dís eile d'aos leighis Thuatha Dé Danann. Ag dul faoin mBrú don triúr lianna luschríonna sin, chonaic sin ann rompu istigh an dea-choinneal déadgheal fir. Folt flannrua a chinn forscaoilte go muin agus meán droma anuas. An léine ar sileadh leis gan chrios gan cheangal. Rud i mbois a láimhe: a shúil féin. Í mar a bheadh bogán uibhe ar nead gan chlúmhach.

'Mochean bhur dteacht, a thriúr lianna,' ar sé, 'agus déanaigí mo shúil a leigheas más féidir sin.'

Is ansin a cuireadh Miach go Tobar Neachtain ag iarraidh baslach fíoruisce chun folcadh agus chun fothrú mhogall na súile ar eagla an othrais. Agus Oirmiach dá réir sin, ba go léana an Bhrú a bhroid agus a bhrostú ag iarraidh lán méaracáin de sheile na mbeach ón gcoirceog ba shine mil cois Bóinne.

Le feabhas a chuid feasa agus a chuid foghlama féin, chuir Dianchéacht luibh le lus agus duille donn le dos i gcomhair na liachta. An cnuasbholg agus an criol beag leathair a bhí faoina chrios aige, bhí a lán den chréachtlus agus den slánlus iontu faoi seach, a lán den airgead luachra agus den lus beathnua, den mhianfhartach agus den mheas torc allta, den ghormdhearc agus den ghlanrosc.

Rinne Dianchéacht an lusra sin a chumasc agus a chómheascadh go dianchúiseach deaslámhach. Chuir sé céirín íocshláinte ar an gcneá, agus nuair a bhí an tsúil athshuite aige go slánchréachtach, scar sé púicín mín éadrom anuas uirthi. An púicín mín éadrom sin, is púicín de theanga coileán toirc ó neamh na seanchoille a bhí ann, agus is déanfasach dea-chothrom a scar Dianchéacht an púicín sin thar chuas na súile. I ndiaidh na híce agus na hoibre sin, cheangail sé an púicín faoi chúil ghruaige Mhidhir.

An t-iall lenar ceanglaíodh an púicín, is iall de shnáth an lín a bhí ann, an lín ba ghoirme bláth dar imríodh fleasc ariamh air faoi ghrian meán samhraidh.

Is ansin a labhair an t-ollamh leighis.

'An púicín teanga coileán toirc seo, fágtar ar an tsúil go ceann bliana é, óir tá airíonna ann, airíonna agus scothúlacht, agus beidh silleadh agus síorsholas sa tsúil i gcionn na bliana arís ach mo chomhairlese a dhéanamh gan frithbheart gan faillí.'

Ní túisce an chaint sin caite ach d'éalaigh Dianchéachta, Miach agus Oirmiach doras an Bhrú amach chun slí.

Chodail Midhir iar n-imeacht don triúr lianna. Arna mhárach, is san eadra agus san iarmhoch a dhúisigh sé. Is ansin a labhair Aonghas Óg leis.

'Is mithid duit fuireach bliana a dhéanamh sa mBrú seo, a oide dhil, agus cuirfidh tú aithne ar an teaghlach, ar lucht fichille agus ar lucht fáistine an leasa, ar chornairí agus ar aos dána an dúin.'

Is beag má ba bhuíoch Midhir.

'B'fhéidir é,' ar sé, 'ach éiric agus aisce a fháil ar an máchail agus ar an mórmhasla a tharla dom.'

B'oth le hAonghas clos na mbrioscbhriathar mioscaise sin, ach is caoin ceanúil a d'fhreagair sé an t-aitheasc.

'Cluintear uait an éiric is dlite duit, dar leat, a oide liom,' ar sé.

Is ansin a labhair Midhir, agus is éard a dúirt: 'Ní beag liomsa d'éiric i ndíol mo mhíchumtha slat óir sé throithe ar fhad.'

'Ní shéanfar sin ort,' arsa Aonghas.

'Slat óir sé throithe ar fhad, agus seachtar banchumhall ag mochfhreastal agus ag mallfheitheamh orm.'

'Ní shéanfar sin ort,' arsa Aonghas.

'Slat óir sé throithe ar fhad, seachtar banchumhall ag mochfhreastal agus ag mallfheitheamh orm, agus carbad caolfhearsaide cruinnrothach cúlfhairsing gona dhá bhromach spadharmhongacha spéiriúla chun taisteal na dúiche seo.'

'Ní shéanfar sin ort.'

'Slat óir sé throithe ar fhad, seachtar banchumhall ag mochfhreastal agus ag mallfheitheamh orm, carbad caolfhearsaide cruinnrothach cúlfhairsing gona dhá bhromach spadharmhongacha spéiriúla chun taisteal na dúiche seo, agus feis i gcionn bliana leis an ainnir is áille in Éirinn, óir nuair a bhainfear an púicín teanga coileán toirc seo de mo shúil, is iad snua

sneachta agus grua griansholais na hainnire sin is
mian liomsa a dhearcadh go cianmhar cúthail
caoinfhollas.'

Lig Aonghas a shainosna.

'Is deacair dofhála an mhian í sin,' ar sé, 'ach cé
ea, is fios domsa cé hí an ainnir úd, agus is fios dom
fós cá cathair agus cá cónaí di.'

'Briathar do chuid feasa liom,' arsa Midhir.

'Chugat fios,' arsa Aonghas Óg, 'agus mo shlán-
aíocht agus mo choraíocht ort i leith mhacra na Mí
ar dtús!'

'Cá slánaíocht, cá coraíocht?'

'Maiteanas don mhacra i gcúis agus i gcaingean
do mhillte agus mhíchumtha-sa: ag sin an tslánaíocht
agus an choraíocht is áil domsa a fháil uaitse sula
n-iarrtar an ainnir is áille in Éirinn chun cumainn
agus chun céileachais leat.'

'Faomhaim sin,' arsa Midhir.

II

Aistear dhá lá ar muin mairc ó Bhrú go Bóinne go
hoirthuaisceart Éireann mar a raibh teach agus áras ag
Ailill Uladh i Maigh Inis. Ar rochtain na háite sin do
theachta Aonghusa arna athmhárach le rinnbhreacadh
na réalt, bhuail sé béim fleisce ar ursain an dorais,

agus chuir urghairm ar an doirseoir dílis mar ba chuí.

'Scéala agam d'Ailill Mhaigh Inis ó Aonghus an Bhrú,' ar sé de ghlór follasghlan foghargheal.

Bhain glór sin an teachta macalla mear-uaigneach as an bhfaiche. Chuaigh an macalla i léig diaidh ar ndiaidh. Gur cluineadh ní: grísc-grúis-gráisc — dorais darach an dúin á oscailt de ghéag-ghíoscán alt-righin tromadhmaid. Isteach leis an teachta.

Ní raibh caite ach trian na fleá an oíche sin nuair a d'iarr Ailill Mhaigh Inis fios agus fáth a aistir ar an teachta ón mBrú. Is é focal a dúirt an teachta gur do dhéanamh cleamhnais agus cumainn a tháinig, cleamhnas agus cumann idir Éadaoin iníon Ailealla agus Midhir Bhrí Léith. Mar thug Midhir grá éagmaise agus searc gan suan d'Éadaoin ar a tuairisc agus ar a hairscéala. Agus ba é Aonghas an Bhrú údar an chleamhnais.

Lig Ailill a shainosna, chas dlaoi agus dual dá fhéasóg faoina mhéar, agus nuair a labhair is éard a dúirt:

'Ní do Mhidhir lámh Éadaoine,' arsa Ailill.

'Fios do bhriathair uait,' arsa an teachta.

'Is de sheanchlanna Thuatha Dé Danann Aonghas Óg. Is mac leis an Daghda féin é, mac leis an Daghda agus dalta le Midhir an tSí. Agus dá n-imreofaí éagóir

nó aincheart ar m'iníonsa, ba shnámh in aghaidh easa
dom cúiteamh na héagóra sin a éileamh. Mar is beag
mo thobar cumhachta-sa mar rí tuaithe agus tríocha
céad, ach an chumhacht atá cois Bóinne, i mBrí
Léith, agus in Uisneach, is tobar mór gan triomú atá
ann. Fill ar Bhrú na Bóinne amárach agus abair sin le
hAonghas.'

D'fhill. Dúirt.

Clos an scéala sin níor bhinn le hAonghas.
Tháinig urú ar a ghnúis. Rinne sé a leormhachnamh.
Is ansin a labhair sé arís.

'Téitear uaim go Maigh Inis athuair,' ar sé, 'agus
fiafraítear d'Ailill cén luach cleamhnais ab áil leis ar a
iníon.'

Chuathas uaidh athuair. Agus an treas uair.
Chuathas agus ceithre huaire ag fiafraí d'Ailill cén
luach cleamhnais ab áil leis ar a iníon.

'Ag seo a luach,' ar sé, 'dhá mhá dhéag a shlighe
agus a shleamhain-chóiriú domsa i m'fhearann féin,
agus an tseanchoill a ghlanadh díobh, ionas go mbeidh
inilt don eallach orthu, treabhadh don treibh orthu,
aonach don slua orthu, dún agus áitreabh orthu.'

Ar chlos na deacra seo d'Aonghas, chuir sé fios ar
an Daghda. Agus sula raibh deireadh ré ná deas-
chorrán gealaí ann, rinne an Daghda an dá mhá
dhéag a shlí agus a shleamhain-chóiriú, orthu sin

Maigh Macha, Maigh Leamhna, Maigh nItha, Maigh Tóchair, Maigh nDula, Maigh Teachta, Maigh Lí agus Maigh Mhuirtheimhne. D'Ailill, áfach, sin níor leor.

'Cá luach cleamhnais fós?' arsa an teachta.

Labhair Ailill Mhá Inis: 'Tá seo fós,' ar sé, 'seacht n-abhainn mhóra a thapú dom as toibreacha na tíre seo, seacht n-abhainn mhóra a éireos ón sliabh agus ón seisceann, ón móinín agus ón mbogach, seacht n-abhainn mhóra a ghluaisfeas chun na mara síos, seal go mear, seal go mallmhaorga, seacht n-abhainn mhóra le tír agus talamh a thaoscadh, seacht n-abhainn mhóra gona seacht n-inbhear iascmhara inseolta, seacht n-abhainn mhóra chun éadáil na dtuath agus na dtreabh a iompar agus a imluchtú. Fill ar Bhrú na Bóinne agus abair sin le hAonghas.'

D'fhill. Dúirt.

Clos an scéala sin níor bhinn le hAonghas. Ar a ghnúis do tháinig urú. Chuir sé fios ar an Daghda. In Uisneach don Daghda an lá úd. Leite á meascadh aige sa gcoire mór le bun a loirg. Ar chlos na hachainí dó ó bhéal an teachta, lig sé osna, chuir tochailt faoina ioscaid, cheangail a sheanchulaith róin ribeach rógharbh ar a dhá ghuaille, agus thug conair agus slí air féin go mugailteach meigeallach.

Sula raibh tús athré ann ná clé-chorrán gealaí, bhí

seacht n-abhainn mhóra tapaithe aige ó thoibreacha oirthuaisceart Éireann, ó shliabh agus ó sheisceann, ó mhóinín agus ó bhogach, orthu sin Fionn agus Sláine, Nás agus Amhnás, Dall agus Banna. Ar fhilleadh ar Uisneach dó, ní raibh an morc mór tine ach ag fuarú ar lár an tí agus an leite chomh ramhar ann le holann i ndabhach fuail. Choigil an Daghda an tine, d'ith a sháith den leite righin ramhar, agus chodail.

Chuathas go hAilill arís.

'Is maith na machairí seo,' ar Ailill, 'is maith na seacht n-abhainn seo. Ach atá seo fós de luach cleamhnais ar m'iníon.'

'Cluintear uait,' arsa an teachta.

'Cothrom a meáchain ina ór, agus a chothrom arís ina airgead. Fill ar Bhrú na Bóinne agus abair sin le hAonghas.'

D'fhill. Dúirt.

Dhá anáil níor tharraing Aonghas. Ach labhair. Agus nuair a labhair is éard a dúirt: 'Ór d'Ailill ós ór is áil leis. Ór dó agus ualach airgid, agus cothrom mheáchan na hiníne faoi dhó.'

Is ansin a cuireadh na giollaí ag giollaíocht. Gléasadh dhá each leo: each nár leasc chun iompar an óir; each nár losc chun iompar an airgid. Gléasadh láir leo chun iompar na hiníne. An láir sin ba leabharmhongach lách, ba luisneach luailchosach. Trí each fós a gléasadh, trí each do thriúr ceithearnach cosanta na seod, triúr ceithearnach gona dtrí chlaíomh dornramhra. Thug an bhuíon sin slí agus sliabh orthu féin, muine agus machaire, móin agus meirgchoill, faoi dhrúcht agus faoi chuisne na dealmhaidine arna mhárach. Imeachtaí na buíne sin ní fios go filleadh dóibh tar éis ceathrú gealaí.

III

Iar ngairm don choileach cois leasa agus cois léana aga beag ama tar éis imeacht do bhuíon na seod, d'éirigh Midhir amach ag gollfhéachaint rinnmhúchadh na réalt agus na reann. Ba chiúin gach dúil de dhúile na cruinne. Is ansin a chuala sé an choisíocht sháil-éadrom ina leith. Chuige Aonghas. Chuimil an óg-ghrian barr méire de dheargbhaithis na díse. Lig lon fead sa tor.

'Comhairle dalta ar a oide!' arsa Aonghas tar éis tamaill bhig.

'Fios na comhairle sin uaidh!'

Ní raibh de réalta ar an mochspéir mhaighdeanda ach aon mhochréalt amháin.

'Tchím an mhochréalt,' arsa Aonghas.

'Is í is gile,' arsa Midhir.

'Tiocfaidh réalt is gile ná í aduaidh,' arsa Aonghas.

'Tiocfaidh.'

'Béarfaidh tú leat í go Brí Léith.'

'Béarfad.'

'Is ann a bheas sí i mbaol a múchta.'

Lig Midhir osna.

'Doiligh liom tuiscint do chomhairle,' ar sé.

'Fuamnach,' arsa Aonghas, 'do chéad bhanchéile.'

'Fuamnach?'

'Nach le Breasal Draoi a hoileadh í?'

'Is ea.'

'Is mór a draíocht.'

'Is mór.'

'Más mór is olc, más olc is urchóideach.'

Ní raibh sa mochréalt feasta ach lagrud i ndeireadh dé.

'Do chomhairle?' arsa Midhir.

'Ar chleas ná bí dall, ar chlaonbheart, ná ar cheilg.'

Réalt ná rinn níor léir faoi seo, ach an spéir ar lasadh agus an lá ar ionradh rabharta.

Tháinig Éadaoin. Má tháinig, ní ar each é ach i gcarbad. An carbad sin ba d'adhmad na fuinseoige é idir chreat agus chlár, idir chuing agus easnacha. Díon ar an gcarbad: díon den bhréid chiartha a rithfeadh braon agus brádán leis. Adhairt faoin ógmhnaoi ar an suí: adhairt de chlúmhach seacht gcadhan. Folach tiubh-olla thar a dhá guaille i gcoinne shíon na haimsire. A lámhthoradh féin lena hais — snáth agus snáthaid chun druine, mionseol agus méaracán, corn dí, cíor agus cíorbholg, an cíorbholg sin agus é déanta as craiceann dobharchon.

Tostach an t-ara, tostach an tiomáint. Freastalaí mná ó lios Mhaigh Inis Uladh ag marcaíocht ar láir cheannann le hais an charbaid. Beirt cheithearnach bhiorshúileacha de theaghlach a hathar ina diaidh sa tslí á cumhdach agus á cosaint ar fhia-mhíolta agus ar ainmhithe allta na bhfásach agus na mothar. Triúr ceithearnach na Bóinne i dtosach na buíne sin. Agus teachta Aonghasa ina cheann feadhna orthu uile.

Chonaic an t-iolar iad agus é ar gaothshnámh i dtoll na spéire. Chonaic an fia fraschrúbach iad ón dún duilliúir a bhí aige féin sa doire. Ar neasú go habhantrach na Bóinne bitháille dóibh, chonaic doirseoir an Bhrú iad céim ar chéim aduaidh.

'Buíon marcach chugainn,' ar sé in ard a chinn agus a ghutha, 'buíon marcach agus carbad feise.'

Dianchéacht: do tháinig athuair don Bhrú. Thug leis a chriol agus a chnuasbholg leathair faoina chrios. A lán den chréachtlus agus den slánlus ann, den airgead luachra agus den lus beathnua, den mhianfhartach agus den mheas torc allta. Dianchéacht: ós é a cheangail an púicín ar shúil Mhidhir, is é a scaoil. Má scaoil, is i ndubh an Bhrú san áit ba mhó dolas a scaoil. Tháinig Midhir amach. Go fardhoras. Go faiche. Go faichilleach. Ba léir dó gach ní tuathal. Gach ní deiseal. An Bhóinn agus an Brú. Grianán na mbláth, an léana agus an luibhghort. Carbad agus ceithearnaigh, láir cheannann, eachra agus eile. Sin ba léir dó. Agus seo: an ainnir a bhí ina fhianaise. Gheit a chroí.

Bhí brat den anairt chluthar léi anuas. Dealg de dhéad muirmhíl ag ceangal an bhrait sin. Fuan agus léine faoin mbrat. Ciumhais de ghorm na bhfraochán agus na n-airní ar an bhfuan. Crios faoina coim fuinseoige. Cochall thar a ceann agus a cúil ghruaige. Coisbheart den mhínleathar ar dhá throith a cos. Muince óir ar a bráid. Dearg a béal. Geal a déad. Caoltanaí a géag. Úr a cneas. Corcra a grua. Réidh a colpa. Cruinn a cíoch. Éadrom a sáil — ubh ní bhrisfeadh fúithi. A dhá súil ar dhath an troim nuair a bhíonn an crann crom faoi ualach na gcaor dúdhearg. Í modhúil mallroscach. Í áilíosach innuachair. Í triopallach támhdheas.

Scaoil Éadaoin an cochall dá ceann. A folt cas

cuachach fite ina sheacht dtrilseán. Samhail ag Midhir do gach trilseán díobh: eas sléibhe tar éis ceatha agus cúrbháistí. Gach ré trilseán díobh fionnscothach floscthaitneamhach. Trilseán díobh fionnrua flannómra. Trilseán díobh ciardhubh. Trilseán díobh chomh bán le cáthadh na mara lá anfa. Dlaoi fáin os cionn a mala. Samhail ag Midhir don dlaoi sin: lúb aitinn os cionn úrshrutháin. Labhair Midhir.

'Mochean Éadaoin, ríon leasa, folt easa, réalt feasa, mochean do theacht.'

An t-amharc a thug an dís ar a chéile, ní amharc gan fhéachaint a bhí ann. An fhéachaint sin ní féachaint gan ghrinndearcadh a bhí ann. An grinndearcadh níor ghrinndearcadh gan tnúthán. An tnúthán níor thnúthán gan tocht. An tocht níor thocht gan údar. Dar le Midhir gur léir dó breacadh na seirce i súil na mná. Amhail bláth mion ag péacadh ar an sceach gheal tar éis an gheimhridh. Nó síol lín ag eascairt in ithir dhubh na ceapaí. Labhair Éadaoin.

'Mochean Midhir, rí ruirtheach, tiarna tréitheach, eo gan aois, mochean Midhir.'

CAIBIDIL III
Fuamnach

I

Brí Leith! Subhach an tír. Taitneamh gréine ann, annamh fuacht. Minic tuar ceatha ann, cneasta gaoth. Braonach earrach ann, Samhain gan síon. Monar na mbeach ann, cumhra na n-úll buí.

Brí Léith! Meas ar chraobh ann, slaodach barr gach crainn. Méith gach muc ann, flúirseach uachtar agus im. Fraoch go glúin ann, féar go huillinn rí. Cruinneacht go hascaill taoisigh ann. Airde fir sa gcíb.

Brí Léith! Dath ar éadach ann: dearg na fearnóige, corcra na gcrotal, buí na ruachan, uaine na luachra, dubh na bpréamh. Síor-óg ann an slua sí. Slua gan aois gan aicíd, gan othras gan easláinte, gan time gan tinneas. Ach spreac agus lúth iontu, brí agus biseach, gealgháire agus greann. Brí Léith! Subhach an tír.

Ar fhilleadh ar Bhrí Léith do Mhidhir, b'áil leis féachaint na dúiche a dhéanamh. Rug sé Éadaoin leis. Carbad acu chun slí. Amach leo ar cuairt. Rud a chonaic siad: meitheal i ngort; seisreach dámh faoi chéachta agus an chuing faoina mbráid; corr éisc ina dealbh leathchoise; coirceoga beach; bólacht á bleán i mbuaile ghlas; ealta mór éan ilbhreac neamhdha faoi luan léirsholais; caoga crann úll faoi bhachlóg; caoga crann úll faoi bhláth; caoga crann faoi úlla; slabhra mínéadrom seanairgid idir gach dhá chrann.

Rud a chuala siad sa bhfearann sin: leoithne láchghaoithe ag baint binn-uaime as na mínslabhraí seanairgid sin; monabhar srutháin; cantain na mban; téada tiompáin á spreagadh i ngrianán aolgheal ildualach; slup slap — bradán breac ballchorcra ag éirí san abhainn. Agus dhá roth an charbaid ag sioscarnach fúthu trasna na mbánta agus na móinéar.

Labhair Éadaoin.

'Leathshúil leat is glas, leathshúil is gorm,' ar sí, 'cén fáth sin?'

Bhain Midhir tarraingt as an srian. Mhoilligh an dá bhromach sa tslí.

'Seal dom i mo bhradán fadó,' ar sé, 'san Eas Rua ba mhinice mo shnámh. Sioc mór an geimhreadh úd. Sioc agus sneachta. Chaitheas léim mhór as an uisce aníos amach. Léim agus ling i mo bhradán glinniúnach. Fuacht! Fuacht! Ar theacht anuas dom, bhí an abhainn ina leac oighir fúm. Fuar mo luí ar an leic sin. Amhlaidh dom ala bheag ama. Gur tháinig iolar. Iolar aille. Bhain an t-iolar sin leathshúil as mo cheann. Ach d'éirigh an ghrian go hard os cionn na talún. Ó d'éirigh sin, ní fada gur leáigh an t-oighear fúm. Leáigh an t-oighear agus domsa ba bheo seal eile. Beo dom seal eile i mo mhaighre bradáin.'

Lig ceann den dá bhromach smuchar smachar as.

'Cé acu súil a leigheasadh?' arsa Éadaoin.

'An tsúil ghlas.'

Bhain Midhir preab as an srian.

'Cá riocht don iolar sin inniu?'

'Riocht mic de mhacra na Mí.'

Chuir an dá bhromach siúl éadrom gan tuairteáil faoin gcarr agus faoin gcarbad arís.

D'Éadaoin ba thostach seal go fóill. Tostach teanntrilseach. Tostach téadchiúin. Dar léi gurbh aithnid di an dúiche. Dar léi gur chlos di seanmhacalla ag ciantathaint ar chéadfaí a croí. Fuinneamh na gréine ag baint gach cluainbholadh ba chumhra ná a chéile as an aiteann agus as an gcreamh sí. Ba mheisce di sin. Meisce agus meath céille. Focal níor chan sí ámh. Ach lig mionosna. Bhí scéal eile ar a haire.

'A Mhidhir,' ar sí, 'cá háit a bhfuil Fuamnach?'

Fuamnach. Í ag triall ar Aonach Bodhbhna. Is ann a bhí Breasal Draoi, a hoide agus a hoiliúnaí féin. Is ar inis a bhí a chónaí. Inis chrannóige. Luibhghort sa gcrannóg. Ráinig Fuamnach bruach an locha ar aghaidh na hinse agus na crannóige sin. Gur lig éamh agus urghairm aisti. Thóg Breasal a cheann. Tamall uaidh amuigh, chonaic sé an fhuinseog chaol mná, í géag-lom gaofar, cochall ar a ceann, agus a gob san aer. Ar aithint a aondalta dó, leag sé uaidh an dornán dea-luibheanna a bhí á chumasc aige.

Dul i dtír ar inis na crannóige, sin é ab áil le Fuamnach. Bhí curach locha ann chuige sin. Curach cruinn. Curach aon seas. Rug Breasal greim ar an súgán fada neantóige a bhí ceangailte den churach, bhain tarraingt shantach as an súgán, agus chuir an barc beag bríomhar ar preab-bhogadh i dtreo na mná agus na mbruach. Shín an bandraoi ar shoc na curaí, tharraing chuici, d'fhliuch leathrúitín, chuir cor aisti, agus lig fúithi ar an seas. Tarraingt súgáin, dhá tharraingt súgáin, trí tharraingt súgain, agus bhí sí istigh ar an gcrannóg.

'Is lán do luibhghort, a Bhreasail,' arsa Fuamnach nuair a bhí a dhá cois go daingean ar fhód na hinse bige.

Níor thug an seandraoi ach lomfhéachaint gan labhairt ar bhean a mholta.

'Deoch ní iarrfainn,' arsa Fuamnach.

Is i ndabhach mór umha a bhí an t-uisce. Shín

Breasal lán coirn chuig Fuamnach. D'ól sí bolgam.

'Lus-sheanchas!' arsa Breasal.

'Maith,' ar Fuamnach.

'Cén lus seo?'

'Sin mínscoth.'

'Craosghlanadh tar éis othras béil!'

'Is fíor.'

'Cén lus seo?'

'Sin lochall.'

'Leigheas dó in íochtar droma!'

'Is fíor.'

'Cén lus seo?'

'Sin é an fuath gorm.'

'Leigheas ar aicíd cneasa, leigheas don té a bheadh faoi gheasa!'

D'éirigh lacha ón luachair agus gach fiotar featar ag eití agus ag cleití.

Lean an dís den seanchas.

'Seo meas torc allta,' arsa Fuamnach.

'Cá bua dó?' arsa Breasal

'Leigheas na drúise,' arsa Fuamnach agus greim aici ar chaor de na caora idir stua-mhéar agus ordóg. 'Leigheas na drúise ach a bhruith i leamhnacht na ngabhar…'

'Agus creamh a chur san anraith.'

Leath aiteal den gháire nod-eolach ar bhéal na díse

draoithe. Bhain Fuamnach bolgam eile fionnuisce as an gcorn.

'Fáth do theachta?' arsa Breasal ar deireadh.

An freagra ba ghiorraisc. Labhair Fuamnach: 'Midhir a d'fhill. Cearc lena sháil aige. Adhaltrach óg.'

'Préamh an éada an phréamh is doimhne,' arsa Breasal.

Thaosc Fuamnach an corn uisce go grian agus go grinneall.

II

Naoi ré, naoi rian, agus naoi roth gréine a bhí curtha ag imeacht aimsire ar naoi gcríoch na spéire nuair a chonaic Éadaoin ag bun na faiche í. A comhchéile. Brat londatha ciardhubh go lorg agus go lomcholpa uirthi. Í géaglom gaofar. A gob agus a geanc san aer. An crios faoina coim chomh teann le hiall ar phocaide lá aonaigh. Cochall ar a ceann. A dhá súil ag glinniúint faoin gcochall sin. Gan samhail dóibh mar shúile ach dhá bhraon drúchta ar starrfhiacla cráin toirc ar chlos an doird seilge di. A dhá mala snoite. A béal fite. Slat ina láimh, slat chaorthainn. Gabhlóg in uachtar na slaite sin. Áit na hordóige sa ngabhlóg. Órnasc ar ordóg na mná, agus cloch bhua ag fuarlonnrú ina cheartlár.

'Fuamnach!' arsa Éadaoin de chogar sceoine.

Tháinig Fuamnach i leith beagán.

'Is maith an teach a bhfuil tú ann,' ar sí.

'Is maith,' arsa Éadaoin.

'Cá háit a bhfuil Midhir?'

'Atá amuigh dar liom.'

Tháinig Fuamnach i leith beagán eile. Faobhar ar a dhá súil. Faghairt agus faobhar a ghearrfadh olann ar uisce. A bhainfeadh an chluais den chú agus é ar a shainrith ar an machaire. A bhainfeadh an chíor den fhuiseog agus í ag tromspalpadh ceoil i bhfearann na néal. Labhair Fuamnach arís.

'Is deas an cuaichín a fuair sé ar a thaisteal,' ar sí. Bhí a béal ar fiar le fonóid.

D'fhreagair an ógbhean í.

'Mé Éadaoin. Mochean do theacht.'

Tháinig Fuamnach i leith de léim.

'Mochean do theacht, ab ea?' ar sí go díomasach.

'Mochean do theacht, ab ea?' ar sí go dásachtach.

'Mochean do theacht, ab ea?' ar sí go díoltasach.

Bhí a dhá súil chomh hiata le cró snáthaide. Tharraing sí an cochall dá ceann. Ba stuacach stoth-ghruagach stiall-ingneach an feic í. Agus is formadach a lig sí a racht feirge leis an éan cuideáin a bhí roimpi ar a tairseach agus ar a teallach féin.

'Mé Fuamnach,' ar sí, 'agus is liomsa an teach

seo, idir chleith agus scolb, idir dhoras agus tairseach, idir thine agus toit, idir ursain agus urlár, idir shorcha agus dorcha, idir shamhradh agus gheimhreadh, idir bheo agus neamhbheo, idir luibh agus lus, idir phréamh agus bhláth, idir thobar agus taisce, idir abhras agus anairt, idir sheol agus snáth, idir mhaith agus mhaoin, idir inné agus amárach, idir fhaiche agus úllghort, idir luí agus lánúnas, idir losaid agus leaba.'

Ní túisce sin ráite ach bhain sí trí chreathadh as an tslat chaorthainn a bhí ina deasláimh aici, trí chreathadh a bhain sian as an aer, trí chreathadh doilfe draíochta a rinne lochán uisce d'Éadaoin lom láithreach ar cheartlár na faiche. Lochán uisce a nífeadh na mionéin clúmh agus cleite ann. Lochán uisce a bhfliuchfadh an mada a bhruas agus a bhéal ann. Lochán uisce a n-aithneodh an ghealach a scáil féin ann oíche spéirghlan uaigneach. Chas Fuamnach ar a sáil. Agus d'imigh.

Aisling a bhí ag Aonghas an oíche sin i mBrú na Bóinne. Chuige bean. Ródheas a dreach. Tiompán aici i leathláimh. Tiompán gan téad. Shín an bhean a mínghéag le hAonghas go maoth. Idir dhá néal suain agus síorchodlata dó, shíl Aonghas breith ar a láimh.

Shín uirthi. Ach an síneadh sin ba shíneadh in aisce é. Ba shíneadh ar cheo. Ba shíneadh ar chúr easa, ba shíneadh ar cháthadh lá gaoithe. D'éalaigh an aisling uaidh. Ba aonraic d'Aonghas dá héis. B'amhlaidh an aisling an oíche dar gcionn. Chuige bean an tiompáin. Tiompán gan téad. An síneadh, an t-éalú. An ceo agus an cúr. An tríú hoíche mar an gcéanna fós. Amhlaidh d'Aonghas go ceann naoi n-oíche. É gan suan. Liath a chneas. Lag a mhisneach. Searg a luí. Íseal a bhrí.

Maidin an deichiú lae, tháinig Dianchéacht á fhéachaint agus á iniúchadh.

'Liath do chneas, a mhacáin,' ar sé.

'Liath sin,' ar Aonghas.

'Neamhchodladh seo,' arsa sé, 'neamhchodladh agus grá éagmaise.'

Ba náir le hAonghas clos na mbriathar sin.

'An galar seo is deacair a leigheas,' arsa Dianchéacht fós.

'Do chomhairle?' arsa Aonghas.

'Misneach!' arsa Dianchéacht. 'Ní luí gan éirí é.'

Agus d'imigh. B'eagal le hAonghas crónú na hoíche, an tiompán gan téad, éalú na haislinge, an dúiseacht aonraic.

Brí Léith. Bhreac an lá arna mhárach. Samhail do ghile na spéire faoi scáth na seanoíche: brollach easóige faoi chrann dubh draighin. B'shiúd anois maidhm dheargsholais ag stealladh anoir gan triomú gan trá. D'éirigh an caor gréine os cionn na mbánta agus na mbeann, os cionn na móinte agus na mearshruthán, os cionn na ndún agus na n-áitreabh.

An ghrian nuair ab ard a dréim, lig sí an chéad anáil leis an tír: is ansin a thriomaigh an drúcht. An dara hanáil: is ansin a ghluais idir bha agus eallach faoi scáth na gcraobh agus na gcrann. An tríú hanáil: is ansin a ramhraigh ceo teaspaigh idir na spéartha agus na tailte. Agus nuair a thriomaigh, nuair a ghluais, nuair a ramhraigh, is ansin a d'éirigh néal gaile den lochán uisce a bhí i gceartlár na faiche tigh Mhidhir, an lochán uisce a rinne Fuamnach d'Éadaoin le mioscais agus le mírún a cuid mórdhraíochta.

D'éirigh néal gaile den uisce, agus i mbruth agus i mbrí na gaile sin is ea a gineadh míol mion mín. Ní fada gur sceith an míol mion mín sin an forchraiceann sleamhain a bhí uime go docht agus go díonach. Agus le teas an aeir agus an uisce, is amhlaidh a rinneadh féileacán gaoithe den mhíol mion mín sin, féileacán gaoithe, féileacán gaile, féileacán gréine.

An féileacán sin ba bhreac ilbhreac a dhá eite. Ba riabhach ilriabhach. Ba scothach ilscothach. Ba

mhaiseach ilmhaiseach. Ba chorcra, ba ghlas. Ba úr
aiteasach éadrom. Ba mhín a dhéanamh. A dhealbh
ba chaol. Dhá shúil an fhéileacáin sin ar dhath an
troim nuair a bhíonn an crann crom faoi ualach na
gcaor dúdhearg.

D'éirigh an banfhéileacán grianghaile sin os cionn
na faiche, agus thug ruaig agus sítheadh chuig an
úllghort áit a raibh Midhir ag beachadóireacht go
bláfar. Gur thuirling i bhfianaise a céile agus a
cumainn. Thóg Midhir a cheann. Agus an chéad
dearcadh dár dhearc sé ar an bhféileacán ilscothach
álainn sin, an chéad fhéachaint dár bhain sé as an dá
shúil mhalla mhodhúla sin, dhá shúil ba dhá lóchrann
sa dorchadas agus sa dúluachair, sin í an uair a thuig
a chroí an díoltas agus an dearbh-olc a bhí imeartha
ag a chéad chéile ar an iníon agus ar an ainnir thar
tír agus thar teorainn, thar tairseach agus thar tobar
isteach. Ní túisce a thuig ach lig sé a shainosna go
dubhach doilíosach ionas gur rith deoir go te, deoir
go tais, agus deoir go trua lena ghrua agus lena
ghiall.

III

Is amhlaidh a bhí seal. Midhir gan bhean gan chéile
gan leath leapan. Ach an banfhéileacán gaoithe agus

gréine ina fhochair de ghréas agus de ghnáth. Is í ba chomhluadar agus ba chuideachta dó. Ba leigheas ar ghruaim í. Ba bhláth í idir úire ghné agus chumhracht. Ba shlán an greann ina gaobhar. B'fhuascailt ón easpa í. Ba mhúchadh tarta agus íota. Bhí seo ann fós: ceo bog braonach ag slíocadh agus ag saibhriú an aeir go caoin cneasta ina diaidh. Bhí leigheas na seacht ngoin agus na seacht ngor sa gceo sin.

Crónán eití an fhéileacáin ba bhinne ná dord na píbe. Foghar agus faí a gutha ba bhinne ná ceolta cruite agus tiompáin. Ba é crónán sin a dhá eite agus foghar sin a gutha a chuireadh suan agus sámhchodladh ar Mhidhir an uair ba mhithid scíth dá cheithre chnámh. An uair ba bhaol dó teacht eascarad nó aoi gan aisce, bhíogadh dordbhíogadh an fhéileacáin chun dúiseachta agus chun deas-labhra é. Agus níl aonach ná oireachtas dá dtéadh Midhir ar aistear nó ar agallamh ann nach mbíodh an bhláthóg ghaoithe sin ag crónán dó lena thaobh. Ba iontach sin le cách.

Cé ea, ámh, foilsíodh d'Fhuamnach gurbh amhlaidh a bhí an dul i mBrí Léith. Foilsíodh di Midhir a bheith suairc sonasach. Foilsíodh di Éadaoin a bheith lena ais de ghréas agus de ghnáth. An grá a bhí ag an slua di; an leigheas a bhí á lua léi; an ceol binn a bhí ina cuid eití ildaite áille, an ceo bog braonach a raibh leigheas na seacht ngoin agus na seacht ngor ann: foilsíodh sin d'Fhuamnach trí bhíthin a cuid feasa agus a cuid foghlama. Agus rinne an fuath nead go domhain i ndiamhair a haigne, an fuath úd a bhí aici don ainnir, don athchéile, don adhaltrach, don fhéileacán.

Fuamnach! Ba bhriathar di feasta gan fos ná fóill a dhéanamh, gan mír a chaitheamh, gan deoch a ól, gan lus a lorg, gan snáth a spíonadh, gan gruaig a cinn a cheangal ná a chíoradh nó go ndíbreodh sí Éadaoin ó Mhidhir, ó Bhrí Léith, óna teach agus óna teallach féin go brách na breithe agus go foirceann na beatha.

Is ansin a chuaigh Fuamnach i muinín trí ní: bua a cuid briocht, cumhacht a cuid cantaireachta, agus dásacht a cuid draíochta. Agus le bua na mbriocht sin, le cumhacht na cantaireachta sin, agus le dásacht na draíochta sin, d'éirigh an chéad leoithne ghaoithe os cionn na dúiche sin, leoithne a bhain lagbhogadh as duilliúr na gcrann. Agus nuair a bhí an lagbhogadh ar ilduilliúr na gcrann sin, den leoithne sin rinne Fuamnach sionnán, sionnán seadghaoithe a bhain luail agus luascadh as leasghéaga na gcrann sin. Agus nuair a bhí an lagbhogadh ar an duilliúr agus an luascadh ar na leasghéaga, den sionnán seadghaoithe sin rinne Fuamnach feothan beag, feothan beag gaoithe a bhain longadáil agus leorshuathadh as lánghéaga na gcrann sin. Agus nuair a bhí an longadáil agus an leorshuathadh ar lánghéaga na gcrann sin, den fheothan beag sin rinne Fuamnach feothan mór, feothan mór a bhain leathchromadh agus léir-chreathadh ní as duilliúr ná as géag, leasghéag ná lánghéag, ach cromadh agus creathadh as na crainn féin.

Agus nuair a bhí an cromadh agus an creathadh ar na crainn féin, den fheothan mór sin rinne Fuamnach cuaifeach, cuaifeach callánach colg-ghaoithe a bhain stangadh agus streachailt as seacht bpréamh na sean-chrann go domhain in úir agus in ithir na talún. Agus nuair a bhí an stangadh agus an streachailt ar sheacht bpréamh na seanchrann go domhain in úir agus in ithir na talún, agus na leasghéaga agus na lánghéaga ag longadáil go leorshuaite, agus an duilliúr ag borb-éalú i mbéal an ghuairneáin, nuair a bhí sin amhlaidh, den chuaifeach rinne Fuamnach spéirling, spéirling shíonghaoithe a bhainfeadh an chraobh den chrann, agus an crann den phréamh, agus an baschrann den doras, agus an doras den dún, agus an adharc den bhó, agus an fhéasóg den easóg, agus an coire den tine, agus sin í an spéirling shíon-ghaoithe a rug ar an bhféileacán álainn ildaite a bhí ag crónán go binn do Mhidhir, agus nuair a rug ruaig, agus nuair a ruaig is ruaigeadh ropánta ró-

chumhachtach a bhí ann, ruaigeadh thar claí agus thar
críoch, ruaigeadh thar críoch agus thar cuan, thar
cuan agus thar toinn, thar toinn agus thar teiscinn.

Agus i ndiaidh na spéirlinge móire sin, Éadoin ba
chloíte, Éadaoin ba chianda, Éadaoin ba choscartha,
Eadaoin ba chráite, Éadaoin ba chaoch ba chríon ba
cheansaithe. Ar aill bheag i meán na mara is ea a
rinne sí an chéad tuirlingt. Gur chan an rosc:

> Mé Éadaoin, mór mo sceoin,
> Orm iomrall de m'ainneoin,
> Orm mearbhall ar muir,
> Orm imeacht ó Mhidhir.

I ndiaidh an roisc sin, rinne sí an dá eite a fhilleadh
agus a dhúnadh ar a chéile. Gur lig uaithi aithne na
cruinne go fóill.

Seacht mbliana. Ag sin an cian aimsire a chaith
Éadaoin ar iomrall ó aill go haill, ó inis go hinis, ó
chríoch go críoch, ó choill go coill. Seal os cionn na
glasmhara glóraí agus screamh sáile ar a dhá eite. Seal
ar chladaí cailce cúrchiumhsacha. Seal ar shléibhte
rúnmhara réimsiúla rua-raithní gan teach gan tóchar.
Seal i ndúichí iargúlta anaithnide gan eolas gan

áitreabh agus gan de chéile ná de chumann aici ach céileachas agus cumann na gaoithe. Gur chan sí an duan:

Gaoth aneas — mo chuach thú!
Gaoth anoir — mo chrá thú!
Gaoth aniar — mo cheol thú!
Gaoth aduaidh — mo chreach thú!

Iar sin, ghluais sí léi arís gan treoir gan tíobhas ar seachrán agus ar síordheoraíocht go haonraic agus go hainnis. Go bhfaca fúithi uair áth agus árthaí, uair eile céide agus ceapach, uair eile fós lios agus longfort, ach cónaí ná oiriseamh níor di ba chinniúint ach uch agus iomrall, iomrall agus uaigneas. Gur chan sí duan beag eile:

Seoid a chaitheas — muince óir,
Seoid eile — dealg fionnóir,
Seoid nach bhfaighead le mo bheo,
Suan gan osna gan anshó.

I gcionn na seacht mbliana, tharla i mBrú na Bóinne í. Agus is ar ghuaille Aonghasa a thuirling sí. Agus ainneoin í ina féileacán gaoithe agus gréine, ainneoin í tréithlag tnáite, ainneoin gan ach rian dá dath féin fágtha ar a dhá sciathán mhaisiúla, d'aithnigh Aonghas an dá shúil mhalla mhodhúla, an dá shúil ba lóchrann sa dorchadas agus sa dúluachair, dhá shúil ar dhath an troim nuair is crom don chraobh faoi ualach na gcaor dúdhearg. Agus nuair a d'aithnigh, chan sé an rosc:

> Mochean Éadaoin, lag do lí,
> trua do ghné, olc do scéal,
> Mochean Éadaoin, tinn do shiúl,
> fuar do luí, bocht do réim.

Is ansin a chuir Aonghas an féileacán bocht lag i dtoll a dhá bhois go ceanúil. Agus rug leis í, ag déanamh liachta agus leighis di.

Bliain d'Éadaoin i mBrú na Bóinne. Bliain gan scéala ó Bhrí Léith. Bliain gan uamhan gan imeagla. Is i ngrianán Aonghasa a chaith sí an bhliain. An grianán sin ba chluthar. Ba chiúin. Ba bhláfar. Crann féithleoige ann agus é féitheach foscúil. Milis boladh an chrainn sin. Crann eidhinn ann gona úrdhuilliúr síorghlas. Gach luibh dá luachmhaire sa ngrianán sin. Gach lus dá réir.

Nuair ba chaite an chéad ráithe den bhliain sin, bhí gné an fhéileacáin slán. Nuair ba chaite an dara ráithe, ba shlán gach dath de sheacht ndath ilbhreaca a dhá sciathán. Nuair ba chaite an tríú ráithe ba shlán do chrónán binn a gutha agus a glóir. Nuair ba chaite an ceathrú ráithe agus an bhliain, ba shlán d'Éadaoin, agus b'ionadh le cách a cuid maise agus a cuid móráille. Iomrá ar Éadaoin dá réir. Sa mBrú. Sa bhfearann. Sa dúiche agus sa tír. Agus bhí Aonghas gan uaignéas. Gan uaignéas gan trom-aisling.

Ach tháinig Fuamnach. Is ar bhéala an Bhrú a bhí Aonghas nuair a chonaic sé banchéile a athar altramais agus a oide féin. Fuinseog mná. Í géaglom gaofar. Cochall ar a ceann. A gob agus a geanc san aer.

'Mochean do theacht, a Fhuamnaigh.'

'Cuireadh agam duit,' arsa Fuamnach go tur.

'Cluintear uait.'

'D'athair altramais agus d'oide féin atá gan tuairisc uait le cian aimsire.'

'Is fíor,' arsa Aonghas.

'Gluais romhat chuig Midhir más ea. Bí leis i mBrí Léith. Is é is déanta.'

Rinne Aonghas ala mhachnaimh. Agus ghéill do bhriathar na mná. Mar ba mhian leis agallamh agus athgháire a oide dhil féin. Ghéill, d'éirigh, agus rinne a théisclim agus a thapa chun conaire agus chun cuarta.

'Gluaisimis linn i bhfarradh a chéile,' arsa Aonghas le Fuamnach.

'Aistear ormsa go hAonach Bodhbhna fós!' arsa Fuamnach go claon.

Le hAonghas ba thrua sin. Ar a ghrua tháinig néal. B'fhearr leis cuideachta an teachta chun cosáin. Mar sin féin, moill ná míog ní dhearna sé, ach chuir a chead agus a cheiliúradh i leith lán an leasa. Gur thug slí Bhrí Léith air féin.

IV

Ní cian gur ráinig Aonghas áras Mhidhir i mBrí Léith.

'Mochean do theacht, a dhalta!' arsa an t-oide, 'Teacht gan choinne ní minic!'

'Teacht gan choinne?' arsa Aonghas, 'Cuireadh uaitse inné ó Fhuamnach!'

'Fuamnach?' arsa Midhir, 'Ar chleas ná bí dall!'

'Cleas?'

'Cleas! Agus abairse liomsa cá háit a bhfuil Éadaoin ó chianaibh.'

Ba náir le hAonghas an t-achainí sin. An chúis ba throm. Lig sé a shainosna.

'Is i mBrú na Bóinne d'Éadaoin,' arsa sé, 'agus is ina féileacán gaoithe atá.'

'Is mairg a thréigfeadh a bhuannacht,' arsa Midhir, 'agus is mithid duit filleadh ar an mBrú, agus gluais leat feasta gan scíth gan oiriseamh!' arsa Midhir.

Ghluais. D'fhill. Agus nuair a d'fhill bhí an grianán folamh.

Folamh an grianán sin. Folamh an Brú. Folamh an lios, an léana agus an luibhghort. Mar níor thúisce Aonghas chun siúil agus chun slí, ach chuaigh Fuamnach i muinín a cuid briocht, a cuid cantaireachta, agus a cuid draíochta. Níor chian gur éirigh an leoithne ghaoithe. An sionnán. An feothan beag. An feothan mór. An cuaifeach. An spéirling. Rug an spéirling ghaoithe sin ar an bhféileacán caoin corcra, agus nuair a rug ruaig, agus an ruaigeadh sin ba ruaigeadh thar claí agus thar críoch, thar críoch agus thar cuan, thar tonn agus thar teiscinn. Agus má ba ropánta an chéad ruaig, an dara ruaig ba ró-ruaigeadh. Agus filleadh ná faoiseamh ní raibh i ndán ach an fuaidreamh faonlag ar lomchríocha sneachta agus seaca i dtuaisceart an domhain. Aon rosc amháin a chan Éadaoin sula ndeachaigh an tocht agus an tost go hinn agus go hearr inti faoi réalta na dubhchruinne:

> Mé Éadaoin: ní heol dom bás.
> Dom is eol aois gan sólás.
> Mo dhídean ní thig le neach,
> Mo dhíbirt dhéanas Fuamnach.

Maidir le hAonghas, nuair a foilsíodh dó feallbheart an bhandraoi, do lean a lorg go hAonach Bodhbhna lámh le hinis Bhreasail Draoi. Is ann a bhí Fuamnach ag folcadh ghruaig a cinn in uisce an locha, a brat ar scaradh ar an trá bheag duirlinge, a crios agus a slat chaorthainn fad a láimhe uaithi, í féin ar a gogaide, gan samhail aici ach cearc odhar ar a nead.

Tharraing Aonghas a chlaíomh as an truaill. Thóg Fuamnach a ceann. Lig scréach uafar as a bráid. Shíl síneadh ar an tslat chaorthainn. Ach d'aon bhéim mharfach mhursanta amháin, scoith Aonghas an ceann dá colainn. Ba dhearg uisce an locha i ndiaidh na béime sin. Tháinig fiach ag ól na fola. Ag sin oidhe na Fuamnaí.

CUID II

Athbhreith

I

Aois iolair ar aill. Aois easa ar abhainn. Aois dearcáin
agus darach: caitheadh trí aois d'aoiseanna na cruinne
i ndiaidh imeachtaí na linne úd in Uisneach, i mBrí
Léith, agus i mBrú na Bóinne. I ndiaidh bhreith
Aonghasa idir lá agus oíche: breith sin Aonghasa, a
oiliúint le Midhir, agus a theacht i réim. I ndiaidh
ghoin Mhidhir le bior ar chluiche-mhá na Mí: goin
sin Mhidhir, a leigheas le Dianchéacht, agus a mhian
de bharr a mháchaile. I ndiaidh thochmharc Éadaoine
iníon Ailealla: tochmharc sin Éadaoine, glanadh na
machairí agus na mothar, a feis le Midhir, agus a
ruaigeadh faoi dhó as Éirinn le draíocht Fhuamnaí. I
ndiaidh dhraíocht sin Fhuamnaí, agus an oidhe gan
oineach gan adhlacadh a fuair sí cois locha in Aonach
Bodhbhna lámh le hinis na crannóige, crannóg sin
Bhreasail Draoi.

Tá! An uair ba chaite an trí aois aimsire sin,
gineadh Éadaoin arís. Agus is i mbroinn mná i gcríocha
Uladh a gineadh í. An bhean sin, is Gormlaith ab

ainm di. Banchéile le hEadar Dubh, curadh agus cathmhíleadh in Inbhear Ciochmhuine.

Agus uair dá raibh fleá á caitheamh i lios Eadair Dhuibh i gcríocha Uladh, tharla féileacán gaoithe os cionn na faiche, agus is caoin corcra an féileacán a bhí ann, ach má ba chaoin, ba lag agus ba leasc. Tharla an féileacán ar chleith an tí. Tharla agus ar an bhforléas. Reacairí an dúin i mbun a gcuid reacaireachta istigh fúithi. Na giollaí ag giollaíocht. Na cruitirí ag cruitireacht. An oíche amuigh go síonchrua suaite.

Agus rug meirfean ar an bhféileacán caoin corcra sin ionas gur thit sí ón bhforléas ard anuas. Agus nuair a thit, is i gcorn meá a thit. Agus ba le Gormlaith an corn sin. Anuas leis an bhféileacán go mall agus go meirbh, go meata agus go maoth. Síos léi sa gcorn, síos sa meá mhilis mheisciúil, agus nuair a bhain Gormlaith taoscadh agus taisbholgam as an gcorn meá céanna, síos leis an bhféileacán i mbolg agus i mbroinn na mná.

Trí ráithe dar gcionn, rugadh an iníon. Agus ar fheiceáil d'Eadar Dubh a dhathúla agus a bhí an iníon sin de dhreach agus de dhealramh, is éard a dúirt gur mhithid Éadaoin a thabhairt uirthi, óir ba dhóigh bantracht Fódla in éad léi ar a cuid dathúlachta ach a dtiocfadh sí in inmhe agus in aois suirí. Agus is amhlaidh sin a tugadh Éadaoin iníon Eadair ar an leanbh. Agus súile an linbh sin, bhí siad ar dhath an troim nuair is crom don chraobh faoi ualach na gcaor.

Oileadh Éadaoin in Inbhear Ciochmhuine. Agus is i measc chlann iníon na dtaoiseach a oileadh cois an inbhir sin í. Leithchéad iníon a líon. Agus is amhlaidh lá a bhí an leithchéad iníon sin á bhfolcadh agus á bhfothrú féin i míntaoille agus i mearuisce an inbhir sin tar éis a dteacht in inmhe ógbhan agus in aois mhacdhachta. Is ansin a chonaic siad ní: marcach ag marcaíocht leis leataobh an inbhir anuas. An marc a bhí faoi, ba cheannbhreac cluasdhearg cruinnchrúbach. Ba bhiorach broinnleathan, b'airgiúil aigeanta. Tháinig an marcach i leith anuas. An leithchéad iníon go tarrnocht taischíochmhar ina fhianaise sa toinn agus sa taoille.

Dhearc an leithchéad iníon an marcach. Thug taitneamh agus tréansearc dó. Sí-bhrat uaine arna fhilleadh uime. Léine chiumhaisdearg faoin mbrat sin. Dhá dhealg óir sa mbrat ar a dhá ghualainn. Sciath airgid ar mhuin a dhroma agus imeall óir ar an sciath sin. Mol óir sa sciath. Greim leathláimhe ag an marcach ar shleá. Cúig bhior ar an tsleá sin. Torc tiarnúil ar a mhuineál. Coisbheart de mhínleathar eilit

bhliana ar dhá throith a chos. A thromchúil ghruaige
ba bhuí fionnbhuí. Snaidhm sa gcúil ghruaige sin
aige. B'fhollas uaibhreach a cheannaghaidh dá réir.
Ráinig an marcach ceartbhruach an inbhir. Sheas.
Gur chan duan. An duan sin ba thuar. Tuar agus
tairngreacht. Ar sé:

> Tchím Éadaoin, iníon Eadair:
> Í óg inniu in uisce inbhir.
> Mór mo scéal, tchím Teamhair:
> Creachfar leo nead mo shinsir.

Tar éis na mbriathar sin, d'imigh an marcach leis mar
a d'imeodh sead nó siolla den cheo. Fios a theachta
ba rún. Fios a imeachta amhlaidh. B'ait le hÉadaoin
an duan a dúirt. Clú agus clos a hainm féin sa duan
sin b'ait léi fós thar aon ní. An naonar ógbhan agus
dhá fhichid eile, is dian a bhí siad á dearcadh. Ba náir
le hÉadaoin sin. Ach an marcach úd a tháinig: glór a
chinn, a dhéanamh agus a dhealramh. Dar léi gurbh
aithnid di é. Ba thostach téadchiúin di dá éis sin.
Chuaigh sí i dtír maille le cách den ógbhantracht.

II

Le linn an ama sin, gairmeadh mac de shaorchlanna
na tíre ina rí i dTeamhair. Eochaidh Aireamh ab

ainm don rí sin. Agus ba leis forlámhas agus flaithiúnas ar chúigí uile na hÉireann, agus is dó ba dhlite
cíos agus cáin na tíre. Ós amhlaidh a bhí, bliain tar éis
a ghairme ina rí i dTeamhair, is é ordú agus urghaire
a rinneadh le hEochaidh fleá a thionól i dTeach
Míchuarta, fleá i gcomhair thaoisigh agus ríthe
tuaithe na tíre, a gcuid reachtairí, a gcuid ollún agus
breithiún, a gcuid saorbhan agus ríona sochineáil.

Fleá sin agus oireachtas na Teamhrach bliain tar
éis ghairm Eachach Airimh ina rí, is ann a bhí cíos
agus cáin na tíre le meas agus le mionríomh go ceann
cúig mblian. Tharla seo ámh: easaontas agus aighneas,
aighneas agus allagar. Nó is éard a dúirt fir Éireann
nárbh intionóil fleá na cánach gan céile mná a bheith
ag an rí. Agus is fear aontumha ab ea Eochaidh
Aireamh, é gan chéile gan chumann, gan ríon ina
fhail ná ina fhochair.

Chuaigh Eochaidh Aireamh i gcomhairle agus i
gcogar le saoithe agus le haos dlí na Teamhrach. Agus
is é comhairle ab fhearr, dar leo, teachtaí a chur chun
na ceithre harda ag lorg mná d'Eochaidh, bean a
bheadh gan aithne fir ná feise go nuige sin, bean nach
raibh a sárú in Inis Fódla ar áilleacht ná ar úire ghné.

Cuireadh na teachtaí chun bealaigh, agus is in
Inbhear Ciochmhuine a frítheadh an bhean sin.
Éadaoin ab ainm di. Agus ní fada dá éis sin a tháinig

Éadaoin go Teamhair. Caitheadh feis ann. Tionóladh fleá agus oireachtas na cánach. Eochaidh Aireamh ba rí i dtús blátha agus buaice, i dtús buaice agus bith-iomrá.

Imirt na Fichille

I

Maidin de chaomh-mhaidineacha an tsaoil, d'éirigh Eochaidh Aireamh amach ar fhaiche mhór bhun-fhairsing na Teamhrach, dhearc uaidh Maigh Bhré agus Maigh Mhuirtheimhne faoi dhrúcht agus faoi chuisne, dhearc uaidh an gleann mar a raibh sean-abhainn na Bóinne ag sníomh léi go rúnchríonna aniar, dhearc uaidh críocha lochánda luachra na Bréifne tamall soir ó thuaidh, dhearc uaidh leithinis Chuailgne sa meath-thuaisceart agus néal ar mullach ann, dhearc uaidh Slí Mhíluachra soir, dhearc uaidh dlús na gcraobh agus fearann beannach na coille.

Bhí múscailt agus moch-chruóg sa dún. Cliotar cleatar cois tobair agus an bhantracht ag líonadh a gcuid feadhnach uisce go tollbhraonach. Géim bó gur lán dá húth. Urchar fáinleoige an cró amach. Púir dheataigh ag fiodrince idir dhá aer. Bró ag meilt na gcrotal, scruch-scrach-scruch.

Is ansin a chonaic Eochaidh fear álainn ildealbhach faoi éadach srólmhaiseach ag druidim go mallda ina leith. Brat uaine uime. Torc tiarnúil ar a bhráid. Coisbheart de mhínleathar eilit bhliana ar dhá throith a chos. Sheas an fear ar thaobh na gréine den Lia Fáil. Loinnir ina shúil. Aoibh gan eascairdeas ar a bhéal.

Labhair Eochaidh: 'Mochean do theacht, a fhir. Cé dar díobh thú?'

Focal níor chan an fear.

Arsa Eochaidh fós: 'Dún na Teamhrach is dúnta ó aréir.'

Ní dhearna an fear ach neamhaird de sin. 'Imrímis ficheall,' ar sé.

Chuir Eochaidh bois le giall. Rinne a mhachnamh. Labhair.

'Atá mo bhanchéile ina suan. Is cois na leapan atá mo chuid fichille.'

'Seo!' arsa an fear.

Leag sé clár ar lom na faiche. Dath cróndearg ródheas air. Lia luachmhar i ngach cúinne. Tiachóg faoina chrios ag an bhfear. Foireann cré umha ar íochtar na tiachóige. D'fholmhaigh sé an tiachóg. Chóirigh an clár chun imeartha.

'Is leatsa an chéad bheart,' ar sé.

'Ní imrímse ach ar geall,' ar Eochaidh.

'Cá geall a chuirfimid?'

'Do rogha féin.'

'Más leat an bua, bronnfad ort caoga each dubhghlas. Iad ceannbhreac cluasdhearg cruinnchrúbach, iad biorach broinnleathan, iad cos-chaol cómhór, iad faobhartha forshiúlach, iad airgiúil aigeanta, iad sodartha soghabhála. Chugat amárach faoin tríú tráth.'

'Is iomchuí sin,' arsa Eochaidh.

Imríodh ficheall. Ba le hEochaidh an bua. D'éirigh an fear, chnuasaigh an fhoireann sa tiachóg, dheasaigh an clár faoina bhrat, agus d'imigh leis gan bhriathar ceiliúrtha mar a d'imeodh sead nó siolla den cheo.

Lá arna mhárach le buídheargadh na spéire, d'éirigh Eochaidh Aireamh aníos ar an ardán aerach iltaobhach adhmaid a bhí ar shúilín na Teamhrach go ndéanadh feitheamh na gcríoch. Go bhfaca ní: a chéile fichille chuige agus leithchéad each dubhghlas i bhfarradh leis. Níorbh fhios cérbh as a thriall.

Ráinig an fear doras na Teamhrach. Srian éadrom airgid ar gach each. A n-eireaball fite ina dtrilseáin.

'Ag seo do gheall, a rí,' arsa an fear.

'Is maith an aghaidh ort é.'

'Tús náire fiacha, deireadh náire a ndíol,' arsa an fear.

Chuir an rí fios ar ghiollaí na n-each.

'Imrímís ficheall,' arsa an fear.

'Ní imrímse ach ar geall.'

'Cén geall ab áil leat?'

'Do rogha féin.'

Labhair an fear arís.

'Más leat an bua, tabharfad chugat leithchéad coileán toirc, iad casbhreac bolgliath muinghlas. Crúba orthu chomh cruinn le crúba each. An lá dar gcionn: dabhach d'adhmad an draighin a mbeidh slí ann don leithchéad torc sin. An lá dar gcionn: leithchéad claíomh órdhoirn. An lá dar gcionn: leithchéad bó chluasdearg gona leithchéad lao cluasdearg fionn agus nasc cré umha ar gach lao díobh. An lá dar gcionn: leithchéad uascán caorach, iad glas ceann-dearg, trí chloigeann orthu, trí bheann ar gach cloigeann. An lá dar gcionn: leithchéad brat bréide le gorscaradh ar leapacha na Teamhrach.'

Focal níor chan an rí. Chuir sé bois le giall. Rinne machnamh. Labhair.

'Bímis ag imirt,' ar sé.

'Leatsa an chéad bheart,' ar an fear.

Imríodh ficheall. Rug Eochaidh an bua ar a chéile comhraic. D'éirigh seisean, chnuasaigh an fhoireann sa tiachóg, dheasaigh an clár faoi fhallaing agus faoi ascaill, agus d'imigh gan cheiliúradh mar a d'imeodh sead nó siolla den cheo.

Maidin lá arna mhárach le bánliathadh na spéire, d'éirigh Eochaidh Aireamh aníos ar ardán aerach adhmaid na Teamhrach gur dhearc an dúiche ina thimpeall. Chonaic ní: fear na fichille chuige. Leithchéad coileán toirc ar iall lena sháil agus lena shainioscaid.

Ráinig an fear doras na Teamhrach.

'Ag sin do gheall,' ar sé.

'Is maith an aghaidh ort é.'

'Chugat mé amárach leis an dara gála,' arsa an fear.

'Is slán t'oineach,' arsa an rí.

Is amhlaidh a bhí go ceann seachtaine. Fear na fichille ag díol na ngeall, gála ar ghála. Eochaidh ag dul chun éadáile.

II

Bhí oide ag Eochaidh, oide le linn a óige, agus fear comhairle dó ó tháinig sé in inmhe fir agus rí. Dairbre ab ainm don oide sin. Ba iontach le Dairbre éadáil agus eallach an rí. Ba chogar cois tobair. Luaidreán cois luaithrigh. Cabaireacht cúl boise ag na doirseoirí.

Tháinig Dairbre go both an rí. Eochaidh roimhe ag dianfhéachaint na fichille agus corn meá ina dheasláimh.

'Mór do chuid éadála, a dhalta liom.' ar sé.

Focal níor chan an rí.

'Fios an scéil chugam, a mhacáin!'

Thug Eochaidh dornfhéachaint gan gháire ar a sheanoide féin.

'Fear a thagann chugam. Fear uasal ildealbhach, fear fionnmhaiseach foltleabhar, fear uaibhreach aduain. Le moch maidine is gnách a theacht. Cuireann dúshlán fichille orm. Rug mé an bua air faoi dhó. An éadáil úd a fheiceann tú, sin é geall an dá chluiche.'

Chrom Dairbre faoi.

'Dar liom gur draíocht agus doilfeacht seo. Is fear maíteach mórchumhachta a tháinig chugat. Bain fios a shloinne de, agus cuir bearta deacra dodhéanta de gheall agus de gheasa air. Is mithid bac air feasta. Ní de ghinealach an duine é.'

D'imigh Dairbre agus d'fhág an rí ag meilt gach smaoineamh ba shuaite ná a chéile. Chuaigh grian i dtalamh. Níor chlos i dTeamhair ach fead an éin oíche ar seilg, siollabadh na lag-ghaoithe ag déanamh a cuid duan, tine á coigilt, agus smuchar smachar na n-each sa mbuaile. Chodail Eochaidh. An ríon lena ais.

Is corrach a chodail Éadaoin an oíche sin. Aisling a tharla di. Aisling agus tromthaibhreamh. Is é seo a taibhríodh di: gail ar uisce, feothan gaoithe; seal gan fothain, seal gan faoiseamh; teas i ngrianán, sioc ar sciathán.

'Uh!'

Lig sí cnead thar a cáir agus bhain cor as a ceann ar an adhairt.

Idir dhá néal is ea a taibhríodh seo di fós: fear cois taoille, dealramh tiarna; folt cas buí air, brat ón sí air. Each faoin bhfear sin, biorach bríomhar. Ealta éan, tiompán gan téad. Gail ar uisce, feothan gaoithe. Is ansin a labhair an marcach. Agus nuair a labhair, do chan a hainm féin go neamhbhalbh.

'Uhh!'

Dhúisigh Éadaoin. Fliuch a léine le hallas.

Le smúidbhreacadh an lae arna mhárach, bhí Eochaidh ina shuí agus ina shainchéim roimh ghairm don choileach crúbach cíordhearg. Crios faoina fhallaing. A bhéal chomh teann le hiall. Go bhfaca ní: fear a dhúshláin chuige ina leith go réimdhíreach rúnmhar. Ráinig an fear doras na Teamhrach. Isteach leis.

'Do chéad fáilte, a fhir imríos ficheall,' arsa Eochaidh.

Focal níor chan an fear.

'Ceist!' arsa an rí.

'Abair leat.'

'Cé dar díobh thú?'

'Is den aos sí mé. Midhir is ainm dom. Brí Léith is flaitheas agus is fearann dom. Ainm eile air Maigh Mór. Má na n-úll agus na sméar. Má na mbeach. Bím seal sa bhflaitheas sin, seal i gcríocha Fódla. I bhFreamhann, i gCruachain. I dTeafa. Seal i dTeamhair.'

Chuir Eochaidh bois le giall. Rinne meandar machnaimh. Labhair.

'An imreofar ficheall?'

'Imreofar,' arsa Midhir.

'Cá geall?' arsa Eochaidh.

'Do roghasa geall.'

'Tá seo,' arsa Eochaidh, 'díchlochadh na Mí.'

Leath an chéad mhac imreasan ar shúil Mhidhir.

'Tá seo fós: tóchar ar chriathrach.'

Leath an dara mac imreasan ar shúil Mhidhir.

'Tá seo fós: luachair ar loch'.

Leath an tríú mac imreasan ar shúil Mhidhir.

'Agus seo: coill ar Bhréifne.'

Leath an ceathrú mac imreasan ar shúil Mhidhir.

Ní fada gur labhair sé.

'Mo thitim agus mo thurnamh ab áil leatsa leis sin. Mo mhilleadh agus mo mharú. Mo dhíothú agus mo dhíchur. Ródheacair dom díol na ngeall sin.

Maith dom ceann díobh.'

'Maithim duit luachair ar loch.'

'Maith leat go fóill.'

'Ní mhaithfead.'

'Níl céile fichille i bhFódla atá inchomhraic liomsa,' arsa Midhir, 'ach tú féin amháin, a rí.'

Ba bhinn le hEochaidh a mholadh féin.

'Maithim duit coill ar Bhréifne,' ar sé.

'Maith leat go fóill,' arsa Midhir.

'Ní mhaithfead. Cuir tóchar ar Chriathrach Lámhraí, agus déan díchlochadh na Mí, nó ní slán t'oineach, agus aorfaidh na filí thú,' arsa Eochaidh.

'Díchlochadh na Mí sula mbí an athbhliain istigh,' arsa Midhir.

'Tóchar ar Chriathar Lámhraí anocht más ea. Má bhuaimse ort.'

Rinne Midhir meandar machnaimh. Neach níor leag troith ná sáil a choise ar Chriathrach Lámhraí ariamh. Ba chriathar. Gan ann ach caochphoill, feallbhogach, agus fód mearbhaill gach re fód. Is é Eochaidh is túisce a labhair arís.

'An imreofar ficheall?'

'Imreofar,' arsa Midhir. 'Is leatsa an chéad bheart'.

Imríodh ficheall. Is ar Mhidhir a chlis. Tóchar le cur aige ar Chriathrach Lámhraí dá réir.

'Achainí agam ort,' ar sé le hEochaidh.

'Fios na hachainí uait!'

'Cathair seo na Teamhrach ná fágadh aon neach roimh éirí gréine amárach.'

'Cén fáth sin?' arsa Eochaidh.

'Saothar mo mhuintire-se ní féidir ach faoi rún,' arsa Midhir.

'Neach ní fhágfaidh an Teamhair,' arsa Eochaidh.

Chuir Midhir an fhoireann fichille sa tiachóg cré-umha, dheasaigh an clár faoi fhallaing agus faoi ascaill, agus d'imigh leis mar a bheadh siolla den cheo.

III

Aoire sléibhe de chuid na Teamhrach a bhí amuigh i mbun na dtréad. Fear Bachaill ab ainm don fhear sin. Chuir Eochaidh teachta chuige san áit a raibh sé ag aoireacht agus ag airneán ar an olluaigneas leis féin. Chonaic an t-aoire an marcach chuige ina chrua-shodar an sliabh siúlach aníos.

'Teachta chugat ó rí na Teamhrach, a aoire!'

'Chugamsa?'

Nocht an teachta fios an scéil d'Fhear Bachaill.

'Tuairisc agus taiscéala uait an tríú tráth amárach faoi imeachtaí na hoíche ar Chriathrach Lámhraí!'

'Mairg an t-aoire thréigeas a thréad!' arsa Fear Bachaill.

Thug an marcach lán an dá sháil don each, agus d'imigh leis sna crúba arda arís.

Iarchoineascar na hoíche. An ghealach ar snámh go héasca faoi dhroichead na scamall. Fia fáilí ag fiossmúrthacht an aeir. Scréach ulchabháin. Agus aoire sínte ar a uillinn agus ar a imleacán ar Thulach na Sceach i gcóngar Chriathrach Lámhraí. A bhachall lena thaobh. Gur chuala an t-aoire an ní: cantaireacht míle glór. Go bhfaca seo: drong mhór ilbhreac álainn ag gluaiseacht go líofa lántapa i dtreo an chriathraigh. Leath an dá shúil ina bhlaosc ar Fhear Bachaill. Stad a chroí. A bhéal do thriomaigh. Taibhreamh? Ní dó ba léir. Scar sé a cheithre chnámh ar an talamh. Amhlaidh dó faoi líonrith agus faoi sceoin ar feadh na hoíche. Trí thráth a mhair an monar sí. Ag seo an rosc a chan siad:

> 'Oirearc linn, oirearc sinn,
> Ní fios leas, ní fios aimhleas,
> Tóchar ar chriathar, tóchar ar chriathar.
>
> Tréan gach damh faoi chuing,
> Luath gach lámh iar fuin,
> Tóchar ar chriathar, tóchar ar chriathar.'

D'éalaigh an slua gan lorg le fáinne an lae. Bhí an tóchar déanta.

Triúr i lios na Teamhrach an tríú tráth arna mhárach. Eochaidh Aireamh, Dairbre, agus Fear Bachaill.

'Céard a chonaic tú, a Fhir Bhachaill?' arsa Eochaidh.

Focal níor chan an t-aoire.

'Abair leat,' arsa Dairbre.

Is macstadach mantsiollach a labhair an t-aoire.

'Slua. Slua gan áireamh. Iad ag cantain. Shroich siad an criathrach. Chaith gach aon a bhrat ar lár. Brat ar bhrat in aon charn amháin. Fear uasal ildealbhach álainn ina sheasamh ar bharr an chairn sin.'

'Midhir,' arsa Dairbre.

'Abair leat,' arsa Eochaidh.

Bhí a dhá shúil fuaite den urlár ag Fear Bachaill.

'An slua á bhrostú ag an bhfear sin,' ar sé, 'á bhrostú agus á bhroideadh. Tús monair díphréamhadh na gcrann. Díphréamhadh. Is ansin a rinneadar carn de bhun na gcrann. Tháinig … na daimh. Seisreach ar sheisreach. Iad á dtiomáint. Iad á mealladh. Rann á chanadh ag lucht a meallta.'

'Abair leat.'

'Iar ndéanamh na claise le treabhadh na ndámh, bun na gcrann chun líonadh na claise sin. Bun na gcrann, bun agus barr na bpréamh.'

D'éist an t-aoire dá thuairisc, ach bhí scáth an iarsmaoinimh i mbeo a shúl.

'Abair leat,' arsa Eochaidh.

'An chuing. Ní ar bhaithis na ndamh a bhí sí i ngreim. Ach faoina mbráid.'

'Faoina mbráid?'

'Is ea.'

D'fhéach an t-aoire ar Eochaidh Aireamh.

'A shoilse,' ar sé, 'na caoirigh. Déanfaidh na mathghamhain ár orthu.'

'Is slán na caoirigh,' arsa Dairbre, 'tá mo ghiolla féin ag feitheamh orthu.'

Lig Fear Bachaill a shainosna. Trom súil ar neamhchodladh.

Ní lá arna mhárach ná an lá dar gcionn ach mí tar éis na haimsire sin a tháinig Midhir arís. Eochaidh ar an ardán aerach ag dearcadh na dúiche. D'aithnigh sé a chéile fichille chuige i leith. Ráinig seisean an doras. Is míbhuíoch maslaithe an dreach a bhí air. Sheas sé taobh na gréine den Lia Fáil.

'Mór an deacair a chuir tú orm, a Eochaidh, a Rí na Teamhrach.'

'Mhaith mé dhá dheacair eile duit.'

'Is tréithlag traochta mo mhuintir tar éis na tógála.'

'Ach is slán t'oineach, a Mhidhir an tsí,' arsa Eochaidh.

Focal eile níor chan ceachtar den dís.

Leag Midhir an clár fichille ar lom na faiche. Chóirigh an fhoireann.

'An imreofar ficheall?' ar sé.

'Leatsa an chéad bheart,' arsa Eochaidh.

'Ní imrímse ach ar geall,' arsa Midhir.

'Cá geall a bheirimid?'

'A rogha geall d'fhear an bhua,' arsa Midhir.

'Maith liom sin,' arsa Eochaidh, 'bímis ag imirt.'

Imríodh ficheall. Ba chrua d'Eochaidh. Má ba chrua ba chúng. Má ba chúng ba chinniúnach. Ní raibh de bheart a fhuascailte aige ach aon bheart amháin. Chuaigh de. Cuireadh an tsáinn air.

'Is leat an bua inniu,' ar sé le Midhir.

'Ba liom an bua ó chianaibh dá mb'áil liom é.'

'Cén geall is rogha leat,' arsa Eochaidh.

Is tur tomhaiste tiarnúil a labhair Midhir.

'Mo dhá láimh faoi choim Éadaoine, agus póg ar a béal.'

Thit socht ar Eochaidh. Ba chlos tiompán a chroí.

A dhá ghéag ar crith. Is fada gur chan sé an t-athbhriathar.

'Bí anseo i gceann na míosa,' ar sé.

D'éirigh Midhir, chnuasaigh an fhoireann fichille sa tiachóg, dheasaigh an clár faoi fhallaing agus faoi ascaill, agus thug bealach an dorais air féin. Gur chas ar a sháil.

'Mo náire thú, a rí. Facthas an t-aoire ar Thulach na Sceach. Tá fabht sa tóchar dá bharr.'

D'imigh.

I rith an ama idir imirt na fichille, díol na ngeall, agus tógáil an tóchair ar Chriathrach Lámhraí, is amhlaidh a bhí Midhir ag tochmharc Éadaoine ar feadh bliain aimsire. Á mealladh. Á bréagadh. Chan sé an duan di:

> A bhé fhinn, an dtiocfá liom
> Go críoch gan léan gan leatrom?
> Milis meá ann, milis fíon,
> Óg ann cách, neach ní róchríon.
>
> Gol ná galar níl sa tír,
> Fial gach fleá ann, a ainnir,
> Úll ar craobh ann, ál ag éan,
> Gach suan is sámh i dtámhnéal.

Éadaoin! Dúirt sí le Midhir nach rachadh sí leis gan cead ó Eochaidh. Rachadh ámh ach cead a fháil.

IV

Nuair ba lán an mhí, dúnadh agus daingníodh cathair na Teamhrach le feascar agus le fuineadh gréine. Cosc amach, cosc isteach. Díorma dea-cheithearnach timpeall an dúin. Iad ag dianfhéachaint na dúiche deiseal. Ag teannfhéachaint na tíre tuathail. Dhá naonúr doirseoirí ar an ardán iltaobhach ag feitheamh go foighdeach gan faí. Uaisle na Mí ag déanamh aoibhnis agus áineasa i dTeach Míchuarta. Na giollaí ag giollaíocht. Na cláirseoirí ag cláirseoireacht. Na cleasaithe ag cleasaíocht. Is í Éadaoin a bhí ag dáileadh na dí. Bua dá cuid an dáileadh sin. Ba stuama a lámh.

Gur facthas ní: Midhir i gceartlár an tí. Chuaigh tormán na fleá i léig. Dá áille Midhir laetha an tsaoil, ba lóchrann fir agus crann soilse an oíche úd é. Folt ómra air. A ghnúis ba chorcra. Ba dhealbh flatha gan easpa é. É muinbhreac coinnealdearc. Labhair Midhir.

'Díoltar liom an geall,' ar sé.

'Cá geall sin?' arsa Eochaidh.

'Mo dhá láimh faoi choim Éadaoine, agus póg ar a béal.'

D'éirigh Eochaidh ina sheasamh.

'Fóill ort!' ar sé.

'Fóill ná fuireach ní féidir,' arsa Midhir.

Is ansin a labhair sé le hÉadaoin.

'Bliain dom dod' thochmharc, a bhé fhinn,' ar sé. 'Cé leis do chroí anocht?'

Dhearg ar Éadaoin.

'Is dearg do ghrua,' arsa Eochaidh.

Bhí tocht ar an mnaoi.

'Is cluain agus is claon uait seo, a Mhidhir,' arsa Eochaidh.

'Díoltar liom an geall.'

Ba chlos cúlmhonabhar an tslua.

'Díoltar,' ar Eochaidh go hainnis.

Triúr i lár an tí. Eochaidh, Éadaoin, Midhir. Iad i bhfianaise lán an leasa. Dheasaigh Midhir a thruaill ar leathchorróg. Chuir a dhá láimh faoi chaolchoim na mná. Ní túisce a phóg sé a béal ach d'éirigh an dís ina dhá eala suas tríd an bhforléas a bhí i ndíon an leasa. Dhá eala ag éalú leo faoi chochall mór na spéire duibhe.

Muintir an rí! Lig siad tromgháir iontais agus alltachta astu. Facthas aon chleite glanbhán amháin ag mallghuairdeall an t-aer anuas go talamh. Neach níor dhrann leis. Neach níor chrom.

I ndídean a ríbhotha féin dó, chuir Eochaidh fios ar

Dhairbre. Ba throm an chúis. Isteach le Dairbre. Na malaí fite air. Labhair Eochaidh.

'Ní buan neach tar éis a náirithe.'

Líon Dairbre dhá chorn meá.

'Fuadach? Nó éalú?'

Óladh dhá bholgam.

'Más fuadach is feall.'

Dhruid an t-oide i leith an dalta.

'Más éalú is adhaltranas.'

Lig Eochaidh a chiall thar a cháir.

'Éalú nó fuadach is cac ar m'oineachsa é.' Bhain sé lán pluice as an gcorn meá. 'Is mithid beart,' ar sé gan ghreann.

Chuir Dairbre glaic le giall.

'Cá comhairle más ea?'

'Tóraíocht?'

'Tóraíocht.'

An Tóraíocht

I

Gléasadh carbad Eachach chun slí agus chun siúil. Creat, cuing, agus fearsaid — ba ghrinn súil an ara á ngrinneadh. An suí agus an brat, an dá roth, an dá dhealg, na téada, na fáinní agus na fithisí — ba stuama lámh an ara á dteannadh agus á gceangal. Chuir sé bealú de shaill na mbroc ar gach alt agus ar gach uille ionas nach raibh samhail ag an gcarbad ach árthach ar an taoille tuile. Tugadh airtheann agus aiteann don eachra, cóiríodh an t-adhastar agus an srian, agus cuireadh slógadh agus sluaghairm ar sheacht naonúr de shluaite na Teamhrach agus na Mí chun aistir i gcuideachta an rí.

I measc an tseacht naonúr sin, bhí naonúr dá theaghlach féin, naonúr dá mhuintir, naonúr giollaí, dhá naonúr ceithearnach, agus dhá naonúr de chosmhuintir na ráthanna agus na roschlochán máguaird. Óir ba gheis don saor sleán, ba gheis don laoch láí, don taoiseach ba gheis tochailt, agus don rí ba gheis rómhar agus rámhainn. Agus is dúr dalba an drong a bhí sa seacht naonúr sin agus iad ag dul ar thóraíocht Mhidhir agus Éadaoine ar fud Inse Fáil.

Is ó dheas i dtreo Shí na mBan Fionn is túisce a thug siad aghaidh agus amas. Tús aistir ar a mian acu. Lámh le habhainn na Bearú ámh, d'éirigh ceo mórthimpeall orthu. Chuir an ceo sin urú ar an lá agus ar an lánsolas ionas gur baineadh fios slí agus siúil d'Eochaidh agus den trí fhichid fear a bhí leis.

Ar a chaoiche a bhí an ceo sin, agus ar a dhorcha a bhí dlúthnéalta an aeir, thiomáin an t-ara creat, clár agus carbad faoi shruth na habhann ionas gur báthadh an dá ghearrbhromach a bhí faoi chuing ag tarrac. Dóbair Eochaidh a bháthadh leis na bromaigh.

Is múisiamach mílítheach a rinne seacht naonúr na Teamhrach fos tine agus fuireach fulachta lámh leis an áit sin. Ní raibh sa dá lasair ach téamh na mbos ar éigean. Fuar gach fear. 'Aduain an ceo seo,' arsa Eochaidh Aireamh.

Lá arna mhárach, ghluais an marcshlua sin leo go misniúil. Tamall ó dheas d'abhainn na Feoire, tharla tréad bó rompu sa tslí. Ba bána. Dearg a gcluasa. Gan neach á sheoladh. Chuaigh an tréad bó ó-dhearga sin faoin muine dhriseogach dhospíonta gan dealg a bhaint den draighean ná duilleog den dair. Ainneoin an fód ina lathach fúthu, lorg na gcrúb níor léir ina ndiaidh. 'Aduain an tréad seo,' arsa Eochaidh. Ar aghaidh leis an mbuíon go fóill.

Tamall ó thuaidh de Shí na mBan Fionn, tharla fear ollmhór aonair anchruthach rompu. Gan samhail aige ach bile crainn ag longadáil lá gaoithe ar shliabh gan fothain. É maoldubh míghéagach. Leathshúil leis i meán a ghrua agus a ghág-éadain. Uachais in áit a bhéil. Léine lachtna lánbhréan go hioscaid air. Méid mullach mic bliana ina dhá cholpa faoi seach. É cosnocht cáidheach. Ar fheiceáil an fhir mhóir uafair sin d'eachra na Teamhrach, thug a lán díobh an bogach agus an riasc orthu féin de ruathar sceoine. Rop an fear míghéagach úd leis d'ábhóga móra naoi n-iomaire agus naoi n-eitre. 'Aduain an fear sin,' ar Eochaidh. Ar aghaidh leis an mbuíon go fóill.

Rángthas Sí na mBan Fionn oíche an dara lae. Naoi lá dóibh ag tochailt an tsí. Nó naoi mí. Níorbh fhios. Is ansin a tháinig neach de lucht an tsí chun agallaimh leo amach. Clúmhach na bhfiach níor dhuibhe ná gruaig an neach sin. Adúirt an dubh-fholtach leo nach sa sí sin a bhí Midhir ná Éadaoin.

Ar sé: 'Is sa rídhún i mBrí Léith dóibh. Téigí ansiúd dá dtóraíocht.'

Chuaigh sin.

Iar rochtain Bhrí Léith dóibh, chrom siad fúthu ag tochailt an tsí. Leithchéad láí, leithchéad lann ag lonnrú. Naoi lá dóibh ag tochailt an tsí sin. Nó naoi mí. Níorbh fhios. Tochailt an tsí ba dheacair. Má ba dheacair ba dhoiligh. Má ba dhoiligh ba dhodhéanta. Bliain dóibh dar leo ag dothochailt ar bhéalaibh Bhrí Léith. Gach dá dtochlaídís sa ló, ba shlán sleamhain úr atógtha arna mhárach. 'Aduain an tochailt seo,' arsa Eochaidh Aireamh, 'aduain an atógáil seo.'

Is ansin a chuathas i gcomhairle lena chéile le himeachtaí na tochailte sin a chíoradh, ós tochailt gan tairbhe a bhí ann, tochailt gan tairbhe ach tuirse na ngéag, tochailt gan toradh agus briseadh na bhfeac.

'Is mithid íobairt,' arsa fear de naonúr teaghlaigh an rí.

'Íobairt?'

'Duine den daoscar a chur sa talamh ina bheatha.'

Cách ba thostach ar chlos na míbhriathar sin dóibh.

'Ní duine den daoscar, ach each d'eachra na Teamhrach.'

Faomhadh sin. Ach is drogallach.

I ndeireadh tochailte arna mhárach cuireadh each odhar uaibhreach ardmhongach d'eachra na Teamhrach faoin bhfód dearg ar bhéalaibh Bhrí Léith ina bheo agus ina bheatha. Ba thrua sin le trian an tslua. Trian ba thoilteanach. Trian idir dhá chogar agus dhá chomhairle. Adhlacadh úd an eich, b'adhlacadh in aisce ámh. Óir gach dar tochlaíodh de Shí Bhrí Léith go ceann naoi lá dá éis sin, ba shlán sleamhain úr atógtha arna mhárach.

Chuathas i gcomhairle athuair.

'Is mithid íobairt!' arsa fear de naonúr teaghlaigh an rí.

Is focal freasúra an focal freagra a fuair:

'Íobairt ní ádhmhar, íobairt ní inmholta, íobairt ní ionraic.'

Ach ba leis an rí an focal scoir. A chroí san ba chráite, a chiall tráite, a chlú agus a cháil báite in éalú agus in adhaltranas, in easonóir agus in éagmais a bhanchéile óig.

'Déantar duine den daoscar a íobairt,' ar sé.

Is mar seo a rinneadh íobairt duine den daoscar: cuireadh ceathrar den naonúr ceithearnach chuig an ráth agus an roschlochán ba neasa don láthair sin. Iar dteacht dóibh i gcóngar an rátha sin, chonaic siad aitheach de chuid na tuaithe sin ina aonar agus é ag tiomsú beart brosna i gcomhair na tine. Rug na ceithearnaigh ar an bhfear sin, chuir cuibhreach agus ceangal air, agus thug leo é i láthair an rí beag beann ar an dlí, beag beann ar an bhfíor fear ná ar an bhfíor flath.

'Anacal agus aisce!' arsa an t-aitheach.

Ainneoin an achainí sin, cuireadh i dtalamh é ina bheo agus ina bheatha.

Líonadh an cuithe agus an caochpholl uime go coim, go hascaill, go bun smige.

'Anacal agus aisce!' ar an t-aitheach.

'Cluintear uait.'

'Leathlámh liom a fhágáil os cionn na talún,' ar sé.

'Cén fáth sin?'

'Greim láimhe a bheith ag mo bhean orm nuair a bheifear do mo chaoineadh.'

Faomhadh sin. Agus carnadh an úir agus an ithir ar mhullach an fhir anuas.

Má lig scread, faic níor cluineadh. Ba lán a bhéal den chré.

'Fear marbh is marbh a chionta,' arsa Eochaidh Aireamh go tur.

Is ansin a d'eitil dhá fhiach as an sí amach. An dá fhiach sin is dath bán a bhí orthu idir ghob, chrúba, agus chleití. D'eitil an dá fhiach bhána leo ó dheas gach ndíreach. 'Aduain sin,' arsa Eochaidh ar fheiceáil an dá bhánfhiach dó. Lean seacht naonúr na Teamhrach na fiacha. Ba go Sí na mBan Fionn a dtriall.

Thug siad faoi thochailt an tsí sin athuair.

Ní cian gur tháinig an neach sí chucu amach arís go dubh.

'Is mór atáir dár gciapadh, a Eochaidh na Teamhrach,' arsa an neach. 'Agus tuig uaimse nach sinne a d'fhuadaigh do bhean. Do bhean ní sinne a d'fhuadaigh, agus duit féin dochar ní dearnamar ná díobháil. Agus céard ab áil leat feasta?'

D'fhreagair Eochaidh an neach sí. 'Ní dhealaím leis an bhfód seo,' ar sé, 'gan fios athghabháil mo mhná uaibh!'

Ag seo comhairle an neach dubh ón sí. 'Beir leat coileáin go Brí Léith. Na coileáin sin, bídís dall. Beir leat ann iad gach lá. Faoiseamh a gheobhair. Sin agat fios athghabháil do mhná.'

'Aduain sin,' arsa Eochaidh.

Ach do rinne amhlaidh. Coileáin con na dúiche, do rinneadh a ngabháil. Ba thrua a ndalladh. Ach dalladh. Ba thrua clos a sianaíle agus a n-uallfairte de dheasca a ndallta. Ach ba chlos.

II

Ag tochailt Shí Bhrí Léith dóibh an naoú lá sin, tochailt gan toradh ach briseadh na bhfeac, tochailt gan tairbhe ach tuirse na ngéag, chonaic siad Midhir ag teacht ina gcoinne agus ina gceartleith. Slat cúig

bhior ina láimh. An torc tiarnúil ar a bhráid. Brat sí-
uaine uime. Ach ba dhubh a mhéin. A bhriathar
agus a bhreac-shúil bhiorach ba dhubh dá réir.

'Cén fáth an drochobair seo ort, a Eochaidh, an
t-éigniú tíre seo, an saothar seo gan séan?'

'Cá háit a bhfuil mo bhean?' arsa Eochaidh
Aireamh.

Is stuama a labhair Midhir.

'D'imir tú ficheall liom, nár imir?'

'D'imir sin.'

'Rug tú an bua orm, nár rug?'

'Rug sin.'

'Caoga each dubhghlas: d'íoc mé an geall leat,
nár íoc?'

'D'íoc sin.'

'Leithchéad coileán toirc, leithchéad claíomh
órdhoirn, leithchéad bó chluasdearg gona leithchéad
lao cluasdearg fionn, leithchéad uascán, leithchéad
brat: d'íoc mé an dara geall leat, nár íoc?'

'D'íoc sin.'

'Tóchar ar Chriathrach Lámhraí: rinne mé sin
duit, nach ndearna?'

'Rinne.'

Tharraing Midhir anáil.

'An ceathrú cluiche — a rogha geall d'fhear an
bhua. Sin mar a bhí. Fíor nó bréag?'

'Fíor,' arsa Eochaidh.

'Mo rogha geallsa: mo dhá láimh faoi choim Éadaoine, agus póg ar a béal. Fíor nó bréag?'

'Fíor.'

'Maith, a Eochaidh,' arsa Midhir, 'cuireadh an cluiche ort, reic tú do bhean liom, agus ná bí do mo chrá-sa feasta gan údar.'

Is feargach a d'fhreagair Eochaidh tiarna Bhrí Léith.

'Reic ná díol mo mhná ní dhéanfainnse go brách!' ar sé. Ailt a dhá dhorn ba gheal um a gha. A bhéal ar crith. Alltacht ina dhá shúil. 'Is tusa a d'fhuadaigh í,' ar sé go fóill.

'Is dá deoin féin a tháinig sí liom,' ar Midhir.

'Dar liom nach ea,' arsa Eochaidh, 'dar liom gur tusa a mheall í le flaithchaint agus le filíocht.'

Lig Midhir a shainosna.

'Maith, a Eochaidh,' ar sé, 'déanam síth agus conradh lena chéile.'

'Cá conradh?' arsa Eochaidh.

'Bí ar bhruach Loch Dairbre an uair is airde don ghréin amárach. Seachtar de do mhuintir bíodh leat. Beidh do bhean romhat cois locha.'

'B'fhearr liom dul go Dún Freamhainn Bhréifne,' arsa Eochaidh.

'Freamhann? Déantar amhlaidh más ea,' arsa Midhir.

Chuir Eochaidh Aireamh coraíocht agus slánaíocht ar Mhidhir i leith a ghealltanais. Agus d'fhill ar an bhfoslongfort a bhí aige lámh le doirse Bhrí Léith. B'fhaoiseamh dó triall ar Fhreamhann arna mhárach, arae bhí a chuid fear i ndeireadh foinn agus foighde, iad ar ghannchuid uisce agus dí, ceannairc agus cantal orthu, iad grúscánach gearánach. Agus filleadh ar Theamhair in éagmais Éadaoine, sin filleadh nach ligfeadh neart, niachas ná náire don rí a dhéanamh. Dhá néal suain ná sámhchodlata níor chaith Eochaidh ó choineascar na hoíche go camhaoir na maidine ach é ag tnúth le hathlánúnas agus le hathghabháil a mhná.

Ar uair na hardgréine arna mhárach, tháinig Midhir go Freamhann. Má tháinig, ní ina aonar a tháinig. Bhí cailleach bhuí lena thaobh. Tiompán gan téad ina láimh aici. Í mantach míolach. Í crom críon. Í scáinte scothghruagach.

Tháinig Midhir. Tháinig cailleach an tiompáin. Agus tháinig leithchéad ban óg i ndiaidh na díse sin i leith. Snáth éadrom airgid idir gach dís bhan. Cúig dís fhichead. Iad ar fad ar aon dealramh le hÉadaoin. Ar aon chúil ghruaige. Ar aon deargbhéal. Ar aon ghealdéad. Ar aon chaolghéag. Ar aon úrchneas. Ar aon ghrua chaoin chorcra. Ar aon réidhcholpa. Ar aon chruinnchíoch. Ar aon tsáil agus ar aon troith. Ar aon mhallrosc caordhaite. Ar aon dreach agus ar aon déanamh.

Ar fheiceáil an leithchéad ógríon aondealraimh dóibh, chuir muintir an rí an dá bhois le grua. Aí anála ná urlabhra ní raibh iontu le ligean. Bhánaigh agus d'aolbhánaigh ar éadan Eachach. Is ansin a labhair Midhir.

'Tá Éadaoin ar bhean den bhantracht seo,' ar sé, 'agus tabhair leat anois í, a Eochaidh, nó roghnaigh ríon de na ríona seo, mar is mithid dúinne filleadh ar Bhrí Léith. Óir an leithchéad ríon seo is den slua sí iad uile, agus ní buan dóibh ach sa sí, agus siolla dá gcanúint féin ní chluinfear uathu abhus i dtír seo na neamhbhuan.'

Is cloíte a labhair Eochaidh lena mhuintir.

'Cá comhairle agaibh dom?' ar sé.

'Comhairle níl againn duit, faraor,' ar siad go bacach.

Ach labhair fear díobh. 'Atá agamsa comhairle duit,' ar sé.

'Cluintear uait!'

'Bua ag Éadaoin: an dáileadh dí. Ag dáileadh dí is ise is fearr in Éirinn. Dáileadh na hógríona seo deoch duit. Déanfaidh an dáileadh sin deimhniú.'

Faomhadh sin.

Is ansin a roinneadh na ríona. Snoíodh an snáth airgid a bhí idir gach dís. Cuireadh cúigear fichead díobh ar dheis, agus cúigear fichead ar chlé. Leastar mór i lár an tí eatarthu. Líonadh an leastar sin le leann. Agus tugadh a chorn féin d'Eochaidh.

'Dáiltear dom,' ar sé.

Dáileadh. Bean ar bhean deas agus clé. Ochtar ban agus dhá fhichid díobh a dháil dó. Níor aithnigh sé Éadaoin.

'Dáileadh an dís dheiridh dom,' arsa Eochaidh Aireamh.

Dháil sin. An bhean leathdheiridh níorbh ise Éadaoin. Tháinig an bhean eile i leith. Níor chlos sa dún ach srólsioscadh a sí-bhrait ag slíocadh uimpi go samhrata. Dháil sí deoch don rí.

'Aithním Éadaoin,' ar sé.

Lig an slua gáir áthais. Ach bhí scáth an amhrais ar aigne Eachach. Focal níor chan sé ámh. Ach is é dath an troim a bhí ar dhá chaorshúil na hógmhná.

'Is mithid dúinne ascnamh agus imeacht,' ar Midhir.

D'éirigh na ríona d'aon éirí amháin. D'éirigh an chailleach bhuí. D'éirigh Midhir. D'éirigh agus d'imigh siad uile mar a bheadh sead nó siolla den cheo.

Maidir le hEochaidh Aireamh, do thug leis ríon dáilte na dí, idir Éadaoin agus amhras, agus d'fhill ar Theamhair maille leis an mbuíon fear a bhí ina fharradh ó thús na tóraíochta ó chianaibh.

Agus is lúcháireach a thug na fir sin cosán agus conair na Teamhrach orthu féin, óir Éadaoin ba shlán dar leo, slán fós oineach an rí, a saothar féin ba leo a leas agus a luach, agus filleadh ar Theamhair b'fhilleadh ar a dteallach agus ar a dtine féin.

CAIBIDIL VII
Díoltas Mhidhir

I

Cheiliúir gealach. Bhreac an lá. Lig smól fead ar chraobh. Agus nocht grian grua os cionn na Mí agus na Teamhrach. Trí ní ba chlos sa dún: cliotar cliotar na bhfeadhnach uisce agus iad á n-athlíonadh go tollbhraonach ón tobar; géim bó gur lán dá húth; agus scruch-scrach-scruch: bró ag meilt na gcrotal. Trí ní ba léir: urchar fáinleoige an cró isteach; púir dheataigh ag éalú idir dhá aer; triúr cnáimhseacha ag triarshiúl trasna na faiche frasdrúchta. An triúr ban cúnta sin, is lá cúraim a bhí rompu, óir bhí an ríon ar a leaba luí seoil.

Cuireadh giolla go cró na n-each. Ba mhithid crúba a bhearradh. An uair ba bhearrtha na crúba, chuir an giolla scamhach na gcrúb i mbolg beag leathair. Theann an ruóigín in uachtar an bhoilg. Chuaigh gan mhoill go háit agus go hionad a raibh an fear bró ag meilt go moch. Is ann a meileadh an scamhach. Nuair ba mhín meilte don scamhach, chuir an giolla an mheilt sa mboilgín leathair, lean lorg na mban glúine trasna na faiche, agus leag uaidh an boilgín i ndoras an bhotha liachta.

Sa ríbhoth rúscbhuí réimsiúil sin, bhí Éadaoin bean Eachach i mbéal breithe. Cuimlíodh ungach de shíol an lín léi ón imleacán go dtí an bhandacht síos.

'Saortar broinn, saortar brú, seoltar seol, beirtear breith,' arsa na mná glúine trí huaire.

Is ansin a meascadh domlas ae bó agus cumasc luibheanna le scamhach na gcrúb. Séimhchruitireacht istigh ag cruitire de chruitirí an dúin agus é ag spreagadh na dtéad. Chuir bean den triúr cnáimhseacha splanc faoin scamhach. D'éirigh trí néal deataigh faoi chaolach an bhotha.

'Saortar broinn, saortar brú, seoltar seol, beirtear breith,' arsa na mná arís.

Leath an deatach anuas ina bhiorthochas súl agus sróine.

Ní fada ina dhiaidh sin gur rugadh an toircheas. Is iníon a bhí ann, iníon gan cháim gan easpa. Snoíodh an gad imleacáin. Ar an ngad sin cuireadh ceangal le snáth olla. Glanadh gach rian den mhaclog den naí, agus rinneadh a folcadh in uisce meath-théite. Cuireadh iar sin in ucht agus in urbhruinne na máthar í, agus sheinn an cruitire ábhann suantraí dóibh.

Tamall de laetha dá éis sin, an uair ab iomchuí agus

ab inmholta an beart, cuireadh an iníon á hoiliúint le beirt bhuimí sa dún i ndeaschóngar na máthar. Ba mhéanar d'Eochaidh Aireamh: cíos agus cáin na hÉireann aige, bean sciamhach, agus a chéad ghin slán.

I ndiaidh imeachtaí na breithe, caitheadh ráithe eile aimsire i gcríocha Fáil agus Fódla, i mBréifne agus i gCuailgne, i dTeamhair na Mí, agus i ngleann na Bóinne.

II

Maidin de chaoinmhaidineacha néalchorcra an tsaoil, d'éirigh Eochaidh Aireamh dá leaba leorleathan úrluachra, d'éirigh dá leaba agus sheas ina rí-bhile ar fhaiche ró-aoibhinn na Teamhrach ag mochfhéachaint na machairí máguaird. Iad faoi chuisne. Iad faoi dhrúcht. Rud a chonaic sé: fear ag druidim go mallda ina leith. Slat cúig bhior ina láimh aige. Brat sí-uaine air. Torc tiarnúil ar a bhráid. Sheas an fear taobh na gréine den Lia Fáil.

'Maith, a Eochaidh Aireamh,' ar sé.

'Maith, a Mhidhir,' ar Eochaidh.

'Bliain gus inniu a bhíomar i nDún Freamhainn.'

'Fíor sin,' arsa Eochaidh.

'Is méanar duit ó shin,' arsa Midhir, 'cíos flatha

agat, cáin na hÉireann agat, bean sciamhach agat, do chéad ghin slán.'

'Méanar sin.'

'Scéala agam duit, ámh,' arsa Midhir.

'Díchlochadh na Mí?'

'Ualach is troime ná sin!'

'Cluintear uait,' arsa Eochaidh.

Is stuama sothuigthe a labhair tiarna Bhrí Léith. Agus nuair a labhair is éard a dúirt:

'Ba thorrach do bhean an uair a d'éalaigh sí liom ó Theamhair go Brí Leith. Is i mBrí Léith a rug sí an toircheas sin. Iníon. Seacht mbliana déag duitse ag tochailt an tsí dá éis sin. Na blianta sin dar leat b'aon bhliain amháin. Agus an bhean a roghnaigh tú bliain gus inniu i bhFreamhann, is í t'iníon féin a bhí ann. Tá seo fós: bhí Éadaoin i nDún Freamhainn an lá sin. Bhí sin. Ach níor aithnigh tú í.'

Leath an dá shúil ar Eochaidh. Bhánaigh agus d'aolbhánaigh air. Bhí crúba céad each ag crúbthoirníl ina chroí agus ina chléibh.

'Is gó do bhriathar,' ar sé, 'gó agus éitheach gan ábhar gan náire!'

Aird níor thug Midhir ar racht an rí.

'Lig tú uait do bhean faoi dhó, a Eochaidh. Agus is í t'iníon féin a bhíonn le t'ais san oíche anseo i nDún na Teamhrach.'

Ní túisce sin ráite ag Midhir, ach d'imigh sé leis arís gan bhriathar ceada ná ceiliúrtha mar a bheadh sead nó siolla den cheo i ndáil na gaoithe.

Iar chlos na mbriathar sin d'Eochaidh Aireamh, rug líonrith mór agus leorbhuaireamh ar a aigne. Má rug sin, rug luail agus leathdhásacht. Má rug sin, rug lagmheirfean agus léanscanradh. Ghléas sé each den eachra ab ansa leis, d'imir an lasc agus bun an dá sháil uirthi, agus rop leis doras an dúin amach gan lón cosáin gan leathmharcach, gan chumhdach gan chosaint. Ba gheis sin do rí. Óir rí gan chosaint, níor shlán luach a oinigh.

Cé ea, ámh, ní cian gur ráinig Eochaidh bruach na Bóinne bitháille. Bhí an tseanabhainn ag sníomh léi go rúnchríonna an gleann aniar. Chuir Eochaidh cois ar lár agus cois ar lántalamh. Lig an t-each ar iníor agus ar innilt. Lean sé féin an abhainn tamaillín le sruth. Rinne machnamh agus cíoradh meanman. Agus is é comhairle a cinneadh leis dul go Dún Freamhainn maille le triúr naonúr dá theaghlach agus dá mhuintir. Go Dún Freamhainn ar dtús. As sin camchuairt na hÉireann. Camchuairt bhliana ag féachaint a chuid flaithiúnais agus a chuid fearann.

Chrom Eochaidh ar bhláth beag bán a bhí ag fás ar bhruach na habhann. D'iadh a dhorn ar an mbláth. D'fháisc. Tharraing. Stoith. Agus rinne cinneadh comhairle fós: an leanbh ráithe a chur chun báis. Leanbh a iníne. A shíol agus a shliocht féin.

III

Ar fhilleadh ar Theamhair d'Eochaidh Aireamh, chuir sé fios ar thriúr dá chuid ceithearnach. Agus is éard a ordaíodh dóibh, an leanbh ráithe a bhreith leo, cuithe agus caochpholl a dhéanamh sa talamh i bhfad ón dún agus ón dea-chathair, i bhfad ón ráth agus ón ros-chlochán, i bhfad ó áras agus ó áitreabh na ndaoine, an leanbh beo a chur sa bpoll sin, agus an chréafóg dhearg a charnadh anuas air, péisteanna na talún agus eile, ionas nach bhfanfadh aí ná anáil na beatha ann.

D'imigh an triúr sin leo, thug seal ag marcaíocht, agus rinne poll ar an tamhnach ar Shliabh Fuaid. Ach ar fheiceáil aoibh an gháire ar bhéal an linbh dóibh, chlis a gcuid misnigh orthu, agus líonadh a gcroí le díograis agus le trua don naí. Óir an triúr ceithearnach sin, triúr curata cathmhara claíomhluatha, ba thriúr iad den seacht naonúr a chaith bliain agus seacht mbliana déag ag tochailt an dá shí, Sí na mBan

Fionn, agus Sí Bhrí Léith. Agus ba thrua leo gabháil agus dalladh na gcoileán le linn na tochailte sin, agus ba thrua leo adhlacadh agus íobairt an eich odhair san úir agus san ithir, agus ba thrua leo fós an éagóir a rinne Eochaidh ar an aitheach a bhí ag tiomsú beart brosna nuair a fuadaíodh go fuarchúiseach fealltach chun íobairte é.

'Maith,' arsa duine den triúr ceithearnach, 'múchadh an linbh seo, sin rud nach féidir, agus cá comhairle feasta?'

'Atá agamsa comhairle,' arsa an dara duine, 'téimis chuig an áitreabh is neasa dúinn ar an tamhnach uaigneach sléibhe seo, agus beirimis linn an leanbh, agus fágaimis ansiúd é, más idir leac agus losaid é, in alt nó in eang, i gcró na gcearc nó na gcon. Agus má éagann éagadh, nó más fóir agus fad saoil atá i ndán don leanbh, bíodh amhlaidh chomh maith céanna.'

Faomhadh an chomhairle sin, agus ghluais an triúr ceithearnach leo.

Ní cian gur ráinig siad teach beag ar an díthreibh ar Shliabh Fuaid. Ní raibh éinne ann. An ghríosach coigilte i lár an tí agus í gan fuarú. Cual adhmaid ag triomú cois na gríosaí. Cuinneog cois dorais. Leastar ar urlár an tí agus bláthach ann. D'ól an triúr trí lán béil den bhláthach úrmhilis. Amach leo arís.

Bhí bó sa mbuaile. Buarach uirthi. Í gan bhleán.

Thál an bhó beagán dá cuid leamhnachta dóibh. D'fhliuch duine díobh binn a léine sa leamhnacht agus chuir an t-éadach fliuch i mbéal an linbh. Chuir agus arís. Agus arís eile nó gur shách don leanbh. Is ansin a d'fhill siad folach agus fuanbhrat anairte uimpi agus chuir i gcró folamh na gcon í ar an tuí. Gur thug aghaidh agus amas ar dhún na Teamhrach arís.

Maidir le hEochaidh Aireamh, tar éis a mhachnaimh cois abhainn na Bóinne ina aonair, do ghairm a theaghlach chuige, chuir lón míosa á thiomsú agus á sholáthar, agus siar leis go Dún Freamhainn arna mhárach amhail gur ar cuairt na hÉireann a bhí sé ag dul. B'ionadh le cách sin. Rinne an scéal cogar cois tobair agus luaidreáin cois teallaigh. Agus an lá ar imigh Eochaidh Aireamh, facthas eala os cionn na Teamhrach. Eala aonair. Iar sin leath brat dorcha ceo trasna na dúiche. B'aduain sin.

IV

Fionnlámh ab ainm don aoire. Casmhaol ainm a bhanchéile. An teach beag ar Shliabh Fuaid, is don dís sin ba dhíon agus ba dhídean. Le fuineadh gréine agus le feascar an lae sin, tharla an cosán abhaile iad. Fannsholas fómhair ann. Miontréad caorach á sheoladh ag Fionnlámh. Dhá chú ag smutchúnamh dó. Isteach leis na caoirigh sa bhfail. B'shiúd Casmhaol ina ndiaidh an cosán anuas. Bhí beart connaidh agus cipíní ar iompar aici. Chuaigh sí isteach. Chuir goic ar a ceann.

'Éalaí nó gadaí, bhí duine sa teach seo inniu,' arsa sí.

Sheas Fionnlámh ar an tairseach.

'Tá an bhó slán,' ar sé.

Bhior sé a chluais. Chuala sian. Sionnach? Éan coille? An gol céanna arís.

'Céard sin?' arsa Casmhaol.

Lig cú den dá chú leath-thafann as. Lean an dís an gol go cró na gcon. Is ann a bhí an iníon ar an tuí. Folach anairte uimpi go teann. Scoir sí don ghol nuair a thóg an bhean í.

'Tugaimis isteach í,' arsa Casmhaol.

Thug. D'fhadaigh Fionnlámh an tine. Is beag a dúirt ceachtar den dís. Scar an oíche a léine ar an sliabh.

Oileadh an leanbh le Fionnlámh agus Casmhaol sa teach díthreibhe sin ar Shliabh Fuaid. Minic méileach ann. Minic glam na bhfaolchon oícheanta siocghealaí.

An srutháin sléibhe ina chaisí ann. Tormán an easa
ann in alt cúng coille. Fead an iolair ag filleadh ar a
nead i Sliabh Cuailgne. Agus ilbhéarla na n-éan.

Caitheadh naoi Samhain. Caitheadh naoi
mBealtaine. Fás agus forbairt, is maith a tháinig sin
ar an iníon. Bláth agus biseach dá réir. Bhí bua
druine aici. Ba luath a méar i mbun snáthaide. Grinn
a súil. A mínlámh réidh ba stuama. Den olann
chaorach rinneadh snáth di. Rinneadh fearsaid
sníomha. Rinneadh coigeal. Rinneadh mionseol agus
méaracán. Dearg, dubh agus buí: de bhun préimhe
agus de bharr luibhe rinneadh dath i gcomhair na
snáth. Dar le Casmhaol gur de shliocht na saor agus
na n-uasal í. Dar le Fionnlámh gur leanbh sí.

'Is mithid ainm di,' arsa an mháthair altramais.

'Uatha ná iolra, ainm ní fhónfaidh di,' arsa
Fionnlámh.

Ba dhóigh leis féin nach fada a bheadh an
ghirseach faoi dhíon an tí.

Caitheadh seacht Samhain eile. Caitheadh seacht
mBealtaine. Tháinig an iníon in inmhe ógmhná. Ba
chaol a géag. Ba réidh a colpa. Ba scuabach a cúil
ghruaige. Ba dhearg a béal. A déad ba gheal, caol a
géag. A grua ba chaomh corcra. A cíoch ba chruinn.
A glór ba shéimh. A dhá súil ar dhath an troim nuair
is crom don chraobh faoi ualach na gcaor dúdhearg.

Agus um an uair agus an aimsir sin, lá de laetha na cruinne, thug an ógbhean an sliabh agus an sean-talamh uirthi féin i ndiaidh na n-uan agus na n-uascán, i ndiaidh na molt agus na mbánchaorach, i ndiaidh na gcorn agus na gcamreithí. Agus ní cian a bhí sí ag siúl an tsléibhe go bhfaca sí ealta mhór ilbhreac éan sa spéir agus iad ag druidim léi. Éan amháin díobh ba bhrice ilbhrice ná a chéile. Labhair an t-éan mór sin léi. Agus nuair a labhair is éard a dúirt:

'Mé Neamhluan, gairim Éadaoin, chuici fios
   ón sí.
De chlann na n-éan sinn, sinne agus Éadaoin,
   chuici fios ón sí.

Conaire an mac a bhéarfar, chuici fios ón sí.
Fiach ar éin is geis don mhac sin, chuici fios
   ón sí.

Mé Neamhluan, de chlann na n-éan mé,
   chuici fios ón sí
Éadaoin, il-Éadaoin, ath-Éadaoin, chuici fios
   ón sí.'

Ní túisce an rosc sin canta ag Neamhluan ach d'éirigh sé ar muin na gaoithe gur théaltaigh leis siar i dteannta leis an ealta ilbhreac éan. 'Conaire' an t-ainm a bhí á thuar don mhac, mar is i gcró na gcon a tugadh aire dá mháthair ina dílleachta linbh di.

Agus le linn na haimsire sin, imríodh éag agus oidhe ar Eochaidh Aireamh. Dún Freamhainn a loisceadh oíche dá raibh sé ar a leaba ann ag néaldearcadh na gealaí agus í ag bolgshnámh ar sheanabhainn na hoíche gan bhréag. Fios a oidhe níorbh eol d'éinne. Sluaite Bhrí Léith a bhain díoltas de i ndiaidh thochailt an dá shí? Drong dá mhuintir féin a d'imir feallbheart agus fionaíl air? Mian báis dá chuid féin a chuaigh in ainseal ina chroí agus ina chléibh? Ní fios ach seo: is i nDún Freamhainn Bhréifne a d'éag Eochaidh Aireamh Rí na Teamhrach an oíche úd.

V

Cé trácht ámh, tar éis loisceadh agus léirscrios Dhún Freamhainn, ní cian gur gaireadh rí eile i dTeamhair. Eochaidh Feidhleach ab ainm dósan. Ba rí fónta. B'oirearc uasal. Is fonnmhar a ghéill clanna Gael dá reacht agus dá riail. An chéad bhliain i dTeamhair ar a mhian aige.

Agus maidin úrdhrúchta earraigh dar éirigh

Eochaidh Feidhleach dá leorleaba luachra, chuir sé air a bhrat agus a léine, chaith baslach fuaruisce lena éadan, agus amach leis faoi na coillte craobhacha ag fiach agus ag seilg ar an bhfia agus ar an torc.

Thug sé leis buíon dá chuid dea-laochra féin, dhá chú go seang siúlach lena thaobh, scoth na marc faoi na marcaigh, dhá shleá an duine acu, agus claíomh dian chun sáite. Ní cian gur scaip ceo agus cuisne, agus ghlan an spéir go smólghorm os cionn na dúiche.

Ag marcaíocht go bríomhar dó féin agus dá chuid fear, ó mhuine go muine, ó dhoire go doire, ó bhán go bán, ó bhreac go breac, ó réidh go réidh, thug Eochaidh Feidhleach suntas agus athshuntas don eala aoibhinn aolbhán a bhí ar snámh ar an aer tamall uaidh. Muince óir faoi bhráid an éin. An muince sin ag lonnrú faoi sholas na gréine.

Thug an rí taitneamh súl don eala. Á féachaint uaidh go cianmhar a bhí sé nuair a labhair an corn seilge go glórach ina ghaobhar. Lig an dá chú glam astu go santach, roinn na fir an lasc leis na mairc, agus thug lán na buíne díobh ling agus léim i ndiaidh na creiche.

Dhruid Eochaidh Feidhleach ar fhód ar leith. Thug cúl le díon na coille. Lámh leis an áit sin ar bhruach an tsrutháin, chonaic sé rud a bhain an réim reatha as a dhá bhonn. Ógbhean sciamhach ag cíoradh ghruaig a cinn cois linne faoi bhun an easa in ógsholas na tréanmhaidine. Caol a géag. Réidh a colpa. Dearg a béal. Caomh a grua. Cruinn a cíoch. Muince óir faoina bráid: bhain an ghrian splanc solais as an muince sin.

Ar chlos na seilge di tamall siúil uaithi, thóg an ógbhean a ceann agus a cruinnmhala. Ar cholbha na coille uaithi suas, b'shiúd Rí na Teamhrach á féachaint, é gan chú gan chomhairleoir gan cheithearnach a chosanta. Tháinig an rí aonair ina leith go stadchéimiúil stuama. Sheas fad trí shleá uaithi. Dhearc an dís a chéile.

'Mochean Eochaidh Feidhleach,' arsa an ógbhean. Gheit croí Eachach. Glór na mná ba shéimh.

'Fios m'ainmse,' arsa an rí, 'cé mar a tharla sin agat?'

'Iomrá ort a chualas, a Eochaidh. Is mór do chlú. Thugas searc duit. Searc agus grá éagmaise. Céile ní mian liom ach thú. Is leat mo lámh thar Feara Fáil.'

Rí na Teamhrach! Do chuala an briathar sin. Ba bhalbh dó ó chuala. Chomh balbh le tiompán gan téad. Fothram an easa ba chlos in aice láimhe. Freagra an tsrutháin. Tafann na gcon ag dul i léig i ndomhain agus i ndiamhair na coille.

Mhúscail an Feidhleach a mhisneach.

'Cé thú féin?' ar sé.

An fhéachaint a thug an ógbhean air ar ala na huaire sin, ní féachaint gan ghrinndearcadh a bhí ann. An grinndearcadh sin níor ghrinndearcadh gan tnúthán. An dá shúil a bhí á ghrinndearcadh, ba dhá shúil iad ar dhath an troim nuair is crom don chraobh faoi ualach na gcaor dúdhearg. Labhair an bhean.

'Mé Éadaoin,' ar sí.

Sin iad imeachtaí agus eachtraí Éadaoine. A céadoiliúint i measc na neamhbhuan i Maigh Inis Uladh. A tochmharc le Midhir. A luach cleamhnais idir mhachairí agus aibhneacha, idir chothom a meáchain ina ór agus a cothrom fós ina airgead. A teacht go Brú na Bóinne, a dul dá éis sin go Brí Léith. An briocht a chuir Fuamnach uirthi, an lochán uisce agus an féileacán caoin corcra. An chéad ruaigeadh, agus an biseach i ngrianán Aonghasa. An dara ruaigeadh, agus an cian mór san iasacht.

Má bhí sin ann, bhí seo: an titim i gcorn meá Ghormlatha, an athbhreith, an oiliúint in Inbhear Ciochmhuine. Duan an mharcaigh cois inbhir ar theacht in inmhe di i measc chlann iníon na dtaoiseach. An céileachas i dTeamhair le hEochaidh

Aireamh. Imirt na fichille agus díol na ngeall. Éalú an dá eala, agus tochailt an dá shí.

Má bhí sin ann, bhí seo fós: dalladh na gcoileán con, íobairt an eich agus íobairt an aithigh; díoltas Mhidhir; an tríú breith agus an dídean ar Shliabh Fuaid; an oiliúint le Fionnlámh agus le Casmhaol; duan an éin mhóir ilbhric agus tuar bhreith Chonaire.

Má bhí sin ann, bhí agus eile: aisling Aonghasa; an tiompán gan téad; an torc tiarnúil agus an brat síuaine; feothan beag, feothan mór, cuaifeach agus spéirling; teas i ngrianán agus sioc ar sciatháin; dhá fhiach bhána. Dáileadh na dí. An chailleach bhuí. Agus bás rí.

Ag sin imeachtaí agus eachtraí Éadaoine in Inis Fódla anallód. Rugadh mac dá éis sin. Ba é Conaire Mór an mac sin. Tar éis bhreith Chonaire, ní cian gur fhill Éadaoin ar an sí. Choill Conaire Mór a gheasa, agus is sa Dún Dearg ar abhainn na Dothra a fuair sé bás agus oidhe nuair a tháinig slua mór na ndíbheirgeach i dtír ar Thrá na Fuirbean faoi Ingéal Caoch mac rí Breatan.

Ní fios cá cor d'Éadaoin ó bhí imeachta agus eachtraí na cianaimsire sin ann. Sa sí is dóichí a cónaí. I measc na mbuan. Ag seo a laoi féin:

ÉADAOIN

Mé Éadaoin, mór mo sceoin,
Orm iomrall de m'ainneoin,
Orm mearbhall ar muir,
Orm imeacht ó Mhidhir.

Mé Éadaoin: ni heol dom bás.
Dom is eol aois gan sólás.
Mo dhídean ní thig le neach,
Mo dhíbirt dhéanas Fuamnach.

Gaoth aneas — mo chuach thú!
Gaoth anoir — mo chrá thú!
Gaoth aniar — mo cheol thú!
Gaoth aduaidh — mo chreach thú!

Seoid a chaithim — muince óir,
Seoid eile — dealg fionnóir,
Seoid a santaím fós a leas,
Suan gan osna gan uaigneas.

Is fras mo gholsa sa ló.
San oíche — is mór m'anshó.
Mé Éadaoin, is sean mo dhán,
Chéasas rí, charas leannán.

— CRÍOCH —

AGUISÍNÍ

AGUISÍN I

Iarfhocal

An scéal atá sa leabhar seo, is scéal é a fáisceadh as ábhar dar teideal *Tochmharc Étaíne*, ábhar atá ar marthain i Leabhar na hUidhre (LU) (c. 1100 AD), agus i *Leabhar Buí Leacan* (LBL) (c. 1400 AD). Maidir leis an ábhar sin, is sleachta agus blúirí atá ann: *Tochmharc Étaíne* ní scéal é a tháinig anuas chugainn ina iomláine sna foinsí Sean-Ghaeilge.

Trí shliocht de *Thochmharc Étaíne* atá i LU. Tá na trí shliocht sin ar fad i LBL chomh maith. Maidir le péire de na sleachta sin (LU líne 10636-10707 agus LU líne 10709-10915 faoi seach, cf LBL lch 143-161 agus LBL lch 174-192 faoi seach), is sleachta iad atá níos faide agus níos iomláine i LBL ná mar atá siad i LU. Dá réir sin, is é LBL príomhfhoinse an amhábhair a bhí ann le h*Éadaoin* a shaothrú.

Maidir le sliocht amháin de na trí shleachta atá sa dá lámhscríbhinn (LU line 10709-10788, cf LBL colún 990-992 agus LBL colún 876), sliocht a bhaineann le deartháir Rí na Teamhrach, is sliocht é nár baineadh úsáid as sa leagan nua den scéal atá sa leabhar seo. Ainneoin gur díol spéise ann féin atá sa sliocht seo, bhí deacrachtaí ag roinnt leis ó thaobh forbairt agus leanúnachas an scéil de, ó thaobh thionchar na gcarachtar ar a chéile de, sin agus ó thaobh athrá móitífeanna agus téamaí de.

Seo a leanas, más ea, an gaol atá idir an dá shliocht eile i LBL agus na caibidlí atá sa leagan nua seo de *Thochmharc Étaíne*. LBL 143-161: is ar na leathanaigh sin atá Caibidil I-III bunaithe, is é sin Cuid I d'*Éadaoin*. LBL 174-192: is ar na leathanaigh sin atá Caibidil IV-VII bunaithe, is é sin Cuid II d'*Éadaoin*.

Is fiú a lua nach bhfuil ach sé mhíle focal nó mar sin sa dá shliocht de *Thochmharc Étaíne* ar fáisceadh an leagan nua seo den scéal astu. Fiche míle focal atá sa leagan nua. Is léir más ea gurbh éigean an t-amhábhar a shaothrú agus a ionramháil go mór. An saothrú agus an ionramháil seo, an spíonadh agus an soláthar ábhair, an cheapadóireacht agus an chumadóireacht, is rudaí iad ba thábhachtaí i scríobh *Éadaoin* ná i scríobh *Conaire Mór* (2017) agus *Tuatha Dé Danann* (2018). Ar na píosaí nua-chumtha is fiú a lua, tá Caibidil I, míreanna II agus III; Caibidil II, míreanna II agus III; Caibidil III, míreanna I agus II; Caibidil V, míreanna II agus III; Caibidil 6, mír I; Caibidil VII, míreanna I, III, agus V.

Is ceart a rá freisin gur nua-chumadóireacht atá sa laoi filíochta *Mé Éadaoin*, laoi atá ina ranna fáin i gcorp an scéil i gCaibidil III, agus in aon téacs amháin i ndeireadh an scéil. Maidir leis an dán 'A bhé fhinn, an dtiocfá liom?', sin dán a bhfuil leagan de sna foinsí. Is athleagan atá in *Éadaoin*. Na ranna filíochta eile atá in *Éadaoin*, is é toradh mo phinn féin atá iontu.

Maidir le téamaí an scéil seo, sin agus gnéithe éagsúla den mhiotaseolaíocht, iarraim go humhal ar an léitheoir an t-iarfhocal atá le *Tuatha Dé Danann* a cheadú (lch 114-116 go mór mór) más mian leis tuilleadh léargais a fháil ar chuid de na cúrsaí sin: cló agus ilchló, an t-am is líne *versus* an t-am is ciorcal, agus rudaí nach iad. Foinsí eile eolais, ábhair, agus inspioráide a bhí agam agus mé ag scríobh an tsaothair seo, tá liosta díobh ar fáil in Aguisín II.

Tá roinnt téarmaí dlí ón tseanaimsir sa leabhar seo, mar

aon le tagairtí do chultúr na nGael anallód, sin agus roinnt focal neamhghnách eile. Tá míniú ar bhunáite na dtéarmaí agus na bhfocal sin sa ngluais (Aguisín III). Na focail eile atá sa leabhar seo, ar scáth roinnt comhfhocal liriciúil de mo chuid féin, tá míniú orthu sna foclóirí atá againn.

BUÍOCHAS

Ba mhaith liom buíochas a ghabháil leis na daoine seo a leanas as ucht a gcuid tacaíochta agus a gcuid tairise, más fadó é nó le deireanas: m'athair Desmond Johnson agus mo mháthair Llinos Morgan; Darach Ó Scolaí (Leabhar Breac), an tOllamh Gearóid S. Mac Eoin, Máirín Mhaitiú Ní Chonghaile (an Cnocán Glas, an Spidéal), Liam Ó Cuinneagáin (Oideas Gael), le Desmond Egan, le hAifric Mac Aodha, agus le Colmcille Ó Monacháin. Buíochas fós le Daniel Büchner (Curach Bhán Verlag), an Dr Gisbert Hemprich (Ollscoil Bonn), agus Irina Wistoff (an Ghearmáin); le Ned Thomas, Glen Peters agus Brenda Squires (an Bhreatain Bheag); leis an Ollamh Katarzyna Dziubalska-Kołaczyk (ollscoil Poznań); le Hervé Dinahet (an Bhriotáin). Buíochas leis an Ollamh Fergus Kelly as ucht na saothar atá luaite leis in Aguisín II. Buíochas leis an gCoimisiún Eorpach as ucht mí ama a chur ar fáil dom le hÉadaoin a scríobh, agus le Foras na Gaeilge as ucht a gcuid féile. Thar aon ní, ba mhaith liom na múrtha buíochais a ghabháil le mo bhean chéile Amanda Reid as ucht a cuid tacaíochta, a cuid taighde, agus a cuid tuisceana.

DJ, an Bhruiséil, Nollaig 2019

AGUISÍN II

Foinsí an Ábhair agus an Eolais

Bailiúchán na Scol (ar dúchas.ie)

Bechbretha, eag. Thomas Charles-Edwards & Fergus Kelly (1983)

Cáin Lánamna: An Old Irish Tract on Marriage and Divorce Law, Charlene Eska (2009)

Commentaires sur la Légende de Maître Manole, Mircea Eliade (1994)

Dress in Ireland — a History, Mairead Dunleavy (2000)

Early Irish Farming, Fergus Kelly (1997)

Early Irish Law, Fergus Kelly (1988)

Flóra Chorca Dhuibhne, eag. Máire Uí Chonchobhair (1995)

Lebor na hUidre (Leabhar na hUidhre), eag. Best & Bergen (1928)

Leabhar Buí Leacan (ar celt.ucc.ie)

Les Druides, Christian J. Guyonvarc'h, Françoise Le Roux (1986)

Pflanzen der Kelten, Wolf-Dieter Storl (2003)

Regemen na Sláinte, eag. Séamus Ó Ceithearnaigh (1942–1944)

The Triads of Ireland, Kuno Meyer (1906)

AGUISÍN III

Gluais I

Adhaltrach — an dara banchéile

Aí — anáil

Airtheann — féar a thugtar do na capaill

Airscéala — clú, cáil

Aitheach — talmhaí, duine den chosmhuintir

Banchumhall — freastalaí mná

Bigireacht — ní fios cén cineál cluiche seo

Bile — crann uasal

Bonsach — camán

Caingean — cúis dlí

Cíorbholg — mála beag le cíor a choinneáil

Criol — mála beag

Cuithe — poll mór sa talamh

Dearbhfhine — an fine is neasa gaol do dhuine

Díchlochadh — baint agus cartadh na gcloch

Druine — obair snáthaide

Eo — bradán

Fithis — fáinne

Foircheadal — teagasc

Fuan — ball éadaigh le caitheamh faoi léine

Imreas — easaontas, conspóid

Innuachair — in aois suirí agus céileachais

Íota — tart

Lámhthoradh — toradh obair lámh (na mban)

Leastar — soitheach (iasacht ón mBreatnais)

Ling — léim

Losaid — mias le taos a fhuint ann

Losc — bacach (capall)

Maclog — fuíoll na broinne i ndiaidh na breithe

Macshlabhra — an chuid de mhaoin na máthar is dlite don
    mhac
Maighre — bradán
Ó-dhearg — cluasa dearga ar ainmhí (i.e. ainmhí ón sí)
Oineach — onóir
Osán — bróg éadrom (iasacht ó Fhraincis na Normanach)
Scamhach — barr na n-ingne agus iad bearrtha
Sítheadh — ruaig, rúid
Tincheadal — briocht, ortha
Tíobhas — tíos, riar tí
Uamhan — faitíos, sceimhle

Gluais II
Na luibheanna a bhí ag Dianchéacht Lia
agus ag Breasal Draoi

airgead luachra — *Filipendula ulmaria*
créachtlus — *Stachys sylvatica*
fuath gorm — *Solanum dulcamara*
glanrosc — *Euphrasia officinalis*
gormdhearc, eithreog — *Rubus caesius*
lochall — *Veronica beccabunga*
beathnua — *Hypericum*
meas torc allta — *Hypericum androsaemum*
mianfhartach, néalfartach — *Potentilla erecta*
mínscoth — *Centaurea nigra*
slánlus — *Plantago lanceolata*

Mé Éadaoin, mór mo sceoin,
Orm iomrall de m'ainneoin,
  Orm mearbhall ar muir,
  Orm imeacht ó Mhidhir.

LEABHAIR EILE LEIS AN ÚDAR

Prós
Éadaoin (Leabhar Breac, 2020)
Tuatha Dé Danann (Leabhar Breac, 2018)
Conaire Mór (Leabhar Breac 2017, 2020)
Pen and Plough (Carreg Gwalch, 2016)
Tro ar Fyd (i bpáirt le Amanda Reid) (Y Lolfa, An Bhreatain Bheag, 2013)
Y Gwyddel (Gomer, An Bhreatain Bheag, 2011)

Filíocht
Rún na mBradán (Coiscém, 2016)
The Birth of Trystan (Curach Bhán, An Ghearmáin, 2014)
The Woods are Growing Younger (Eikon, An Rómáin, 2013)
Der Vogel und andere Gedichte (Curach Bhán, An Ghearmáin, 2013)
Súil Saoir (Cló Iar-Chonnacht, 2004)

Aistriúcháin liteartha
Washing My Hair with Nettles (dánta Rómáinise le Emilia Ivancu) (Parthian, 2015)
Vatilan the Dish Thief (Y Dŵr Mawr Llwyd, Robin Llywelyn) (Parthian, 2009)
Sarah Eile (Sarah Arall), Aled Islwyn (Cló Iar-Chonnacht, 2005)
Coinnigh do Mhisneach (Yfory Ddaw, Sioned Wyn Jones) (Cló Iar-Chonnacht, 2004)
Dafydd ap Gwilym (i bpáirt le J-C Lozac'hmeur) (Wodan Books, An Fhrainc, 1994)

Tuatha Dé Danann

Diarmuid Johnson

€16 (crua), 96 lch; ISBN 978-1-911363-23-1

Is le misneach mór, le héirim aigne, agus le feabhas a gcuid draíochta a bhain Tuatha Dé Danann seilbh na hÉireann de na Fir Bolg fadó, agus is le dícheall agus le díograis na dtréanfhear agus na ndeithe a shéan siad ceannas an oileáin ar na Fomhóraigh lá ab fhaide anonn. Athinsint bhreá bhríomhar atá sa leabhar seo ar theacht Thuatha Dé Danann, scéal a bhaineann le dúchas na nGael agus le flaitheas na hÉireann.

Scéal flaithiúnais, scéal dúchais, scéal ársa agus scéal nua — sin é atá i scéal na n-eachtraí faoi mar atá inseacht agus aithris orthu sa leabhar beag eipiciúil seo. Cé mar a baineadh an ghéag de Nuadha, cérbh é Lugh Lámhfhada, cén tairngreacht do Bhalar na Súile Nimhe, agus cén bhandáil a bhí ag an Daghda cois Éirne?

Ghnóthaigh an leabhar seo gradam 'Leabhar Gaeilge na Bliana' ag an An Post Irish Book Awards.

Conaire Mór

Diarmuid Johnson

€16 (crua), 100 lch; ISBN 978-1-909907-92-8

Is athinsint bhríomhar bheoga atá in *Conaire Mór* ar an eipic Sean-Ghaeilge *Togail Bruidne Da Derga* — scéal a thosaíonn le rí á ghairmeadh de Chonaire agus a chríochnaíonn lena mharú brúidiúil ar bhruach na Dothra. Na hiontais ar fad atá i dtraidisiún na seanscéalta, tá siad ar fáil go flúirseach in imeachtaí an scéil, idir mhacghníomhartha Chonaire agus a theacht i réim, na blianta a raibh Éirinn faoi bhláth lena linn, agus an tuar báis nárbh fhéidir a shéanadh. Seo scéal nár insíodh i nGaeilge le beagnach míle bliain, ach tá Conaire Mór i réim anois arís ar deireadh.

"**Leabhar an-shuaitheansach. Athinsint shamhlaíoch chruthaitheach ar cheann de na scealta is tábhachtaí dá bhfuil aqainn ó litríocht na Sean-Ghaolainne.**"
— *Breandán Ó Cróinín, Léirmheas Leabhar TG4*

Ghnóthaigh an leabhar seo Gradam Uí Shúilleabháin 'Leabhar na Bliana' 2017.